WOMAN AGAINST HER SEX
A Critique of Nawal el-Saadawi

WOMAN AGAINST HER SEX

A Critique of Nawal el-Saadawi

Georges Tarabishi
With a Reply by Nawal el-Saadawi

*Translated by Basil Hatim
and Elisabeth Orsini*

Saqi Books

Library of Congress Cataloging-in-Publication Data

Ṭarābīshī, Jūrj.
    Woman against her sex.

    Translation of: Unthá ḍidda al-unthá.
    Bibliography: p.
    Includes index.
    1. Sa'dāwī, Nawāl — Political and social views.
2. Sexism in literature. I. Sa'dāwī, Nawāl.
II. Title.
PJ7862.A3Z8913   1988   892'.736   87-23346

British Library Cataloguing in Publication Data

Tarabishi, Georges
    Woman against her sex: a critique of
    Nawal el-Saadawi.
    1. Sadawi, Nawal — Criticism and
    interpretation
    I. Title   II. Sa'dāwī, Nawāl   III. Untha
    Dod al-Unutha. *English*
    892'.78609   PJ7862.A3Z/

ISBN 0-86356-143-8
     0-86356-082-2 Pbk

First published 1988 by
Saqi Books, 26 Westbourne Grove, London W2 5RH
and 191 Atlantic Avenue, Brooklyn, NY 11201.

© Saqi Books 1988

Typeset by Theatretexts, London

Printed in Great Britain by
Billing & Sons Ltd
Worcester

Contents

Introduction

This study is the third in a series. The first book, *The Oedipus Complex in the Arabic Novel*,[1] subjected the novels of Ibrahim Abd el-Qadir el-Mazini, Tawfiq el-Hakim,[2] Amina el-Sa'id and Suhail Idris to a critical analysis from the standpoint of psychoanalysis. This was followed by *Manhood and the Ideology of Manhood in the Arabic Novel*,[3] which examined the novels of the two major representatives of the 'manhood' school in Arabic literature: Muhammad Dib and Hannah Minah. The present work is devoted to the novels and short stories of the principal exponent of the Arabic feminist novel, Nawal el-Saadawi.

Surprisingly perhaps, it is this task that has proved the most difficult, or rather the most intractable. In the case of Tawfiq el-Hakim, for example, it was relatively easy to adopt a radical critical stance in the face of his blatantly anti-feminist sentiments. His literary works occupy a prominent place in the Arab literary tradition and are based on a philosophy of demeaning and scorning women. Our critical task was somewhat more difficult in the case of Muhammad Dib, on the other hand, and even more so in that of Hannah Minah: in both these authors, a subconscious 'anti-women' ideology is interwoven with that of a conscious, confident social realism.

In the case of Nawal el-Saadawi, however, not only were we faced with what was a consciously pro-feminist ideology, interwoven with one that was subconsciously anti-feminist. There was a further complication. It is relatively easy to adopt a critical stance over the works of Tawfiq el-Hakim or the representatives of the 'manhood' school (though they have conflicting ideological positions), since they all belong to the sex of the 'oppressor' — in this instance, the male sex. The author of *Woman at Point Zero, Memoirs of a Woman Doctor, Two Women in One* and *The Absentee*,[4] however, belongs to the sex of the 'oppressed'. How, then, can we criticize her heroines' vision of the world without severing our bond of solidarity with them as members of the same oppressed sex, and without losing sight of the fact that the oppressed, even when wrong, are more in the right than their oppressors? Indeed, can't we go further and say that it is impermissible if not illegitimate to criticize the colonized who labour under the yoke of the colonizer? It is sometimes said that women are man's 'colony'. How then can we criticize woman without aligning ourselves with her colonizer — playing his game, as it were?

There is perhaps a way out of this impasse. It is to stress that what we criticize in this particular woman's vision of the world is not a product of her inner self, nor the outcome of her rebellion against her colonizer, but, on the contrary, the result of her having identified with her colonizer and internalized man's hostile ideology. In other words, our criticism will be biased in favour of the woman who is inside the woman, so that the criticism can better focus on reaching the man who is inside the woman.

Once an imported ideology has been internalized, it also becomes 'exportable'. One proof will suffice here. One of the oldest and most frequent claims made by traditional anti-feminist authors is that woman is like a flower — her beauty and freshness enliven human existence. They also warn, however, that, like all flowers, woman bears the thorns of evil[5] and divisiveness within her. As it happens, Nawal el-Saadawi adopts both this image and the same duality. In the dedication setting out the framework of the novel *Two Women in One*, she says:

> when flowers first bloom in the sun they are assaulted by swarms of bees that suck their tender petals, and... if they do not fight back they will be destroyed. But if they resist, if they turn their tender petals into sharp protruding thorns, they can survive among hungry bees.

It is not difficult to detect where the leanings towards masculine ideology lie: the image of 'sharp protruding thorns' leads us straight into the world of the male and of masculine hostility. Only a masculine, warlike logic could conceive of the relationship between the bee and the flower as a battle. It is simply untrue that the flower is 'destroyed' when the bee sucks out its nectar; indeed, it is this very act that enriches nature and maintains the ecological balance. On the one hand, it turns the nectar into honey, and on the other, it spreads the pollen to many other flowers which would otherwise never have bloomed.

Of course, there have always been aggressive males who treat the relationship between the two sexes as a war and use the penis as an instrument of aggression. In fact, if women have any mission at all, it is to win the war by annulling it and not by arming themselves in their turn with thorns and a gun. The feminist militant Germaine Greer maintains that women must tame and humanize the penis so that it becomes not a weapon of steel but one of flesh. To this we would add: Women must also humanize the world.

It's not destructive, it's mutualistic.

Penis envy should be penis taming.

1
Woman at Point Zero

'We here come face to face with one source of both the conscious and unconscious impulses of prostitution in women.

'Frigidity is practically a *sine qua non* of prostitution. The experiencing of full sexual satisfaction binds the woman to the man, and only where this is lacking does she go from man to man, just like the continually ungratified Don Juan type of man who has constantly to change his love object. Just as the Don Juan avenges himself on all women for the disappointment which he once received from the first woman who entered his life, so the prostitute avenges herself on every man for the gift she expected from her father and never received. Her frigidity signifies a humiliation of all men and therefore a mass castration to her unconscious, and her whole life is given up to this purpose.'

Karl Abraham[1]

The first point to strike us in the 'biography' of the prostitute Firdaus, the heroine of *Woman at Point Zero*,[2] is the 'biographer's' overwhelming desire to identify with her subject. In both the preface and the conclusion to the novel, the author not only stresses that Firdaus is a 'real woman' she 'met in the Qanatir Prison a few years ago', and that hers is a true story, but she couples this with the conviction that this murderess, 'who, in ten days' time, would be led to the gallows', is 'better than all the men and women we normally hear about, or see, or know'. Indeed, she is even 'better' than the narrator herself, to the extent that she makes the woman psychiatrist (whom we may regard as a guise for the author) feel, in comparison, 'nothing but a small insect crawling upon the land amidst millions of other insects'.

In so-called 'real-life stories', authors often claim that the tale we are about to read, though true, is stranger than fiction; that the person whose story is to be told has left an indelible impression on the author, just as he or she doubtless will on the reader. In spite of these conventional gambits, the story usually remains firmly in the realm of fiction and it is difficult to tell whether it has been dreamed up by the author or is in fact based on real life.

This is the kind of cliché which the narrator of *Woman at Point Zero* is careful to avoid as she introduces the biography of Firdaus. Both the preface and the last chapter of the book (a story related from Firdaus's point of view) betray an intensely personal tone. The female psychiatrist, who has been entrusted with the task of carrying out 'research on the personalities of a group of women prisoners and detainees convicted or accused of various offences',[3] is taken aback when told by the prison doctor that this woman who 'had been sentenced to death for killing a man' is 'not like the other murderesses held in the prison. "You will never meet anyone like her in or out of prison."'

Although remarks such as these might be considered clichés, a 'personal tone' immediately emerges when the narrator adds:

I was supposed to examine some other women prisoners that day, but instead I got into my car and drove away. Back home I could not do anything. I had to revise the draft of my latest book, but I was incapable of concentrating. I could think of nothing but the woman called Firdaus who, in ten days' time, would be led to the gallows.

If Firdaus's refusal to see the female psychiatrist is itself one of these standard clichés, the effect of this refusal is personal in the extreme:

I returned to the prison several times, but all my attempts to see Firdaus were of no avail. I felt somehow that my research was now in jeopardy. As a matter of fact, my whole life seemed to be threatened with failure.

The dependency established by the writer between her life and that of the woman whose days are numbered is particularly striking in the preface and final chapter of the novel. Not only is it the mechanism by which the reader is led to believe that Firdaus's story is true and somehow close to the 'heart of life'; it also expresses the writer's desire to identify and empathize with her heroine.

(Christ said, 'What shall it profit a man, if he shall gain the whole world and lose his own soul?') In both the preface and the final chapter, the writer's alter ego seems to be saying, 'How would I benefit if I won myself and lost Firdaus?' The exaggeration is not ours but Saadawi's. She is the one who tells us that when Firdaus refuses to meet her, she feels rejected not by 'one person amongst the millions that peopled the vast world, but by every living being or thing on earth, by the vast world itself'.

It is also the author herself who tells us that, with this rejection:

A strange feeling of heaviness weighed down my heart, my body, drained my legs of their power. A feeling heavier than the weight of the whole earth, as though instead of standing above its surface, I was now lying somewhere beneath it.

On the other hand, when at the last minute Firdaus agrees to meet her, 'a wonderful feeling, proud, elated, happy' sweeps over her, a feeling that makes her breathe deeply and her heart pound violently, so that she feels, in her own words, as if she is holding the whole world in her hands and that the whole world is hers.

This need to empathize with Firdaus and, in the final analysis, to identify with a prostitute and killer is perhaps the first thing to attract the reader's attention in the preface. (The final and lasting impression at the end of the book, however, is the total lack of moral or ideological justification behind this desire to identify with Firdaus, and thus with prostitution and murder.) The reader can thus never wholeheartedly empathize with the woman who will shortly 'be led to the gallows'.

In spite of her overwhelming desire to be a carbon copy of Firdaus, the psychiatrist-narrator is unable to match Firdaus's achievements. Firdaus has reached the ultimate state — beyond the reach of any ordinary mortal. She has practised prostitution wilfully, and murdered wilfully. In a world in which men are what they are, a woman who wants to be true to herself can only become a prostitute and murderess. But there is a high price to be paid for such integrity. And Firdaus is the only person in the world who can pay it. In this respect, she is the ultimate example, the unreachable cry for the impossible identification.

It is for this very reason that Firdaus is fated to die at the hands of the law. The most any other woman could do, even the psychiatrist-narrator herself, is dream of empathizing with Firdaus. This is precisely how *Woman at Point Zero* ends. This eulogy to a woman whose desire to be true to herself pushes her to become a prostitute and murderess concludes with a satirical look at another woman who is not honest enough with herself to follow suit:

> the door was thrown open, revealing several armed policemen. They surrounded her in a circle, and I heard one of them say:
> 'Let's go... Your time has come.'
> I saw her walk out with them. I never saw her again. But her voice continued to echo in my ears, vibrating in my head, in the cell, in the prison, in the streets, in the whole world, shaking everything, spreading fear wherever it went, the fear of the truth which kills...
> I got into my little car, my eyes on the ground... I felt ashamed of myself, of my life, of my fears, and my lies. The streets were full of people bustling around, of newspapers hanging on wooden stalls, their headlines crying out. At every step, wherever I went, I could see the lies, could follow hypocrisy bustling around. I rammed my foot down on the accelerator as though in a hurry to run over the world, to stamp it all out...
> And at that moment I realized that Firdaus had more courage than I.

Who then is Firdaus? And what, as prostitute and murderess, has she done to become an example to be emulated and a paradigm to be revered? As she begins her confessions on the psychiatrist's couch, her first statement is that she has never looked at a man's picture in a newspaper without literally spitting on it, leaving 'the spit where it was to dry'. She has never met a man without wanting to 'lift [her] hand and bring it smashing down on his face'. Her

16

last statement before departing to the hereafter is, 'They know that as long as I am alive they will not be safe, that I shall kill them. My life means their death.' It goes without saying that 'them' here refers to men.

Thus Firdaus is a woman who wants to challenge the biological laws of nature. Humanity was not created male and female[4] so that the two sexes can know and love each other. Nor was a human being created half-male and half-female, with each half eternally protecting the other. Instead a man was created to be a man and a woman a woman, with all interaction between them eternally condemned to strife and war.

Firdaus is equally intent upon challenging social laws. Far from accepting the man–woman relationship as entirely natural, she sees it as the most hostile and belligerent relationship of all. Men and women are two tribes, two classes, two nations, separated by a yawning chasm of unabating strife. Any contact between them is only to create destruction, not life.

Thus Firdaus is a fighter, and her battlefield is the two sexes. Her slogan is that, far from complementing each other, the sexes actually repel each other, like the Manichaean principles of good and evil. It is a war without truce and without exception. Every man is the enemy, whether he be father, brother, uncle, husband, judge, policeman, doctor, journalist or whatever.[5] And while all men are criminals, 'No woman can be a criminal. To be a criminal one must be a man.'

So long as the criminals are all in one camp and the innocent in another, it follows that what lies between the male and the female is not love but hatred, and what lies between the female and the male is not mutual attraction but fear:

> I continued to look straight at him without blinking. I knew I hated him as only a woman can hate a man, as only a slave can hate his master. I saw from the expression in his eyes that he feared me as only a master can fear his slave, as only a man can fear a woman.

But if this terrifying war admits of no exceptions because it is conducted between two abstractions — the man *qua* man, and the woman *qua* woman — the abstraction *per se*, particularly as far as

17

human relations are concerned, is not very illuminating. By the same token, such abstractions do not make for good literature.

Both Firdaus and the psychiatrist-narrator are well aware of this fact. Indeed, Firdaus does not engage in her war of attrition, the war of one sex against the other, in an imaginary cosmos; she acts it out on earth in a realistic, conscious way. Before she generalizes her hostility towards an abstraction called man, as the logician or apologist would do, and before she upgrades this hostility to the degree of the absolute formulated in some global law ('I might not kill a mosquito, but I can kill a man'), she has known and explored man. In fact she has, as it were, read man in her father, uncle, husband, lover, pimp and client.)

For example, to be reduced to the only dimension — that of a man — the father has first to be stripped of the dimension of father, even if it means denying his fatherhood. Thus we find the image of the 'non-father' in *Woman at Point Zero* — a father who is not a father, but a mere individual in a generic herd whose members are known as men:

> I was still young at the time, and my breasts were not yet rounded. I knew nothing about men. But I could hear them as they invoked Allah's name and called upon His blessings, or repeated His holy words in a subdued guttural tone. I would observe them nodding their heads, or rubbing their hands one against the other, or coughing, or clearing their throats with a rasping noise, or constantly scratching under the armpits and between the thighs. I saw them as they watched what went on around them with wary, doubting, stealthy eyes, eyes ready to pounce, full of an aggressiveness[6] that seemed strangely servile.
>
> Sometimes I could not distinguish which one of them was my father. He resembled them so closely that it was difficult to tell. So one day I asked my mother about him. How was it that she had given birth to me without a father? First she beat me...[7]

The father here is denied his fatherhood not only physically but also morally. This father whose fatherhood is questioned in terms of both descent and lineage is also the embodiment of a selfishness that is anything but fatherly, as it appears particularly in relation

[handwritten margin note: Allah's "male" aspect is emphasized]

to the children:

Our hut was cold, yet in winter my father used to shift my straw mat and my pillow to the small room facing north, and occupy my corner in the oven room...

Like most people, I had many brothers and sisters. They were like chicks that multiply in spring, shiver in winter and lose their feathers, and then in summer are stricken with diarrhoea, waste away quickly and one by one creep into a corner and die.

When one of his female children died, my father would eat his supper, my mother would wash his legs, and then he would go to sleep, just as he did every night. When the child that died was a boy, he would beat my mother, then have his supper and lie down to sleep.

My father never went to bed without supper, no matter what happened. Sometimes when there was no food at home we would all go to bed with empty stomachs. But he would never fail to have a meal. My mother would hide his food from us at the bottom of one of the holes in the oven. He would sit eating alone while we watched him. One evening I dared to stretch out my hand to his plate, but he struck me a sharp blow over the back of my fingers.

I was so hungry that I could not cry.

This stark picture of fatherly selfishness becomes increasingly repulsive. It shades into the image of an anal man. As he is eating, from his mouth emanate all the sounds we would normally associate with another orifice when excreting:

I sat in front of him watching as he ate, my eyes following his hand from the moment his fingers plunged into the bowl until it rose into the air, and carried the food into his mouth. His mouth was like that of a camel, with a big opening and wide jaws. His upper jaw kept clamping down on his lower jaw with a loud grinding noise, and chewed through each morsel so thoroughly that we could hear his teeth striking against each other. His tongue kept rolling round and round in his mouth as though it was also chewing, darting out every now and then to lick off some particle of food that had stuck to his lips, or dropped on his chin.

At the end of his meal my mother would bring him a glass of water. He drank it, then belched loudly, expelling the air from the mouth or belly with a prolonged noise. After that he smoked his water pipe, filling the room around him with thick clouds of smoke, coughing, snorting and inhaling deeply through his mouth and nose. Once over with his pipe he lay down, and... the hut would resonate with his loud snoring.

The picture of the father is followed by that of the uncle. Although this alternative father who gives Firdaus refuge after the death of her parents is not as despicable as her original father, he is nevertheless a man. And as such, he is one of those who have 'in common an avaricious and distorted personality, a never-ending appetite for money, sex and unlimited power'. Neither the ties of kinship nor his el-Azhar University background deter him from trying to seduce her, a mere child. And when she comes of age, he does not hesitate, driven by his greed for money and his desire to get rid of another useless mouth to feed, to marry her off to Sheikh Mahmoud — a man much older than her and, moreover, suffering from a sickening facial deformity:

The day came when I departed from my uncle's house and went to live with Sheikh Mahmoud. Now I slept on a comfortable bed instead of the wooden couch. But no sooner did I stretch out my body on it to rest from the fatigue of cooking and washing and cleaning the large house with its rooms full of furniture, than Sheikh Mahmoud would appear by my side. He was already over sixty, whereas I had not yet turned nineteen. On his chin, below the lip, was a large swelling with a hole in the middle. Some days the hole would be dry, but on others it would turn into a rusty old tap exuding drops red in colour like blood, or whitish yellow, like pus.

When the hole dried up, I let him kiss me. I could feel the swelling against my face and lips like a small purse, or a water skin, full of a stagnant greasy fluid. But on days when it was not dry I would turn my lips and face away to avoid the odour of dead dogs which emanated from it.

This ugly, disgusting husband whose malodorous lips ooze blood and pus belongs to the race of anal fathers through possessing their distinguishing trait, namely avarice.[8] Sheikh Mahmoud's meanness, however, cannot be summed up in one word. Indeed, it is of the type that has provided one of the classic themes of Arabic literature since the earliest days:

He never went out of the house... lest he be obliged to pay a few piastres for a cup of coffee. All day long he remained by my side in the house, or in the kitchen, watching me as I cooked or washed. If I dropped the packet of soap powder and spilled a few grains on the floor, he would jump up from his chair and complain at me for being careless. And if I pressed a little more firmly than usual on the spoon as I took ghee out of the tin for cooking, he would scream out in anger, and draw my attention to the fact that its contents were diminishing much more rapidly than they should. When the dustman came to empty the refuse from the bin, he would go through it carefully before putting it out on the landing. One day he discovered some leftover scraps of food, and started yelling at me so loudly that all the neighbours could hear. After this incident he got into the habit of beating me whether he had a reason for it or not.

He beats her until she bleeds, then has sex with her. Her only means of defence is to offer herself as a body totally devoid of life, just like that offered by the prostitute to the client:

He leapt on me like a mad dog. The hole in his swelling was oozing drops of foul-smelling pus. I did not turn my face or my nose away this time. I surrendered my face to his face and my body to his body, passively, without any resistance, without a movement, as though life had been drained out of it, like a piece of dead wood or old neglected furniture left to stand where it is, or a pair of shoes forgotten under a chair.

When Firdaus runs away from the marital home, she is to fare no better at her lover's. It is true that the café-owner Bayoumi takes her in off the street, gives her refuge and feeds and clothes her. But no sooner does she express a desire to be independent and look for work (she has a secondary school certificate) than the 'man' inside Bayoumi erupts, standing up and slapping her in the face, saying, 'How dare you raise your voice when you're speaking to me, you street walker, you low woman?'

He begins to lock her in the flat when he goes out, and when he comes back at midnight he pulls back the covers, slaps her again and throws himself on top of her. Once again, her only means of defence is that of the prostitute, offering up a lifeless, unresisting body, a body that 'lay there under him without movement, emptied of all desire, or pleasure, or even pain, feeling nothing. A dead body with no life in it at all, like a piece of wood, or an empty sock, or a shoe.'

Simulating the role of a prostitute, Firdaus soon finds herself actually playing the part:

Then one night his body seemed heavier than before, and his breath smelt different, so I opened my eyes. The face above me was not Bayoumi's.

'Who are you?' I said.

'Bayoumi,' he answered.

I insisted, 'You are not Bayoumi. Who are you?'

'What difference does it make? Bayoumi and I are one.' Then he asked, 'Do you feel pleasure?'

'What did you say?' I enquired.

'Do you feel pleasure?' he repeated.

I was afraid to say I felt nothing so I closed my eyes once more and said, 'Yes.'

Like a gramophone record when the needle's stuck, Bayoumi's friends who take turns at having sex with her night after night keep putting the same question to her, while her lips mouthe the same answer. Even after she escapes from Bayoumi's house to the flat of the procuress Sharifa,[9] it is only the decor and the atmosphere that are different — the tune doesn't change. The fingers of the men who caress her body are white and smooth, whereas Bayoumi's nails were black as 'the colour of black tea'. But the differences in the colour of their skin, their fingers and their nails and the stench of their sweat do not cancel out their common identity and their membership of one clan, that of men: 'They're all the same, all sons of dogs, running around under various names. Mahmoud, Hassanein, Fawzy, Sabri, Ibrahim, Awadain, Bayoumi', from the 'stupid' to the 'dog-like'.)

I never used to leave the house. In fact, I never even left the bedroom. Day and night I lay on the bed, crucified, and every hour a man would come in. There were so many of them. I did not understand where they could possibly have come from. For they were all married, all educated, all carrying swollen leather bags, and swollen leather wallets in their inner pockets. Their swollen heavy paunches hung down with too much food, and their sweat ran copiously, filling my nostrils with a foetid smell, like stagnant water, as though it had been held back in their bodies for a long time. I turned my face away, but they insisted on pulling it back, on burying my nose in the smell of their bodies. They dug their long nails into my flesh and I would close my lips tightly trying to stifle any expression of pain, to hold back a scream, but in spite of my efforts they would part and let out a low, muffled moan. Often the man would hear it and mutter stupidly something in my ear,

'Do you feel good?'

In answer I would purse my lips and prepare to spit in his face, but he would start biting them with his teeth. I could feel his thick saliva between my lips and with a push of the tongue sent it back into his mouth.

This is not the passive professional frigidity of the prostitute; it is an aggressive frigidity. It is not the sort that allows a prostitute to practise her profession, but rather a type that makes prostitution desirable in its own right. To the prostitute, frigidity is secondary; to Firdaus, by contrast, it is a primary condition. The prostitute becomes frigid in order to practise her profession; Firdaus, on the other hand, has chosen to be a prostitute in order to practise frigidity, because, to use Karl Abraham's terminology, it is 'castrating'.

The prostitute is unique among women in her ability to 'castrate' the largest possible number of men. Even the most masculine of men becomes impotent in the face of a prostitute's frigidity. The impotent man is characterized not by his failure to have an erection or to penetrate the woman, but rather by his failure to bring her to a climax. Male impotence only becomes an issue when seen in relation to the female. Masculinity means nothing unless it is viewed in relation to femininity. The male who empties himself into a prostitute as if into a 'hole in the sand'[10] withdraws from her just like an ox pulling in its horns.

As the scene of collective castration unfolds in the prostitute's bedroom, Firdaus's claim that she feels neither pleasure, pain nor any other emotion is shown to be untrue. The gloating manner in which she describes her stay in the bedroom, frequented day and night by troops of men, leaves us in no doubt that even if she has suppressed all feeling in her body she still feels pleasure. The pleasure, felt both consciously and subconsciously, is that of stripping men of pride in their masculinity. It is the pleasure of the female who deprives man of what lies at the very core of his manhood. In a word, it is the pleasure of rejecting man as man.

In addition, the prostitute plays a second game of revenge. In his relations with a prostitute, a man is reduced to a mere sexual organ; his only hallmark is his sexual desire, and this desire is both basic and brutal. In confronting this primitive need, the prostitute's frigidity is proof of her spiritual sensitivity and moral superiority. The man who wallows in the mire of the brothel is reduced to the personification of animal desire, that is, a sex organ. The prostitute, on the other hand, is living proof that a woman cannot be reduced to a mere sexual being. Her frigidity is precisely the proof of the female rising above man's animalism.

Thus prostitution is no longer a special case or an individual social phenomenon born of sexual and social problems, but rather a general behavioural attitude, a total principle, a precept which should guide the life of every woman, as a woman. Firdaus states, 'All women are prostitutes of one kind or another.' Rationalizing this law which she has declaimed, she says, 'A woman's life is always miserable. A prostitute, however, is a little better off — or rather freer and more noble. Since every woman is a prostitute, whether she likes it or not, she might as well ask for 'the highest price' rather than selling herself short like wives who are 'the lowest paid' prostitutes of all. And since prostitution is a condition imposed upon women by men, it is better for the woman — whatever her position or profession — to be 'a free prostitute' than

24

'an enslaved prostitute'.

Any other route to the liberation of women is a dead-end, even having a job — seen by armchair feminist theorists as the way to woman's freedom and independence. The working woman is also a prostitute but, unlike the professional, she is not respected. Work is a male value and a male system. Under male domination, there is no respect for women even if they work. Firdaus herself demands respect after she has been rich and successful in the world of prostitution. She decides to use her secondary school certificate and find a job. But what is the result of her attempt?

After I had spent three years in the company, I realized that as a prostitute I had been looked upon with more respect, and been valued more highly than all the female employees, myself included. In those days I lived in a house with a private toilet. I could enter it at any time, and lock the door on myself without anybody hurrying me.[11] My body was never hemmed in by other bodies in the bus, nor was it a prey to male organs pressing up against it from in front and behind. Its price was not cheap, and could not be paid for by a mere rise in salary, an invitation to dinner, a drive along the Nile in somebody's car...

I felt sorry for the other girls who were guileless enough to offer their bodies and their physical efforts every night in return for a meal, or a good yearly report, or just to ensure that they would not be treated unfairly, or discriminated against, or transferred. Every time one of the directors made me a proposition, I would say to him,

'It's not that I value my honour and my reputation more than the other girls, but my price is much higher than theirs.'[12]

I came to realize that a female employee is more afraid of losing her job than a prostitute is of losing her life. An employee is scared of losing her job and becoming a prostitute because she does not understand that the prostitute's life is in fact better than hers. And so she pays the price of her illusory fears with her life, her health, her body, and her mind. She pays the highest price for things of the lowest value. I now knew that all of us were prostitutes who sold themselves at varying prices, and that an expensive prostitute was better than a cheap one.

Love, like work, is merely a dead-end. In fact, love is a threat to woman's very femininity. It can make her forget all about herself as a woman, and may give her the false impression that she is a human being. This is mere illusion. In love a woman remains a woman, that is a prostitute, but a deluded prostitute. It would be better for her to be a professional prostitute, aware of all that this involves, rather than one who is emotionally involved and at the same time deceived:

I had never experienced suffering such as this... Perhaps as a prostitute I had known so deep a humiliation that nothing really counted. When the street becomes your life, you no longer expect anything, hope for anything. But I expected something from love. With love I began to imagine that I had become a human being. When I was a prostitute I never gave anything for nothing, but always took something in return. But in love I gave my body and my soul, my mind and all the effort I could muster, freely. I never asked for anything, gave everything I had, abandoned myself totally, dropped all my weapons, lowered all my defences, and bared my flesh. But when I was a prostitute I protected myself, fought back at every moment, was never off guard. To protect my deeper, inner self from men, I offered them only an outer shell. I kept my heart and soul, and let my body play its role, its passive, inert, unfeeling role. I learnt to resist by being passive, to keep myself whole by offering nothing, to live by withdrawing to a world of my own. In other words, I was telling the man he could have my body, he could have a dead body, but he would never be able to make me react, or tremble, or feel either pleasure or pain. I made no effort, expended no energy...

This extract does not give us the truth, however, or at least not the whole truth. First, it fabricates an experience of love that is doomed to failure from the outset, in order to establish the categoric generalization that the path of love is always a dead-end. Second, it is judgmental, putting all men without exception, including the 'revolutionaries', into the category of the enemy with whom no truce can be made and no deal struck. Third, it refuses to recognize variety and confines each sex to its own domain (the woman is a

26

woman and cannot become a human being even through the miracle of love, and the man remains a man and cannot become a human being even though he is a revolutionary[13]). Finally, the text is essentially untrue because it is saying that what governs the relationship of the prostitute to the man is absolute passivity, and that Firdaus as a prostitute never becomes excited or trembles with pleasure, nor does she experience pain or indeed any emotion at all.

In actual fact, despite the claims in the novel, Firdaus does become excited and is overwhelmed by such intense feelings of pleasure that she trembles. Again contrary to the book's claims, she not only gives but also takes. She gives men a corpse and in return she takes the essence of their masculinity. By her own admission, her whole body shakes with ecstatic violence almost to the point of pain at what she is taking from men:

The sun was shining brightly that day. I walked with a quick, energetic step, my right fist clenched tightly over something in my palm, something really valuable, not just a piastre this time, but a whole ten pound note. It was the first time I had held such a big note in my hand. As a matter of fact, it was the first time my fingers had even touched a note of that kind. The sudden contact sent a strange tautness through my body, an inner contraction as though something had jumped inside me and shaken my body with a violence which was almost painful. I felt as if something was pulsating out from a wound buried deep in my guts. When I stretched the muscles of my back, stood upright and breathed deeply it hurt. I could feel it rising up to my belly like a shiver, like blood beating strongly through the veins. The hot blood in my chest rose to my neck, swept through to my throat, to become a flow of warm, rich saliva, bringing with it a savour of pleasure, so strong, so poignant that it was almost bitter.

What is this magical 'thing' that makes the sun shine and suffuses the body with vitality and strength right down to the fingertips? What is this 'valuable thing' which, for the first time, attains such dimensions that when it touches the body it shakes it with a 'violence' that is 'almost painful', as if something is 'pulsating out from a wound buried deep in [the] guts'?

It is a banknote. That may very well be so, but ever since Freud discovered anal eroticism we have known that the equation *money = penis* is one of the principal symbolic equations governing the anal complex. It is Firdaus, not us, who wonders, 'Was it possible that a mere piece of paper could make such a change?' It is Firdaus, not us, who associates the banknote with the genitals and forbidden pleasure:

> The waiter was still standing upright by my side. His half-closed lids drooping over the eyes, his stealthy way of glancing aside were the same. I held the ten pound note in my hand, and he watched it through the corner of one eye, while his other eye looked away as though shunning the forbidden parts of a woman's body. I was seized with a feeling of wonder. Could it be that the ten pound note I held in my hand was as illicit and forbidden as the thrill of sacrilegious pleasure?

It is Firdaus, not us, who compares the secret of the banknote with that great riddle of life, the Sphinx. If man, like Oedipus, could only solve the riddle, he would be able to turn over the page and move on from his childlike prehistory to the beginning of his mature history:

> I ceased to bend my head or to look away. I walked through the streets with my head held high, and my eyes looking straight ahead... The rest of the ten pound note nestled safely in my pocket. My footsteps on the dark tarmac road struck the ground with force, with a new elation, like the elation of a child that has just pulled a toy to pieces and discovered the secret of how it works.

It is Firdaus, not us, who associates the ecstasy (let us call it 'phallocentrism') she comes to understand through the possession of the banknote with the ecstasy she knew as a child when she reached puberty, solved the riddle and for the first time was rewarded with a piastre by her father:

> It was as if he had lifted a veil from my eyes, and I was seeing for the first time.[14] The movement of my hand as I clasped the

ten pound note solved the enigma in one swift, sweeping movement, tore away the shroud that covered up a truth I had in fact experienced when I was a child, when for the first time my father gave me a piastre...

Why had I not realized this before? Was I really unaware of this throughout the years? No. Now that I thought about it I could see that I had known it for a very long time, right from the start, when I was born and opened my eyes to look at my father for the first time. All I could see of him was a fist, its fingers closed strongly over something in the palm of his hand. He never opened up his fingers, and even when he did, he always kept something behind in his hand.

Money is a symbol. And like all symbols, it speaks here on behalf of the subconscious. If any doubt remains, this will be dispelled by Firdaus herself some thirty pages further on. This woman who has lived a 'quarter of a century' before finally taking charge of her 'body' and her 'self' still has to fight one last battle to win the war. After the scales have fallen from her eyes and she has identified the secret of her father's piastre, there is another veil to rend. It is not enough for her to see: all men must be blinded. If they are still able to see, they will only see her as blind. Just as their sight is her blindness, so her sight should be their blindness:

With every movement he kept repeating the same stupid question:

'Do you feel pleasure?'

And I would close my eyes and say, 'Yes.'

...and just when he was on the point of repeating the same stupid question again, I snapped out angrily,

'No!'

When he held out his hand with the money, I was still wildly angry with him. I snatched the notes from his hand and tore them up into little pieces with a pent-up fury.

...The movement of my hands as I tore the money to pieces, tore off the veil, the last remaining veil from before my eyes, to reveal the whole enigma which had puzzled me throughout, the true enigma of my life. I rediscovered the truth I had already discovered many years before when my father held out his hand

Freud → money = penis

to me with the first piastre he had ever given me. I returned to
the money in my hand and with a redoubled fury tore the
remaining bank notes into shreds. It was as though I was
destroying all the money I had ever held, my father's piastre,
my uncle's piastre, all the piastres I had ever known, and at the
same time destroying all the men I had ever known, one after
the other in a row: my uncle, my husband, my father, Marzouk
and Bayoumi, Di'aa, Ibrahim, and tearing them all to pieces
one after the other, ridding myself of them once and for all,
removing every trace their piastres had left on my fingers...
ensuring that not a single vestige of these men would remain
at all.

This collective castration is accompanied by a 'massacre' on the
level of values. In the same way as the notion of 'value' in human
society (patriarchal since the beginnings of recorded history) is a
male, father-oriented value, the prostitute *qua* prostitute — that
is, as an embodiment of 'non-value' — represents a living denial
of the fatherhood of fathers and the manhood of men, at whatever
level of existence.

It is true that, taking other prostitutes as a model, the prostitute
is retrievable and can be reintegrated within the value system of
patriarchal society, given that she is considered a sort of 'safety
valve' for virtue. But taking Firdaus as an example, the prostitute
is scandal personified. It is the system which is flouted or, to be
more precise, it is the system which is violated as a system.

Some other women may be forced into prostitution by
circumstances. It is this pressure that perpetuates the value system
of patriarchal society, despite the partial violation represented by
the prostitute's behaviour. But Firdaus has chosen this profession
voluntarily, and by this choice she embodies the total violation of
the laws and value system of patriarchal society. She completely,
wilfully and consciously seeks to drain herself of 'the last drop of
sanctity in [her] blood'. Her total contamination is a sullying of
their 'heroism and nobility'. In this sense a prostitute such as
Firdaus, like Marx's proletarian, is stateless: 'I knew nothing about
patriotism... my country had not only given me nothing, but had
also taken away anything I might have had, including my honour
and my dignity.'

The value system of the patriarchy

But at the heart of this scandal and chaos, of this total denial of values and deliberate and total violation of the law, a new value is established — that of freedom. And a new joy bursts forth — that of non-belonging:

A gentle breeze was beckoning softly from the Nile. I walked along, enjoying the peace of the night... The gentle breeze caressing my face, the empty streets, and the rows of closed windows and doors, the feeling of being rejected by people and at the same time being able to reject them, the estrangement from everything, even the earth, and the sky and the trees. I was like a woman walking through an enchanted world to which she did not belong. She is free to do what she wants, and free not to do it. She experiences the rare pleasure of having no ties with anyone, of having broken with everything, of having cut all relations with the world around her, of being completely independent and living her independence completely, of enjoying freedom from any subjection to a man, to marriage or to love; of being divorced from all limitations whether rooted in rules and laws in time or in the universe.[15]

This joy is not difficult to interpret. The intrinsic value is not really harmed; it is left intact. There has merely been a change of value, a process of reacquisition. What once belonged to all fathers, all husbands and all men has become the monopoly of Firdaus. She has risen through their inferiority, transcended their degeneracy, acquired riches through their impoverishment, grown strong through their fragility and been honed fine through their nullity.

The Nile had something almost magical about it. The air was fresh, invigorating. I walked down the street, my head held high to the heavens, with the pride of having destroyed all masks to reveal what is hidden behind. My footsteps broke the silence with their steady rhythmic beat on the pavement... They were the footsteps of a woman who believed in herself, knew where she was going, and could see her goal...

No one would have easily recognized me... Perhaps they thought I was a princess, or a queen, or a goddess. For who would hold her head so high as she walked? And who else's footsteps could resound in this way as they struck the ground? They watched me as I passed by, and I kept my head high like a challenge to their lascivious eyes.

'A princess, a queen or a goddess'. Here we are still within the confines of the hierarchical values of patriarchal society. In fact we are at its summit, as is all too obvious. It may be difficult to deny Firdaus the description of 'militant', but it is also clear that her struggle is aimed at liberating not her female sisters, but herself. Despite her being a self-styled legislator for her sisters,[16] this elitist attitude is a point zero from which she began and a point zero at which she ends:

> And one day the whole school went out on the streets to join a big demonstration against the government. Suddenly I found myself riding high up on the shoulders of the girls shouting,
>   'Down with the government.'
>   When I got back to school my voice was hoarse, my hair in disarray, and my clothes were torn in several places, but all through the night I kept imagining myself as a great leader or head of state.
>   I knew that women did not become heads of state, but I felt that I was not like other women, nor like the other girls around me who kept talking about love, or about men... What seemed of importance to them struck me as being trivial.

Whatever the nature of the liberation struggle, the path of elitism is inevitably a dead-end, blocked by individualism and nihilism. In fact, when Firdaus imagines that she has finally regained her freedom and 'escaped men' by moving from the level of 'the enslaved prostitute' to that of the 'free prostitute', she is descended on by a new man who confronts her with a truth of which she has so far been unaware, namely that the law regulates even the alleged freedom of a prostitute, since all prostitutes have to have a pimp to protect them 'from other pimps, and from the police'.
  The only way out is through murder. Firdaus kills the 'dangerous pimp' whose very profession sums up 'the profession of all men'. After she has been sentenced to death, she refuses to

appeal for a pardon: 'If I go out once again to the life which is yours I will never stop killing. So what is the use of my sending an appeal... to be pardoned?'

In the annihilation of death, Firdaus tells us she has finally regained her freedom: 'I have triumphed over both life and death because I no longer desire to live, nor do I any longer fear to die. I want nothing. I hope for nothing. I fear nothing. Therefore I am free.' But regardless of her bravery, which makes her 'biographer' say, 'I felt ashamed of myself, of my life, of my fears, and my lies,' we may ask what sense there is in regaining one's freedom if a pre-condition is that one should desire nothing, hope for nothing, and that life and death are all the same.

This nihilistic asceticism may be one way of rejecting reality, but it is not the only way to change it. Firdaus's story is undoubtedly worth telling. However, presenting it as an individual, isolated case is one thing; and elevating it to the level of a theoretical issue is quite another. *Positing this Lifestyle as one means of attaining Freedom is a stretch*

Moreover, the narrator's theoretical rationalizations fail miserably to disguise Firdaus's neurotic bent. Neurosis can be defined as the lost ability to adjust to reality, whether positively or negatively, by accepting or rejecting it, perpetuating or changing it. Can we then imagine a more neurotic condition than that of a woman who chooses to be a prostitute and a murderess in order to wage a war of the sexes, reassert herself and win 'the crown of a princess' in a society of men?

The paradox is that the narrator of Firdaus's tale has placed herself in the role of 'psychiatrist'. In so doing, it is as if she were deliberately denying any possible psychological interpretation of Firdaus's condition. It is not Firdaus but society that is sick, we are told. Indeed, the psychiatrist herself feels as insignificant as an insect face to face with the supreme example of Firdaus:

> I went through difficult moments. It looked to me as though this woman... was a much better person than I. Compared to her, I was nothing but a small insect crawling upon the land amidst millions of other insects.

A far more coherent interpretation would have been as follows: Firdaus is a sick case in a sick society (or rather, in a society afflicted by many ills). However, the problem lies in the very logic of the rationalization itself. In order to deny one woman's illness (as if it were somehow wrong to single her out), 'millions of human beings' are put in the dock, having been reduced to the ranks of 'insects' which 'crawl' on the ground. This is a major pitfall for every individualistic philosophy, particularly when combined with an elitist attitude.

2
Memoirs
of a Woman Doctor

In spite of her 'biographer's' desire to identify with her, Firdaus is only superficially a heroine. In *Memoirs of a Woman Doctor*,[1] however, heroine and narrator become one. There is no longer any gap between them. The two merge when they speak. There is no need even for names. The events in this autobiographical novel are recounted in the first person without the mediation of a name: a name would only create a sort of 'distanciation' between author and narrator and one would no longer be the spokesperson of the other.

> The conflict between me and my femininity began very early on, before my female characteristics had become pronounced and before I knew anything about myself, my sex and my origins, indeed before I knew the nature of the cavity which had housed me before I was expelled into the wide world.

This sentence, typical of the world of Nawal el-Saadawi's heroines, not only opens the novel, but is also the key to understanding it. Despite all the subsequent ideological rationalizations which attempt to elevate the struggle against femininity to a social level, this opening salvo leaves us in no doubt that the struggle grinds on first and foremost (i.e. before any social considerations) on the biological or even the anatomical level.

It is clear that the struggle against socially determined femininity can only begin simultaneously with the acquisition of awareness. However, it is the narrator herself who tells us that, for her, the struggle began 'very early on', not only before the emergence of her femininity but before she could even tell the difference between 'the wide world' and the womb from which she had emerged.

The second key is provided in the following sentence: 'All I did know at that time was that I was a girl. I used to hear it from my mother all day long. "Girl!" she would call, and all it meant to me was that I wasn't a boy and I wasn't like my brother.'

Femininity for someone who struggles against it even before she is aware of its existence can hardly be seen as positive. It is definable only in negative terms, by what it is not. It is a deficiency or lack, 'an empty wound' in the words of one of Kafka's heroes, or 'the forbidden parts' as our glorious heritage tells us.

The result of this struggle, fought on the basis of defining something by its opposite, is a foregone conclusion. Deficiency never turns into its opposite — completeness. The wound will never heal. The girl who struggles to become a boy like her brother will no longer be a girl if she becomes like her brother. Her identity will always be usurped and her validity always judged by false criteria. She will always be referred to as something other than herself.

From start to finish, the struggle is futile. The one who is no longer a girl at the end of the struggle (assuming that such a struggle can have an end) can still only be defined in negative terms, similar to the one who is not a boy at the beginning. Negative identity in the case of sexual identity is a vicious circle: the opposite defines itself, not the reverse.

The third key is provided by the third sentence of the novel:

My brother's hair was cut short but otherwise left free and uncombed, while mine was allowed to grow longer and longer[2] and my mother combed it twice a day and twisted it into plaits and imprisoned the ends of it in ribbons and rubber bands.

My brother woke up in the morning and left his bed just as it was, while I had to make my bed and his as well.

My brother went out into the street to play without asking my parents' permission and came back whenever he liked, while I could only go out if and when they let me...

My brother played, jumped around and turned somersaults, whereas if I ever sat down and allowed my skirt to ride as much as a centimetre up my thighs, my mother would pierce me with a glance like an animal immobilizing its prey and I would cover up those shameful parts of my body.

The anatomical differences between the sexes here take on a glaring social significance. A male chauvinist society such as ours establishes a correlation between femininity and inferiority. But this social aspect of sexual inequality (which forms the basis of the conscious critical ideology of Nawal el-Saadawi, the author of *Woman and Sex*, *The Female is the Origin* and *Woman and Psychological Struggle*[3]) is not what occupies the attention of the heroine of *Memoirs*...

She lives this injustice, at least at the subconscious level, as a narcissistic castration, reiterating, magnifying and translating into the language of the conscious the imagined castration of the subconscious, at the level of the sex organs. Our evidence for this is that the heroine adopts to suit herself the very accusation of inferiority with which she identifies femininity in patriarchal society. Indeed, she does so to the extent of sadistic aggression.

She uses all sorts of ways and means to fabricate new calumnies, accusations and arguments to add to the dictionary of words demeaning women, a practice handed down and elaborated from one generation to the next. She does not come up with anything new when she says, 'I was filled with a great contempt for womankind: I had seen with my own eyes that women believed in worthless trivia. And in her turn she provides wounding images in her caricatures by announcing that she wants no part in 'the ranks of common women', 'the miserable world of women', 'the hateful, constricted world of women with its permanent reek of garlic and onions'.

By brutally severing her solidarity with members of her own sex, the heroine has, knowingly or unknowingly, established the framework of her struggle against her femininity. It is not a struggle against the social injustice which hierarchically legalizes and standardizes anatomical differences between the sexes: it is a struggle against anatomical destiny, against femininity as a physiological concept, against the natural law which deems that a human being is born, or behaves, as half-man and half-woman. In a word, it is a struggle that is against nature and not against society:

I locked myself in my room and cried. The first real tears I shed in my life weren't because I'd done badly at school or broken something valuable but because I was a girl. I wept over my femininity before I even knew what it was. The moment I opened my eyes on life, a state of enmity already existed between me and my nature.

A sadistic attitude towards members of a given sex is the obverse of a masochistic attitude towards oneself. The woman who sees members of her own sex as nothing but a common herd will, body and soul, stamp out both femininity and sex. Moreover, she will adopt the very attitudes towards her sexuality that patriarchal society adopts towards women in general. In other words, she will internalize oppression and end up becoming her own oppressor.

She will also adopt a fearful, guilty attitude towards some aspects of femininity, particularly menstruation. This brings to mind the attitudes of certain primitive tribes who used to isolate menstruating women, putting them in quarantine for the duration of their menstrual period, believing that the blood was taboo and seeing the woman as possessed by evil spirits until purified. Indeed, most religions have considered women to be unclean during menstruation.[4] Once our heroine is aware of her role in the 'bloody history of women', she puts herself in quarantine and voluntarily assumes that she is soiled and shamed, treating herself in the same way as outcasts in closed sectarian societies:

> Fear gripped my heart and I left the game. I ran back to the house and locked myself in the bathroom to investigate the secret of this grave event in private.
>
> I didn't understand it at all. I thought I must have been struck down by a terrible illness. I went to ask my mother about it in fear and trembling and saw laughter and happiness written all over her face. I wondered in amazement how she could greet this affliction with such a broad smile...
>
> I took to my room for four days running.[5] I couldn't face my brother, my father or even the house-boy. I thought they must all have been told about the shameful thing that had happened to me: my mother would doubtless have revealed my

new secret. I locked myself in, trying to come to terms with this strange phenomenon. Was this unclean procedure the only way for girls to reach maturity? Could a human being really live for days at the mercy of involuntary muscular activity?[6] God must really hate girls to have tarnished them with this curse. I felt that God had favoured boys in everything.

The text here reveals all. It is not the social reaction to menstruation that has caused the girl's terrible shock. On the contrary, the mother receives the news of 'the terrible affliction' with laughter and rejoicing. It is the girl herself, ashamed of being female, refusing to be female, or rather of collapsing under the burden of the fear of being female, who chooses to isolate herself for four days and who judges the matter for herself, voluntarily accepting it as taboo, 'unclean' and 'shameful'.

The explanation behind this episode probably lies in the sentence in which she says, 'My mother would doubtless have revealed my new secret.' Femininity is a secret, and one which must be closely guarded; any revelation is a scandal. Menstruation is a scandal precisely because it announces to everyone that the girl, deny it as she may, is a girl. It is a scandal because it brings her face to face with the fact that she is a girl, despite the fact that during her period of hiding, she denies this to herself and others.

In fact menstruation *is* a scandal, not to others but to oneself. Throughout her period of hiding, this girl convinced herself that she was not a girl, and that she could play with the boys in the street in the same way as they played, running as fast as they could and jumping as high as they did. Yet here she is faced with the fact that her femininity is a physiological fate, a fate branded into her body, in her very flesh, ineradicable and inevitable.

But is this the end of the great denial? It would be more correct to say that it is the beginning. Before puberty, the girl does not feel the anatomical differences between the sexes so strongly. After puberty, however, they can no longer be hidden. The female's battle against her femininity becomes much fiercer when this femininity is out in the open rather than hidden.

This war becomes so ferocious that all the criteria are reversed. Let us take the example of the breasts. When a girl develops breasts — or 'mounds', to use the expression adopted by the heroine of

Memoirs... — she usually sees them as a source of pride or as
providing important narcissistic compensation. The word
'compensation' here may appear abhorrent. So it should. But
unfortunately, in our patriarchal society, it is of real significance.
Our calculating society translates 'possessions' into 'value' and
distinguishes selfishly between 'what is mine' and 'what is yours',
indeed it establishes a hierarchical ranking order between 'to possess
and not to possess'.[7] In such a society, the male merely by being
male feels superior to the female because he 'has' and she 'has not'.

Similarly, the female feels that merely by being female she is
inferior to the male because she 'has not' while he 'has'. As soon
as the day of puberty dawns and the girl sprouts two 'mounds',
however, she will be able, in her turn, to say 'I also have,' indeed
to rebut the boys by saying, 'I may not have what you have, but
neither do you have what I have.'

This narcissistic compensation is what the heroine of *Memoirs...*
emphatically rejects. The rejection is not only motivated by the
negative overtones of the word 'compensation'. Nor is it a rejection
of the calculating logic of patriarchal bourgeois society. She simply
refuses because she sees the growth of her breasts as another sign of
inferiority, another attempt at exposing femininity and what she
considers to be its shame:

> I got up... and dragged myself over to the mirror and looked
> at the two little mounds sprouting on my chest. If only I could
> die! I didn't recognize this body which sprang a new shame on
> me every day, adding to my weakness and my preoccupation
> with myself. What would grow on my body next? What other
> new symptom would my tyrannical femininity break out in?

She is not only a female who wants to be equal to the male;
she also wants to *be* male. Thus, in the final analysis, she is a
female who does not wish to be female. Her breasts are no longer
the object of narcissistic pride. On the contrary, they are the source
of a new narcissistic wound. It is not a sign that she is equal and
that this equality must be proclaimed but, on the contrary, another
pointer to a diminished identity which must be hidden:

> I hated them, these two protrusions, these two lumps of flesh

which were determining my future! How I wished I could cut them off with a sharp knife! But I couldn't. All I could do was hide them by flattening them with a tight corset.

She then reiterates the theme of the breasts, this time using the analogy of hair. For the female in patriarchal society, long hair is usually another source of narcissistic compensation. For the heroine of *Memoirs...*, however, it merely represents one more of those resented distinctive features, a mark or stamp of disgrace:

The heavy long hair I carried around everywhere on my head held me up in the morning, got in my way in the bath and made my neck burning hot in summer. Why wasn't it short and free like my brother's? His didn't weigh his head down or hinder his activities...

For the first time in my life I left the house without asking my mother's permission. My heart was pounding as I went down the street, though my provocative act had given me a certain strength. As I walked, a sign caught my eye: 'Ladies Hairdresser'. I had only a second's hesitation before going in.

I watched the long tresses squirm in the jaws of the sharp scissors and then fall to the ground. Were these what my mother called a woman's crowning glory? Could a woman's crown fall shattered to the ground like this because of one moment of determination? I was filled with a great contempt for womankind: I had seen with my own eyes that women believed in worthless trivia. This contempt gave me added strength. I walked back home with a firm step and stood squarely in front of my mother... I looked in the mirror and smiled at my short hair, the light of victory in my eyes.

For the first time in my life I understood the meaning of victory...

But the heroine's self-oppression does not extend to the aspects and symbols of femininity alone but also has to reach its essence, that is as a sexual function. Sex is a natural, functional and pleasurable activity deriving from the instinct to reproduce and founded on the different but complementary aspects of the two sexes. Sexual activity, in both the human and the ideal sense, implies that the woman accepts herself as the object of the man's desire and that the man accepts himself as the object of her desire.

This is not only the law of nature but the law of man as a bipolar, bisexual creature — a male and a female. Unless we reduce man to absolute narcissism or reduce him to the level of a worm whose head copulates with its tail, there is no other path than Plato's definition of love as being the yearning of the two halves of man to unite. But this complementary nature of the two halves implies a mutual recognition of the distinction of the other. It is on the basis of this mutual recognition that the act of love is founded and in which the two halves achieve the highest possible degree of union.

It is precisely here that the tragedy of the heroine of *Memoirs...* lies. Here we have a female who denies her femininity, a female who does not want to see herself as female through the mirror of the male, a being who cannot participate in the act of love, at least in its qualitative or complementary sense. This does not mean that such a female is without desire, but only that whatever desire she has must be repressed. Our heroine never tries to hide the fact that repressing her desire has become a routine practice:

Still panting, I looked up at him and saw him staring at me in a funny way which made the blood rush to my cheeks. I watched his arm reach out in the direction of my waist...

I was convulsed by a strange violent trembling. For a moment which passed like lightning through my feelings, I wished he would stretch out his arm further and hold me tight, but then this odd secret desire was transformed into a wild fury.

My anger only made him more persistent and he held on to me with an iron grip. I don't know where I got the strength, but I threw off his arm and it flailed in the air while I brought my hand down across his face.

The repression we read about in the text (or which the text makes us read into it) is not the kind of objective repression which is imposed upon the sexuality of women and their more intimate desires by fathers or men in patriarchal male society. It is self-repression chosen from within. It is the repression of a female who hated being female. I felt as if I was in chains — chains forged from my own blood... and produced by the cells of my own body, chains of shame and humiliation. I turned in on myself to cover up my miserable existence.'

It is the repression of a female who wants to base her right to equality not on the basis of being different but on the basis of her being identical with the male. To her, being a man's equal means being his equivalent. But a female who wants to be a man denies herself *a priori* the right to belong to herself and to be what she is. If human beings deny themselves the right to be what they are, then what is the sense of equality or the right to equality? Equality between two beings presupposes the existence of those two beings. If their very existence is denied, between whom is this equality to be established?

Who is talking about equality anyway? The female in *Memoirs...* denies her right to distinctiveness and wants nothing to replace it but 'identicality': this is because she demands not only equality but superiority. Her refusal to be a woman is not in order to prove that she is a man: she wants to be a 'better' man and to *prove* that she is a better man:

> I would prove to my mother and grandmother that I wasn't a woman like them... I was going to show my mother that I was more intelligent than my brother.... than any man, and that I could do everything my father did and more.

This comparative stance, with all its elitist overtones, almost constitutes in itself a plan of action, even a plan bordering on the infinite. Indeed, our heroine announces in the introduction to her plan that her horizon is fixed on infinity: 'It seemed to me that whatever heights I reached, I wouldn't be content, the flame burning within me wouldn't be extinguished.'

In the final analysis, however, the question is not one of logic or differential calculus; it is a question of struggle. A woman who has decided to repress her sexuality in order not to be a woman, or in order to prove that she is not a woman, is first and foremost a woman embarking on a constant, continuous and ceaseless struggle. (This is because continuous renewal is in the nature of desire, much as the skin of the denizens of hell is continually scorched by the fires.) Every time a particular desire is repressed, it is replaced by another. It is like the phoenix rising from the ashes. (If the way to fulfil a desire is blocked, the desire will inevitably find another outlet.) If its flames are extinguished in the conscious, it will be rekindled in the cauldron of the subconscious. If it is prevented from any form of expression, it erupts as a neurosis:

I pulled the covers tightly over my head to shut out my strange dream but it crept back, so I put the pillow over my head and pressed it down as hard as I could to suffocate the stubborn ghost, until sleep finally overtook me.

I opened my eyes the following morning. The sunlight had chased away the darkness and all the phantoms that prowled in its shadows. I opened the window and the fresh air blew in, scattering the last dying traces of the night's dreams. I smiled scornfully at the cowardly part of me which trembled with fear at the stronger part when I was awake, but then crept into my bed at night and filled the darkness around me with fantasies and illusions.

But the struggle against the desire for self-renewal is not only continuous but recurrent. Its recurrence is proof of its compulsion and also of its futility. Doesn't our heroine liken it to a daily, or rather nightly, bickering with phantoms: 'The nights grew longer as the fantasies and illusions gathered round my bed.'

Even the word 'phantom' seems inappropriate. Although it can perhaps be used to mean those desires which one cannot quite put one's finger on, or which cannot totally be repressed, it cannot express the strength of the desire. Later on, this forces our heroine to talk not about 'phantoms' or 'illusions' but about 'the giant asleep in [her] depths'.

A woman who, in order not to be a woman, or in order to prove that she is not a woman, has decided to repress all desire and individual identity is, moreover, a woman who by her own choice has sentenced herself to exile from pleasure. Desire is one of our most natural needs, and its satisfaction is an abundant source of pleasure and joy. (To repress sexuality or bury it alive is a futile exercise in asceticism.)

A life stripped of the principles of pleasure (with all that pleasure represents as a liberating experience) is one in which every passing leaves a sigh and the future holds no promise. From it we inherit only the bitterness of the self. Such a life can only be filled with hatred, not with love. It is here that the heroine of *Memoirs...* feels that her life has been merely a series of burnt bridges: 'My childhood was over, a brief, breathless childhood. I'd scarcely been aware of it before it was gone, leaving me with a mature woman's body carrying deep inside it a ten-year-old child.'

These words about her childhood as she stands on the threshold of adolescence will be repeated when talking about her adolescence as she stands on the brink of adulthood:

Twenty-five years of my life had passed without my feeling what it was to be a woman. My heart hadn't once beaten faster because of a man, nor had my lips tasted that wondrous thing known as a kiss. I hadn't passed through the glowing heat of adolescence. My childhood had been wasted fighting against my mother, my brother and myself. Textbooks had consumed my adolescence and the dawn of my womanhood. And so here I was, a child of twenty-five...

But a woman who, in order not to be a woman, or in order to prove that she is not a woman, has decided to repress her desires and sexuality, is not only a woman who has decided that her entire life should be a battlefield. She has also, essentially, sentenced herself unknowingly to fight battles she is destined to lose.

The odds are against her from the start. The entire deal is spurious. A woman who has decided to bury her sexuality alive is someone who has, so to speak, decided to live without sex organs. And here is the vicious circle: a human being struggling against an imaginary castration complex by actually behaving as if castrated. Moreover, castration is a direct result of the sadism of others, while the person who imagines himself to be castrated suffers from this condition due to his own masochism.

The imaginary castration complex[10] defines a type of behaviour which largely repeats the behaviour of the child. In a society of 'uniqueness', of superlative forms, and where possession is taken to mean identity, the child feels the absence of all those characteristics which others have but he himself does not: he feels this absence as a narcissistic wound. What the child, the narcissistic being *par excellence*, does possess is an organic extension of himself. What is possessed by others, and not by him, is an inferior amputated organ of his own body.

It is here that childish jealousy takes on such dimensions that adults are surprised. The child is not content with showing blatant hostility, full of envy, towards those who possess what he does not; he actually tries to strip them of their possessions in order to impound and repossess them for himself. If he fails in this attempt, he resorts to revenge: he inflicts on them an injury which is equivalent to the injury they inflicted on him, albeit unintentionally.

This spirit of revenge, born of unsatisfied envy and jealousy,[11] sheds light on the infantilism that governs the behaviour of the heroine of *Memoirs...* Even after she has bidden childhood farewell and moved from adolescence to maturity, the feeling remains that she is still a baby wrapped inside the skin of 'a mature woman's body'. This is because the child that she was has never had the opportunity to satisfy its desires, and an unsatisfied desire is an eternal desire. It is a call which echoes until it finds a response. It is the spirit of the slain which hovers in the atmosphere until revenge is wreaked.

There is one difference, however. The desire which is not satisfied in childhood, and around which the whole personality revolves, becomes a rapacious desire that cannot be satisfied.[12] Any future satisfaction will be only partial. It constantly renews itself, with increasing violence. In other words, an unsatisfied desire turns into a force of nature which, as Napoleon said, is destiny. Our heroine herself sums up her nature as follows: 'I began to search constantly for weak spots in males to console me for my sense of powerlessness, derived from the fact of being female.'

In a sense, her life at the approach of adolescence and throughout her youth and maturity will only be a repetition of the game she played as a child:

I no longer went out in the street... I fled from those strange creatures with harsh voices and moustaches, the creatures they called men. I created an imaginary private world for myself in which I was a goddess and men were stupid, helpless creatures at my beck and call. I sat on my high throne in this world of mine, arranging the dolls on chairs, making the boys sit on the floor and telling stories to myself.

When she finishes secondary school 'top of her class' and sits down to think about her future, she finds all her thoughts turning towards medicine. But why medicine in particular? Perhaps because medicine is a 'terrible thing' that could become a tool of revenge in her hands:

The faculty of medicine? Yes, medicine... The word had a terrifying effect on me. It reminded me of penetrating eyes moving at an amazing speed behind shiny steel-rimmed spectacles, and strong pointed fingers holding a dreadful long sharp needle. I remembered the first time I'd ever seen a doctor: my mother was trembling with fright, looking up at him beseechingly and reverently; my brother was terrified; my father was lying in bed begging for help. Medicine was a terrifying thing. I would become a doctor then, study medicine, wear shiny steel-rimmed spectacles, make my eyes move at an amazing speed behind them, and make my fingers strong and pointed to hold the dreadful long sharp needle.[13] I'd make my mother tremble with fright and look at me reverently; I'd make my brother terrified and my father beg me for help.

When she goes into the dissecting room for the first time and stands before a man's corpse with a scalpel in her hand, she has none of those feelings which a normal human being experiences at a scene of death, or faced by a corpse. She feels neither fear, pity nor disgust. Indeed her thoughts do not go as far as death or man's inevitable fate as represented by the body. Instead she experiences feelings of hatred, gloating and revenge, not towards the corpse itself but towards the man it entombs:

This was my first encounter with a naked man, and in the course of it men lost their dread power and illusory greatness in my eyes. A man had fallen from his throne and lain on the dissecting table... naked, ugly and in pieces. I hadn't imagined that life would... give me my revenge in this way over that miserable man who'd looked at my breasts one day and not seen anything

else of me besides them. Here I was slinging his arrows straight
back into his chest. Here I was looking at his naked body and
feeling nauseated, tearing him to shreds with my scalpel.

Was this a man's body, the outside covered with hair and
the inside full of decaying stinking organs, his brain floating in
a sticky white fluid and his heart in thick red blood? How ugly
man was, both inside and out, as ugly as could be![14]

But the corpse of the man is not yet the man himself. Tearing
at it with her scalpel may provide an outlet for her feelings of
hatred, but it remains a symbolic, revengeful act of castration, or
rather an act of substitution. Nevertheless, this way of treating the
body provides a pattern for treating men: every man must be
reduced to a corpse while he is still alive. This means stripping
him not of life but of his identity as a man, in a word of his
manhood.

Without his manhood, a man is but a corpse. And as his
manhood is only meaningful in relation to the woman's femininity,
the only recourse left to the woman, if she is intent on turning
men into corpses, is to refrain from being a woman. This is the
secret behind our heroine's choosing wilfully and consciously to
let twenty-five years of her life pass without ever once 'feeling
what it was to be a woman', without her heart ever once 'beating
faster because of a man'.

It is not difficult to see this indifference to men repeated in a
negative form and performing the same function as that of the
prostitute's frigidity in *Woman at Point Zero*. In *Memoirs...* the
relationship, or rather the non-relationship, which brings together
the medical student and the professor is a blueprint for any
relationship the heroine may have with a man. The up-and-coming
young doctor accepts the professor's invitation to his house. She
goes there despite having seen the lust in his eyes, or perhaps
because of it. She goes not in order to respond to this desire but
in order to kill it. She lets him delude himself into thinking that
she is an easy prey, about to fall into his trap.

When he comes near enough for his 'hot breath' to 'sting' her
face, she backs away. He comes after her 'on his hands and knees'.
She stands up and keeps her distance. With a sense of triumph
reminiscent of Firdaus in *Woman at Point Zero* when talking about

the stupidity of men asking her continually 'Do you feel pleasure?' the heroine of *Memoirs...* asks:

> What was going on? Why did a man crumble in the face of his desire? Why did his willpower vanish the minute he was shut in with a woman so that he turned into a wild animal on four legs? Where was his power? Where was his strength? Where were his authority and qualities of leadership?

She is not content to play the role of Delilah cutting off Samson's hair:[15] she has to reduce him to the level of his desire and turn him into an animal, thus keeping a monopoly on human superiority for herself. After thus killing two birds with one stone, she feels too superior even to deign to take part in 'the battle between men and women':

> I looked at him, at his eyes, his fingers and his toes. I turned the searchlights of my gaze on him and looked closely into the depths of his heart and mind only to find hollow, empty wastes, a shallow mind and a false heart... I looked at him with pity and contempt. I felt sorry for him so I withdrew from the confrontation, despising myself for having considered a fight with someone so much weaker than me.

She feels superior only because he is 'weaker' than her. And when she chooses the first man in her life to be her husband, her choice is dictated by the fact that he is weaker than her. The only qualification possessed by the man who has called her to treat his dying mother is 'an expression of weakness and need'. His 'weak, beseeching glances failed to arouse [her] femininity'. But in return, they 'aroused [her] maternal instincts'. He is not a man, nor is he looking for a wife. He is a child, 'an orphan child', looking for a mother. He calls her quite openly 'Mummy', and tells her that after his mother's death 'the world seemed empty... but I found you and it was full again'.

Although the word 'Mummy', by her own admission, 'sounded out-of-place and incongruous coming out from under his thick luxuriant moustache', she feels that his need for her draws her closer to him, uniting them. She 'looked at him tenderly'. Quickly and easily she accepts the roles of mother and child between them, as this means that he will not be a man, nor she a wife. A man who adopts this passive, child-like, indeed effeminate attitude towards his wife is the only type of man she can accept as a husband because he is the only man who will not require her to be a 'wife'. 'My husband! These words which I'd never spoken before! What did they mean to me?'[16]

Despite all these protestations, and the realization that she is marrying a man who is weaker than her, indeed 'a small baby' who by his weakness confirms her strength, and who by the pathetic look in his eyes satisfies her overwhelming desire for superiority, she feels from the moment she signs the marriage contract as if she has 'signed her death warrant'.

As soon as he becomes a husband, the man starts to demand a husband's rights: 'The look of weakness and need was gone from his eyes and the thread that had been binding me to him was severed.' From a little baby he changes into a man. He sees himself as a man with the attributes of a man: 'a deep voice, a bushy moustache... a hard, rough hand'. When his manhood eventually blossoms, he becomes unrecognizable: 'Who was this stranger beside me? Who was this lump of flesh I called my husband?'

In fact as soon as his manhood blossoms, the 'babyishness and naivety' vanish from his eyes and he begins to project a new and despicable image, that of the anal man, heir to the base father on whom the hatred pertaining to the anal-sadistic phase has been fixated in the phase of pre-sexual organization:

A hefty body, taking up half the bed. A gaping mouth which never stopped eating. Two flat feet which dirtied socks and sheets. A thick nose which kept me awake all night long with its snorting and whistling... How could I live with him?

She does not. Instead, by a daring decision that is true to herself but surprising to others, and indeed arouses their indignation, she leaves her husband. She becomes 'free... completely free! ...For the first time in my life, a heavy burden was lifted from my heart, the burden of living in a house shared by others.'

A question poses itself. Here we have a man who is passive, babyish, dependent and looking for a mother in a woman. If it is impossible for him to behave like a human being without sex organs, then how is it *possible* for an active, lively, self-reliant woman like the heroine of *Memoirs...* to do so? It is more logical to assume the contrary and say that the strength of the desire to live without sexuality and with people without sex organs betrays a strength and not a weakness in terms of the functioning of the sex organs.

The heroine of *Memoirs...* tells us frankly that no sooner has she regained her independence than, 'The spectre which had haunted the nights of my youth began to visit me again. The nights grew longer and the bed wider. Solitude no longer seemed attractive.' In fact, as we have seen, she herself tells us not about a spectre but about 'a giant sleeping in her depths'. Will this giant stop being a giant once imprisoned in a cell? Isn't the opposite more true — that the imprisoned giant will be more volatile than the free giant?[17]

But if the road to homosexuality is blocked by this 'giant' under the pretext that 'femininity is fettered and servile', and if the way to heterosexuality is similarly blocked under the pretext that the male is intolerably 'haughty and arrogant', then how can the giant erupt? Unquestionably through the medium of narcissistic sexuality. When it lacks interest in the object, the libido regresses towards the self. If the road to others, whether homosexually or heterosexually, is blocked, the only possible escape route is that to the ego. The energy which is not utilized outside is utilized within. The sexual pleasure which is repressed will bear narcissistic fruit.

However, despite inflation being the first principle which governs the egoistical world of the narcissists, the source of 'narcissistic nourishment' remains the outside world. Narcissism, unless it lapses into hallucination, does not negate the objective relationship with the outside world. On the contrary, it demands it. It is impossible to conceive of Narcissus without his mirror. The outside world is this mirror, that is, the source of social values without which the driving element of an exaggerated self-estimation (which is narcissism) becomes non-functional.

This is the secret behind the great transition of the heroine of *Memoirs...* from the biological and psychological sphere to the sociological. This woman who perceives her femininity as wanting and as a blow to her narcissism has no choice but to embark on a compensatory war in the external world. Through social transformation, anatomy will no longer be predestined and the struggle against it will no longer be some form of hallucination.

This is what she means when she says, 'The struggle in my depths has gone beyond the limits of femininity vs masculinity to include humanity in its entirety.' This is the far-reaching significance of what she terms her battle with 'society at large'. Her life must be made up of 'a series of endless battles' and she must fight 'a new battle' every day, otherwise her reserves of narcissistic sustenance will run out.

We can see immediately that the narcissism of this permanent battle is defined not only by its goal but also by what we will call its morphology. To begin with, it is a battle 'against' society, not 'for' it. The battlefield is the only thing which is social. Its goal, however, is not concealed nor does it conceal its egoistic membership: 'I would fight, looking to myself for protection, looking to my strength, my knowledge, my success in my work.'

What is more remarkable about this battle, however, is that it is waged along legendary-heroic lines. The heroine not only feels that it is beneath her to fight someone weaker than herself, but the urge to exaggerate her narcissistic self-worth pushes her to the extreme of fighting only those who allow her to stand 'all alone against the entire city'. But a magnified opponent acts as a magnifying glass for the person who fights: 'Here I was up against a new [battle] with society at large: millions of people, with millions more in front and behind.' The enemy is not only numerically superior, it also possesses superior resources:

The battle between a man and a woman: that odd, artificial contest in which the woman faces the man alone, but the man stands barricaded by tradition, laws and creeds, backed up by generations and aeons of history, and row upon row of men, women and children, all with sharp tongues extended like the blades of a sword, eyes aimed like gunbarrels and mouths blazing away like machine-guns. [18]

In such an unequal battle, the only way a woman can win is to rely on her own inner strength:

I felt stronger than him in spite of the barricades he dragged along with him, the barriers he surrounded himself with, the armoury supporting him. I didn't need any of this: my strength was inside me, in my being.

To dispel any confusion which might belittle narcissistic omniscience, this inner strength is characterized as being totally wanton, free of all relationships. It is to be looked at in isolation even from 'work', seen by most feminists as women's primary strength in the battle for liberation.[19]

He'd reached the conclusion that it was my work which endowed me with the strength that prevented him controlling me. He thought that the money I earnt each month... was what made me hold my head up high. He didn't realize that my strength wasn't because I had a job, nor was my pride because I had my own income, but both were because I didn't have the psychological need for him that he did for me. I didn't have this need for my mother, my father or anyone else because I wasn't dependent on anyone, whereas he'd been dependent on his mother, then had begun to replace her with me.[20]

Narcissistic utilization not only takes the self as object, but also includes all its extensions and tools. The heroine of *Memoirs...* chooses the path of medicine to overcome the 'powerlessness' imposed on her 'by the fact of being female'; scientific knowledge allows her to metamorphose into 'a mighty, powerful god who knows the secrets of everything'. For when she decides to 'face society on feet of iron', challenge its traditions and customs and practise abortion counter to its laws, she does not get hanged or stoned as she has expected, but turns her surgery into a spectacular place to demonstrate her inner powers:

My surgery filled up with men, women and children and my coffers with money and gold. My name became as famous as that of a movie star and my opinions circulated among people as though they were law. Strangers suddenly claimed a relationship with me, enemies became friends and confidants. Men swarmed round me like flies and their attacks turned into a defence of my position and gestures of support. The drawers of my desk filled up with testimonials, requests and pleas for help.

I sat on my lofty peak looking down on society at my feet. I smiled at it pityingly. Society — that mighty monster which seized women by the scruff of the neck and flung them into kitchens, abattoirs, graves or the filthy mire — was lying in my desk drawers, weak, subdued and hypocritically begging for mercy. How small mighty society looked now!

And what of love, defined by philosophers as the melting of one self into another, and seen as a breaking up of the narcissistic siege around the human being? The objective choice which imposes itself on the heroine of *Memoirs...* is the narcissistic one. An 'ego going it alone', like that of this particular heroine, is incapable of loving and can only be loved narcissistically. She is unique in this huge universe; her soulmate must also be unique among 'the million millions' who make it up. It is here that the search for a love object by such an ego becomes something akin to an epic:

I decided to search for him everywhere: in palaces and caves, in nightclubs and monasteries, in the factories of science and the temples of art, in bright lights and in pitch dark, on lofty summits and down deep chasms, in bustling cities and in wild deserted forests.

In the jungle of the millions upon millions of ordinary human beings the extraordinary man is to be found:

I left the crush and stood in a quiet corner. I half turned and found a man standing there. An ordinary man wearing ordinary clothes and standing in an ordinary way. He was neither short nor tall, thin nor fat, but I felt that something out of the ordinary hung about him.

Naturally this extraordinary man is an artist: a musician who is frustrated by the fact that the public is appreciative of those of his works with which he is dissatisfied and uncomprehending of those he is pleased with. In the mirror of this extraordinary man, in the deep pool of his 'unfathomable' eyes, she sees herself as an extraordinary woman, a unique human being. Does he not tell her, 'I've never met a woman like you before'? And does he not couple these words with action, or rather with inaction, when the man within him refrains from acknowledging the woman in her?

He was talking to me, looking into my eyes all the time. I never once saw him stare at my thighs or glance stealthily at my breasts. We were alone. The four walls closed around us. But I didn't feel that he was seeing the walls or feeling them. He was on another plane and I was beside him in flesh and blood. Yet I never felt he was addressing my body. He was directing himself to my heart and mind.

I closed my eyes, feeling calm and secure.

Yes, indeed! When she is secure in the knowledge that she is not a woman like all others and he is not a man like millions of others, and after she has thus reached the peak of narcissistic satiety, she is content for the general law applicable to all men and women to be applicable to her too. For the first time in her life, after thirty years, she understands the meaning of love: 'He held me close and embraced me until all my being melted into his and his whole existence was lost in mine.' Is this an unexpectedly happy ending? We would have said so were there not more to add in our analysis of the novel.

Erich Fromm holds the view that a minimum amount of narcissism maintains life and a maximum destroys it. *Memoirs of a Woman Doctor* actually seems to be governed by two alternating themes, love of life and love of death. And since it is in the nature of living to tend towards a continued existence, as Spinoza maintains, we may assume that love of life is primary, while love of death is secondary. The essence of existence is to be alive and to stay alive. It is only at a later stage that death materializes, whether involuntarily or by choice.

In *Memoirs...*, moreover, life appears to be the root, and death the branch. In other words, love of life is nearer to a biological phenomenon, while love of death is closer to a psychological phenomenon. This is the very crux of the struggle depicted in the novel: the biological versus the psychological. The heroine's

Biological vs psychological

biological destiny has cast her as a female. On the other hand, her psychological destiny, which she herself has chosen, is to prove that she is not female. It is here that life becomes a constant war against her nature. But isn't a war against nature also a war against life?

What is nature or, to avoid confusion, what is instinct? More precisely, what is sexuality? It is the capacity of life for life, and even though bipolar, male and female, this is only so that there may be mutual attraction and union. It is no coincidence, as Fromm says, that nature has made the union of these two poles a source of the most intense ecstasy. As a result of this union, a new creature is born, and nature, like life, is partial to reproduction. In fact the female in *Memoirs...* who rejects her biological destiny until death, seems not only to be rejecting her femininity but also the force of life itself: she wants no part of union; she passionately hates men, and if it was left to her, she would kill them;[21] and she does not want the experience of birth and hates motherhood *per se*. She has this to say about her mother's childbearing:

> Why did [giving birth to me] give her some special merit? She went about her normal life like any other woman and conceived me involuntarily in a random moment of pleasure. I'd arrived without her knowing or choosing me, and without my choosing her. We'd been thrust arbitrarily on one another as mother and daughter. Could any human being love someone who'd been forced upon them? And if my mother loved me instinctively in spite of herself, what credit did that do her? Did it make her any better than a cat which sometimes loves its kittens and sometimes devours them?

She returns to the analogy of the cat to generalize on the motherhood of all women: 'How could... a woman with your intelligence and learning waste her life breastfeeding like an illiterate peasant, or worse, like cats and dogs?'

Finally, she rejects the idea of reproduction. She hates society. She hates its 'vastness'. In particular, she hates its being made up of 'millions of people, with millions more in front and behind'.[22] In fact it is not difficult to discern, in this tripartite programme she sets herself, a charter for death and not for life, governed by the law of Thanatos and not the law of Eros:

> What could I do, given that I hated my femininity, resented my
> nature and wanted nothing to do with my body? All that was
> left for me was denial, challenge, resistance! I would deny my
> femininity, challenge my nature, resist all my body's desires.

What gives us pause for thought this time is not the anal–sadistic
significance (hatred, revenge, denial, challenge) in the programme,
but the ultimate stance it reveals: the practice of death, or more
precisely, putting to death. Desires which can be repressed are
desires which can be stifled: 'I put the pillow over my head and
pressed it down as hard as I could to suffocate the stubborn ghost,
until sleep finally overtook me.'

A body which is resisted is a body imprisoned and condemned
to death:

> I'd prove to nature that I could overcome the disadvantages
> of the frail body she'd clothed me in, with its shameful parts both
> inside and out. I would imprison it in the steel cell forged
> from my will and my intelligence.[23] I wouldn't give it a single
> chance to drag me into the ranks of illiterate women.
> ...I had charted my way in life, the way of the mind. I had
> carried out the death sentence on my body so that I no longer
> felt it existed.

If femininity is so despised, then death is the only alternative.
She looks at the 'two little mounds sprouting on my chest. If only
I could die!' If long hair is a distinctive feature of such femininity,
let it be cropped with 'sharp scissors', let that 'woman's crowning
glory fall shattered to the ground' and let the locks fall into a 'filthy
bin along with other unwanted bodily matter and scraps of flesh'.
And if her remaining distinctive features are two breasts, let these
also be rooted out with a 'sharp knife'. If this proves to be
impossible, let them be flattened by a 'tight corset'. Nothing could
be sweeter than the sight of these two lumps of flesh 'shrivelled
and dried up like a piece of old shoe leather'.

Hasn't medicine itself been chosen as a profession because it
allows the practitioner the opportunity to face death daily and

stand day and night on the threshold between life and death? And doesn't this obsession with death reach its climax precisely in the dissecting room of the faculty of medicine?

I stood at the door of the dissecting room: a surprisingly penetrating smell... naked human corpses on white marble slabs. My feet carried me in fearfully. I went up to one of the naked corpses and stood beside it. It was a man's body, completely naked. The students around me were looking at me, smiling slyly and waiting to see what I would do... I turned my gaze back to the man's corpse and examined it steadily and unflinchingly...

Would my mother ever believe that I'd stood with a naked man in front of me and a knife in my hand, and opened up his stomach and his head?

If death can be defined as a regression from human to animalistic behaviour, doesn't the world of medicine and dissection exert an irresistible attraction since it is precisely a world in which man is reduced to an animal?

A vast new world opened up before me. At first I was apprehensive, but I soon got a taste for it as the fever of knowledge gripped me. Science revealed the secrets of human existence to me... and proved to me that women were like men and men like animals. A woman had a heart, a nervous system and a brain exactly like a man's, and an animal had a heart, a nervous system and a brain exactly like a human being's. There were no essential differences between them...

I was delighted with this new world which placed men, women and the animals side by side...

And if the definition of death is of a dynamism reduced to mechanics, does not, then, the world of medicine and anatomy have its own irresistible allure precisely because it is a world in which the living body is reduced to a set of machine parts and reflexes?

The body of a living person lost all respect and dignity and became exactly like a dead body under my gaze and my searching fingers, and disintegrated in my mind into a jumble of organs and dismembered limbs.

And if the definition of death is that that which is organic becomes inorganic and that which is composite disintegrates — a secret that can no longer be hidden — then surely the world of medicine holds an irresistible fascination precisely because it is a world in which secrets are laid bare, compounds are dissolved and the organic body becomes inorganic, emptied of movement and life:

Human beings appeared to be insignificant creatures in spite of their muscles, their brain cells and the complexity of their arterial and nervous systems. A small microbe, invisible to the naked eye, could be breathed in through the nose and eat away at the cells of the lungs. An unidentifiable virus could strike at random and make the cells of the liver or spleen or any other part of the body multiply at a crazy rate and devour everything around them... A single drop of blood could clot in one of the brain cells and result in paralysis... One random air bubble could infiltrate the bloodstream by accident and the body would become a motionless corpse like a stinking, putrefying dog or horse.

This arrogant, proud and mighty man, constantly strutting and fretting, thinking and innovating, was supported on earth by a body separated from extinction by a hair's breadth. Once severed — and severed it must inevitably be — there was no power on earth which could join it together again.

This acceptance of the primacy of death — which is here invoked to condemn man as 'trivial' and 'arrogant' and which is separated by a hair's breadth from fascism (characteristically generated by a tendency towards necrophilia) — does not, however, lapse into anti-humanism. Indeed, this is a point we must concede to the heroine of *Memoirs*... As stated above, the novel is governed by two themes rather than one: parallel to the love of death there is the fear of death. While love of death is a secondary and regressive reaction, fear of death, by contrast, is a primary stance. The human being, who by nature wants to continue to exist, equally naturally fears death. If, despite his fear of death, he is fated to love it, then this death wish must be considered a sign of illness rather than a normal biological reaction.

The heroine of *Memoirs...* is as afraid of death as she is fascinated by it (or perhaps her fear is even greater than her fascination). We can therefore jump ahead in our analysis and say that from now on it is health rather than sickness which wins out at the end of the novel. But it is not only the conclusion that is important. If the final verdict were delivered only at the conclusion, we might then be able to talk of a compulsive acquittal at the eleventh hour by the conscious ideology.

But *Memoirs of a Woman Doctor* is in fact a tale of struggle. The alternation of the two themes determines the sequence of events right from the first line. The love of death never once generates hostile or quasi-fascist poisons without the fear of death, or the love of life, manufacturing antidotes. The pores of the novel might be said to exude moisture. The clean air of the humanitarian tendency expels the foul miasma of anti-humanism until the exhalations of life finally overcome the inhalations of death.

Each scene of fascination with death and its attendant hatred is followed by a scene of infatuation with life and the practice of love. It is therefore clear that the mechanism behind this breathing in of life and breathing out of death approximates, as in life, to a feeling of suffocation. The atmosphere of death stifles everything, even love of death, as this is, in the final analysis, a form of love.

The infatuation with death reaches its peak in the dissecting room scene, where the medical students' necrophiliac tendencies are exposed as nakedly as the body of the man whom the heroine is mercilessly carving up with her scalpel. This scene leaves behind only an intolerable feeling of suffocation and a pressing need to escape to the outside world to breathe the pure oxygen of life.

All this is accomplished with an involuntary movement like that of the thorax, forced to contract as it expels contaminated air and to expand as it inhales fresh air:

> I felt a sour taste in my throat and spat out the piece of meat from my mouth... I tried to swallow and felt the bread scraping against the walls of my larynx... I seemed to be choking. My

lips stopped moving, I couldn't stretch out my arms, the muscles of my heart weren't contracting and my veins were no longer throbbing with blood.

Ah, I'd died! I jumped up in fright...

No, I wasn't going to die! I refused to join all the corpses stretched out in front of me on the tables. I put down my scalpel and raced out of the dissecting room. In the street I looked around me in astonishment as people walked and moved their arms and legs without a moment's thought... opening their mouths, talking and breathing without the slightest difficulty.

I calmed down... I was still alive. I opened my mouth wide and filled my lungs with the air of the street and breathed in deeply. I moved my arms and legs and walked in the midst of the surging mass of humanity. Ah, how simple life is when one takes it as it comes!

'Take it as it comes!' But where then is the programme of denial, challenge and resistance to nature? And how has 'the surging mass of humanity' turned into a haven after being a lair for 'millions of insects'? Isn't the first night the medical student spends in the hospital (where the sick and half-dead present a scene of disintegrating life before death, and where living existence takes on the colour and taste of metal, pervaded by the smell of alcohol, ether and iodine) an announcement of the imminent arrival of the inorganic angel of death?

The night was cold and desolate, the darkness dead and still. The great hospital with its lighted windows crouched in the darkness like a wild hyena. The patients' groans and racking coughs tore at the curtains of the night. I stood alone at the window of my room, staring at the little white flower opening in the vase beside me. As I touched it, I shuddered as if I was a corpse touching a living thing for the first time. I brought it close to my face and inhaled its perfume, feeling like a condemned prisoner pressing his nose against the iron bars of his cell to breathe in the fragrance of life. I put my hand up to my neck and my fingers brushed the metal arms of the stethoscope — it encircled my neck like a hangman's noose. The white coat hung round my shoulders reeking of ether, disinfectant and iodine.

What had I done to myself? Bound my life to illness, pain and death; made my daily occupation the uncovering of people's bodies so that I could see their private parts, feel their swollen sores and analyse their secretions. I no longer saw anything of life except sick people lying in bed dazed, weeping or unconscious; their eyes dull, yellow or red; their limbs paralysed or amputated; their breathing irregular; their voices hoarse or groaning in pain. Could I bear this life sentence for the rest of my days?

If the crux of the first theme is an obsession with the secret of death in life,[24] the crux of the second must be the obsession with the secret of life in death. The miracle is not that death is born of life, but that life is born of death. This is the meaning behind the realistic but highly symbolic scene of the mother who dies in childbirth:

Wasn't it extraordinary that this lump of live flesh had come out of that stiff dead body lying on the cold metal table? ...How could a young woman's heart stop for ever? How could a dying woman give birth to a living child, a tiny spark of life emerge from dead matter? ...Whence does man come from and whither does he go?

From this very moment, the regressive journey begins. Science, with its microscopes, viruses and so on, can explain the secrets of death, yet finds itself unable to explain the secrets of life. The journey which began with the body's imprisonment in a 'cell of reason' and reached its destination in the medical college and the dissecting room has ended in a cul-de-sac: 'Science toppled from its throne... I realized that the path of reason which I had pledged to follow was a short, shallow one ending at a huge, impenetrable barrier.'

It is not difficult to predict where this new voyage will begin and how it will proceed. When the mind is assigned to one pole, then feelings must occupy the other. When man restricts his existence to a cell, a hospital, a dissecting room, that is to an inorganic, artificial world, the alternative world must be natural, organic and animate. The heroine of *Memoirs*... shows little originality when she chooses to leave the world of the 'contaminated' city for the 'pure' world of the village, but we will not subject this exodus to a romantic interpretation. We will, instead, interpret it as a healthy, freedom-loving response to the unhealthy exudations of the anal-sadistic phase.

Under the domination of this phase it seemed as if the entire world had become a claustrophobic cesspit, where everything was suffocating from the penetrating stink. In the lap of nature, on the other hand, repressions are not only cast off and repressed elements regain their rights, but it seems that life can be purged of its filth through a non-toxic, uncontaminated redigestion process. This will lead to a reaffirmation that the great secret is not the capacity of living matter for death but the capacity of dead matter for life:

I packed my few belongings and boarded the train which was to carry me far away from the city... away from the science professors and their laboratories...[25]

In a remote, peaceful village I took a little house. I sat on the balcony of my country abode, shifting my gaze from the wide, peaceful green fields to the clear blue sky. The sun's warm rays fell on my body as I sprawled on a comfortable couch...

I stripped myself bare of thoughts and began to feel...

For the first time in my life I was feeling without thinking, feeling the warm sun on my body, feeling that beautiful placid greenness which clothed the earth... Face to face with nature, I saw its enchanting magic unspoilt by the hollow clamour of the city...

I felt my heart beating fast and this filled my spirit with strange currents of sentiments and emotions... There was a new language to my heartbeats which neither science nor medicine could have explained, a language I understood with my newly awakened feelings but which would have been incomprehensible to my old experienced mind. I felt that emotion was sharper-witted than reason. It was more deeply rooted in the human heart, more firmly bound to the distant history of the human race, truer and more responsive to its nature...

It is not only the emotions which regain their rights, however, but also the body. And not any 'body' but precisely the 'female's body':

> I stretched out further on the couch, flexing my legs and abandoning myself to the new rush of emotions which swept through my body. A sudden thought occurred to me: this was the body that I'd once sentenced to death, the female body of the woman I'd mercilessly sacrificed at the feet of the god of science and reason, and it was coming to life again.

Nor is it the body alone, but also its 'forbidden parts'. The body has previously bound her in 'chains of shame and ignominy'; she has experienced it as incomplete and deficient, an open wound, a contaminated vessel. The denial of this body has been given priority in her daily routine. Yet this same body is now accepted in its very nakedness, indeed with its forbidden parts, if one can still speak in such terms:

> A gentle breeze lifted my skirt up over my thighs but I felt none of the alarm I would have done in the past whenever my thighs were exposed. How had my mother managed to instil in me this notion that my body was something shameful? Man was born naked and he died naked. All his clothes were mere pretence, an attempt to cover up his true nature.
>
> As I let the breeze lift up my clothes, I felt that I had been reborn.

It is, then, a rebirth, a return to the source. All the dams have been breached, all the predispositions towards 'denial, challenge and resistance' have tumbled, all the regressive formulations razed to the ground. The primary instinct has been reinstated to its former pre-eminence. All mental ruminations, ideological rationalizations and other psychological constructs and artefacts have become secondary. In a word, neurosis has given way to health:

> I was about to leave it all behind and begin afresh, start from the cradle of life, with the primitive flat land which yielded crops with spontaneous benevolence; with virgin nature which

had covered the earth for millions of years; with the simple country people who ate the fruits of the earth and followed their instincts under a canopy of trees, and ate, drank, bore children, sickened and died without ever asking how or why.

But the biggest question here is: are we faced with a final radical transformation or is the visit to the country, with all its blossoming of repressed feelings, simply a recreational intermission after which the struggle will be resumed as fiercely as before? The heroine's immediate response to this question is that, on returning to her home, work and surgery, she experiences a great reconciliation with life which she begins to 'love with every cell of my being, body and soul'. When she is with her family:

I opened my arms to life and embraced my mother, feeling for the first time that she was my mother. I embraced my father and understood what it meant to be a daughter, and embraced my brother and knew the feeling of brotherly love.

She is even reconciled with her femininity:

A violent longing swept through me, body and soul — the yearning of a soul thirsty for love and set free by reason, and of a virginal body newly let out of its iron cell. I wondered what an encounter between a man and a woman was like. The nights grew longer as the fantasies and illusions gathered round my bed... the chatter of the girls at school floated to the surface of my memory. I sighed and moaned and had the fantasies of an adolescent girl; it was as if I'd never dissected a man's body or stripped it naked and been repelled by its ugliness.

Had I forgotten? ...I don't know... But I had forgotten... And now the mystery and wonder of the living human body was restored for me... Perhaps my womanhood had emerged defiantly from its prison, dismantling on its way all the memories stored in my mind. Perhaps the stormy yearnings of my soul had uprooted the ugly images of the body from my imagination...

Dawn no longer broke. The warmth of my bed turned into a blazing furnace...

Can we then say that narcissism has retreated from its maximal to its minimal limits, from being a factor of death to being one of life? In fact, rather than 'development', we should talk of 'alternation'. For if we return to the analysis of the first failure in 'the search for love' we find that there are purely narcissistic reasons behind it. The heroine's choice of a 'weak' man for her first husband is motivated by the belief that his weakness arouses her maternal instincts and snuffs out her femininity. Yet right from the start, the marriage contract seems to her a 'death warrant': it constitutes an attack on what is effectively an ideal object for inflated narcissistic investment, in other words her 'name', which sums up her entire egoistic being and is her alter ego:

I might as well have signed my death warrant. My name, the first word I ever heard, and which was linked in my conscious and subconscious mind with my existence and very being, became null and void. He attached his name to the outside of me. I sat at his side, hearing people call me by my new name. I looked at them and at myself in astonishment as if they couldn't really be addressing me. It was as if I'd died and my spirit had passed into the body of another woman who looked like me but had a strange new name.[26]

The closed circuit of narcissistic existentialism is intolerable. It is akin to diabolic possession, that is to the invasion by a strange body. So the husband becomes an intolerable intruder, even before he moves from 'weakness' to 'strength' or before he manifests his hidden complexes and 'base traits':

My private world, my bedroom, was no longer mine alone. My bed, which no one had ever shared before, became his too. Every time I turned over or moved, my hand came into contact with his rough tousled head or his arm or leg, sticky with sweat.

This woman has defined herself as 'belonging to no one'. Having rid herself of the intruder whom she finds it impossible to call 'my husband', she is quick to reformulate the definition in an even more radically narcissistic fashion. She belongs to herself, to the world of the self:

The little world that I used to build out of chairs and dolls when I was a child became a reality. In my pocket was the magic key. I could come and go whenever I wanted without having to ask anyone's permission. I slept alone in a bed without a husband, turning over from right to left or from left to right as I fancied. I sat at my desk to read and write or to ponder and think or do nothing at all.

I was free, completely free in this little world of mine. I shut my door and cast off my artificial life with other people along with my shoes and clothes and pottered around the house at will. I was completely alone there. I couldn't hear voices or people breathing and I didn't have to look at other people's bodies. For the first time in my life, a heavy burden was lifted from my heart, the burden of living in a house shared by others.

She prefers to leave the countryside and return to the city because she can no longer cope with being enclosed within 'that desolate isolation'. She makes this choice now that she is beginning to love life with every cell of her body and to pick up the meaning of her existence from the grains of sand she finds on the earth, 'like a pigeon picking up grain with its beak', and now that she has begun to feel an 'overwhelming desire' to hold onto life.

But her self-imposed isolation in the city is immeasurably more cruel than that which she experiences in the country. In the latter, her isolation is voluntary. In the city, on the other hand, it is involuntary. Seeking sociability in the desolation of the countryside is one thing; finding desolation in the sociability of the city is quite another. In the former, isolation overflows with an overwhelming desire for life. In the latter, isolation seems to be a prelude to and a foretaste of death.

Success changes nothing in the taste for death, which is the taste for isolation from 'society at large', particularly if this success builds on a narcissistic base: 'I would fight, looking to myself for protection, looking to my strength, my knowledge, my success in my work.'

In fact, from the pinnacle of success, the world appears as distant as life from death. The higher the pinnacle, the colder it becomes and the more deathly iciness it accrues to itself:

In the street outside, people were clinging to one another, talking, laughing, scowling. I looked at myself and found that I was looking down on them from a great height.

I felt a chilling cold as though I was sitting on a snowy mountain top. I looked above my head and saw only clouds and sky. I looked beneath my feet and saw the great distance separating me from the... low-lying plains warmed by the breath of humanity.

But what is the secret of this success? Now that this woman doctor has chosen to embark on a battle with society and its millions from a position of stark inner strength, what has made her surgery fill up with 'men, women and children' and filled her 'coffers with money and gold'? What has made her name 'as famous as that of a movie star' and made her look down from her pinnacle at society below and remark, 'How small mighty society looked now!'

Here again we find ourselves face to face with that maximal level of narcissism which creates death rather than promotes life. The basis of this astounding success is the practice of abortion, which in the final analysis is the killing of life. Needless to say, we are aware of all the ideological justifications. The first person she aborts is a girl from Upper Egypt. Without an abortion, this girl will inevitably face death at the hands of her father, brother or uncle — not forgetting that any one of these three may have been the person who seduced her.

There is no doubt that many of those she aborts would have to pay with their lives for their 'shame' did she not operate on them. Just as clearly, the feminists' demand for a woman's right to choose whether or not to be a mother is just and legitimate. Finally, there is no doubt that legislation could save the lives of a number of women who pay dearly for an abortion, risking their lives to go ahead with the operation in secret and under unhygienic conditions. An abortion is also expensive, both physically and psychologically, unhealthy and ultimately unpredictable.

But all this is one thing and the regular, constant and ultimately unrestricted practice of abortion is another. Medicine is by definition the science of preserving life not destroying it. When a doctor's surgery turns into an abortion clinic, it is certain that not every women there is always and categorically threatened with death unless she rids herself of her 'shame'. Even if we accept this to be the case, the doctor's duty here is not to renege on his Hippocratic oath and carry out an abortion, but to struggle within the existing legal and medical structures to legalize and legislate for abortion. This is the democratic and radical solution to the problem.

On the other hand, the elitist solution opted for by the heroine of *Memoirs...* is only the answer for a necessarily limited number of individual cases. Moreover, it leaves the door wide open for quacks and other unethical doctors who, in their turn, violate the Hippocratic oath and amass huge fortunes from the practice of illegal abortion.

As far as the question relates to the present study, we can finish this aside by saying that, whatever the ideological underpinnings and rationalizations on grounds of conscience, an abortion clinic is by definition, in the strict biological sense of the word, a clinic for the manufacture of death, not the creation of life. Thus the heroine of *Memoirs...*, whose life as we have seen is governed by these two alternating themes, life and death, cannot have chosen this specialization by accident. Indeed, she originally opts for medicine not because it is the ultimate humanitarian profession but because it is 'a terrifying thing'. However, any criticism we might level against her is made superfluous by the criticism she levels at herself.

When she finally experiences for the first time the emotion of love (even if it is, as we have argued above, with a man chosen along narcissistic and elitist lines), she also realizes for the first time that all her past life has been spent in contestation and conflict. It was a life in which she saw 'the other' as an alien body, a source of irritation, creating difficulties and problems, contributing to the degradation of the ego rather than enriching and complementing it. It was a blind narcissistic life in which she saw only herself and where relationships with 'another', all others, were nothing but a 'battle', a 'war', and a source of unabiding hostility.

If financial gain (the uncrowned king of the anal-sadistic phase) is the end result of all her success, her critical attitude to money at the conclusion of her memoirs means that she is aware, albeit unconsciously, that her past life was as much a hoarding of riches as a maximal hoarding of excremental hatred and the remnants of death in the strongbox of overwhelming narcissism:

> How had I held out my hand all these years and taken money from my patients? How had I sold health to people in my surgery? How could I have filled my coffers from the blood and sweat of the sick?
>
> ...I didn't understand anything. I was blind. All I could see was myself. The battles I was fighting hid the truth from me.
>
> ...I hadn't achieved a thing. Being a doctor wasn't a case of diagnosing the illness, prescribing the medicine and grabbing the money. Success didn't mean filling the surgery, getting rich and having my name in lights. Medicine wasn't a commodity and success wasn't measured in terms of money and fame.
>
> Being a doctor meant giving health to all who needed it, without restrictions or conditions, and success was to give what I had to others.
>
> Thirty years of my life had gone by without my realizing the truth, without my understanding what life was about or realizing my own potential. How could I have done, when I'd only thought about taking? — although I couldn't have given something which I didn't have to give.

The self-criticism with which the novel ends does not mean that biophilia has finally won out over necrophilia. It means, rather, that the heroine's conscious ideology is that the love of life must be victorious over the love of death. However, since this is a novel, the book is not entirely directed by a conscious ideology. Thus it has two voices, two streams of consciousness, just as it has two themes. In addition to the narcissistically inflated ego, there is the critical ego which is akin to the alter ego. The constant confrontation between these two egos, though it manifests itself as a type of schizophrenia, is what saves the novel from lapsing into what could otherwise have been an anti-humanist doctrine, and brings it closer to what could be called a counter-tendency to anti-humanism.

3
Two Women in One

The heroine of the novel discussed in the previous chapter 'chooses' to remain anonymous. In *Two Women in One*,[1] on the other hand, she has a name: Bahiah Shaheen. But apart from this detail, there are many similarities between the two heroines of *Memoirs of a Woman Doctor*[2] and *Two Women in One*. First, there are the actual events. Bahiah, like her unnamed counterpart, is a first-year medical student. Her first marriage has failed as has the subsequent affair with her teacher at the university. Like her spiritual sister, she can only fall in love with 'an extraordinary man' able to pluck her from 'the grave of ordinary days'.

Apart from their similar circumstances, the two young women share a markedly similar psychological make-up. For example, they both have an undying hatred for members of their own sex. Ever since Bahiah has been aware of anything, she has become ever more firmly convinced that 'they were one species and she was from a different mould'. When she looks at her 'female sisters' and sees their 'beaten eyes' and their 'fat, tightly-bound legs' which force them to walk with 'a strange worm-like reptilian movement', it 'made her angry, and she was sure that she did not belong to this sex'.

How could she ever belong to this animalistic sex?

They walked like reptiles, legs together, and if their thighs happened to separate briefly, they would quickly snap together again. The girls pressed their legs together as if something valuable might fall if they separated... None of the female students could walk alone. They always went in groups, like gaggles of geese.

Their 'animal' nature is not only apparent from their appearance, but also extends to their essence: they have 'a brain soft like a rabbit's, knowing nothing of life except eating and reproduction'. Even before her refusal to belong to this inferior sex, full of the others — 'her female sisters' — she rejects it deep down as an individual: 'The word female sounded like an insult to her, like the first exposed genitals she had ever seen.'

Bahiah's alter ego continually repeats, 'Who told you that I'm a female?', 'Who told you that I'm a girl?' Like her counterpart in *Memoirs...* who feels 'God has sided with the boys in everything' and if he had not 'hated girls' why 'would he tarnish them with this shame' Bahiah says loud and clear that she 'hated God' because it is he who created her a girl.

If the sex organs determine gender, making a female a female and a male a male, it is small wonder that her hatred revolves around this part of her body. 'Bahiah came to hate bath-days' because then her body confronts her with a view of these organs. 'When she undressed she looked with loathing at her sexual organs.' This is originally one of the reasons for her early dabbling in theology, and for her invention of a novel theory in the realm of anti-creationism: if it is true, as her mother says, that 'God creates only beautiful things', 'who [then] created those bad organs?'

Her hatred of her sex organs even makes her wish she were circumcised:

The cries of her sister Fawziah still rang in her ears: there was a red pool of blood under her. Every day she waited for her turn. The door would open and Umm Muhammad would enter with the sharp razor in her hand, ready to cut that small thing between her thighs. But Umm Muhammad died and her father was transferred to Cairo and that small thing between her thighs remained intact.

Sometimes she was afraid of it, thinking that it was harmful, that it had been forgotten or left inside her body by mistake. She would long for Umm Muhammad to rise from her grave and come with her razor.[3]

But this hatred of her own sex organs is, as it were, merely theoretical. By contrast, her hatred of the male sex organs in general is highly charged emotionally, to the extent where it could be described as motivated anal hatred:

> she was disgusted when she saw men's sexual organs bulging under their trousers; she wanted to throw up when a man dug his elbow into her chest as she waited for the tram. She hated men with their trousers, their ugly protruding organs, their greedy, shifty eyes, their smell of onions and tobacco, and their thick moustaches which looked like black, dead insects flapping over their lips.[4]

In fact this hatred of the sex organs, whether male or female, reveals a suspension of the sexual function. The protagonist of *Memoirs...* does not experience this suspension as deeply as Bahiah: she resorts to suppressing her desire by burying her head desperately in her pillow in order to suffocate 'that stubborn giant' and to free her bed of the 'nocturnal phantoms'. Bahiah, on the contrary, does not need to wage war on the giant asleep in her depths. The warmth of her bed never kindles a flame, whether by night or by day. The giant here is a mere dwarf. She not only lacks sex organs; she also lacks sexual desire:

> She had always known that her eyes lied and that they hid her sexual desires, but not by choice. Her sexual desire was shrinking despite her. She could feel it withdrawing from her, leaving her body on its own. Sometimes when she felt the need for it she would try to summon it up, but it refused to respond and never settled in her body.

Even having known her one great love and chosen one extraordinary man from among millions to rescue her from the purgatory of her mundane life — after 'thirty seconds they knew each other in a way that would have taken another man and woman fifty years' — the ultimate ecstasy Bahiah experiences with him is far from sexual. With Saleem Ibraheem, 'She was not even aware of being female. She did not consider Saleem male... When she was with him, she lost... her sexual appetite. She would become a human being without instincts and without those familiar desires.'

Thus Bahiah presents the paradox of a circumcised female who is not actually circumcised, of a female whose sex organs are excised without actual excision. In fact, this is a fundamental question which the heroine of *Two Women in One* never asks herself. Given the slithering movements of her reptilian sisters, whose 'fat, closely-bound legs and... beaten eyes betrayed their everlasting frigidity', their excuse could at least be that it is impossible for 'those parts that have been cut away' to return, and for 'that murdered, dead and satiated desire' to be 'revived'.[5]

But how can the girl who has escaped Umm Muhammad's razor explain that 'she does not feel like a woman' and is 'incapable of sexual desire', even during adolescence, a time of the flowering and eruption of desire? Indeed, how can she explain that, 'Since the time her mother had smacked her when she was three, she felt disgusted by the sight of her sexual organs'? Is it sufficient explanation that her mother smacked her hand at the age of three for touching herself?

It is undeniable that the sexual life of a child, particularly a female child, is repressed in most societies today, particularly in the Arab world. But the repression of sexual desire can only increase the likelihood of its breaking out. As it happens, Bahiah complains not of the repression of her desires but of their total absence: of their shrinking, withdrawal and non-existence, as she puts it. While not denying the influence of the current hierarchical nature of patriarchal society, Bahiah's lack of sexual desire can only be explained in terms of the subconscious or psychological infrastructure, which is in turn linked to the Oedipus complex.

The most striking aspect of Bahiah's case is that her sexual desire only recurs or expresses itself by reference to a fatherly Oedipal attitude. It is in relation to her father, and her father alone, that her sexuality seems to burgeon. When she goes to Saleem's flat to make love for the first time, all her fantasies revolve around her father:

Her brain started churning at dream speed, hurling up image after image. She imagined her father in his bamboo chair in the sitting room, sipping his morning coffee. He opens his newspaper, and finds that the naked body of his daughter Bahiah has been found in a bachelor's flat in al-Muqattam. Her father thought the road between home and the college delineated Bahiah's world... that she... studied four hours a day... He thought she was unlike other girls, that her body was unlike other girls', in fact, that she had no body at all, no organs, especially no sexual organs liable to be aroused or stirred by someone of the opposite sex.

Her mind baulked at imagining her father's shock on seeing his polite, obedient daughter's body naked, not in her own bedroom but in a young man's flat.

When she returns to the paternal house and spends the first night after losing her virginity, her father is again the pivot of her dream-like fantasies:

'Bahiah!' ...Her father's voice rang in her ear like a shot, like the sole voice of truth...

She pulled the bedclothes over her head and feigned sleep as she heard her father's footsteps coming toward the bed. His big fingers lifted the blankets and he stared at her and discovered, thunderstruck, that she was not Bahiah Shaheen after all: she was not his daughter, nor was she polite, obedient and a virgin; she had actually been born with sex organs, not only clearly visible through the bedclothes but moving as well, like the very heartbeat of life. By moving, she had removed the barrier in her way. She had torn away the membrane separating her from life.

What gives us pause for thought in both these extracts — and they are the only two in the novel in which Bahiah, and consequently the reader, discovers that she was created 'without sexual organs' — is not the Oedipus complex *per se*, or its negative or positive nature, but that she actually lives this complex situation at a subconscious level which is very close to the conscious mind.

This is unique to Bahiah Shaheen. Under normal circumstances, the taboo Oedipal feelings are repressed to the deepest layers of the subconscious, allowing sexual desire or the need for erotic satisfaction to occupy the entire conscious space. In the case of Bahiah, however, almost the opposite is true. With Oedipal feelings consciously to the fore, and these being sinful by definition, the denial of sexual desire becomes a compulsory exit as the only way out of this impasse.

This is how Bahiah comes to believe that sexual desire is 'abnormal', rejects 'the sexual interpretation' of behaviour in adolescence, refuses to admit that she has any sexual desires and insists that her relationship with Saleem is 'something different'. As we have seen, this denial is extended to the sex organs themselves: when she accidentally catches sight of them in the bathroom, she 'would quickly avert her eyes'. This is why she cannot bring herself to imagine herself naked or possessing sex organs unless she fantasizes that she is either dead or somebody else.

Crucial as this is, it is no less important than the subconscious becoming conscious. In this case it is not only sexual desire which is forced to withdraw, but the ego itself which fades away. When faced with a new experience for which it is unprepared, the ego may choose to withdraw to the pre-ego phase. The unresolved Oedipus complex, heavily charged with taboos and feelings of guilt, is the worst possible experience for the ego if these feelings become conscious.

The ego, the acknowledged king of the realm of feeling, may reach a stage where it is constantly besieged and crowded in on by an intolerable guest, day and night, an intruder forcing its way into the kingdom. In the face of this, the ego may relinquish its very egocentricity. It will no longer be the ego. In other words, in defending its narcissistic entity against injury, the ego may have to negate its own identity in the interests of survival. The ego may tolerate being a non-ego more easily than becoming a wounded ego.

The regressive model represented by Bahiah Shaheen is almost unique; it is unparalleled among the heroes and heroines of the Arabic novel. For a large number of male heroes, regression may never go beyond the penile phase of pre-sexual organization (the castration complex). As we have seen, the heroines of *Woman at Point Zero* and, to a greater extent, *Memoirs...* present us with models of a female regression towards the anal-sadistic phase of the development of the libido.

Although we can also detect the legacy of anal-sadistic tendencies in the heroine of *Two Women in One*, her regression seems far more critical as it goes beyond the various pre-sexual phases of the growth of the libido to reach the stage of the development of the ego itself. Bahiah wants to regress not only to the phase of the non-ego but beyond it. She often dreams of returning to the state of a foetus in her mother's womb, not in a metaphorical but in a real sense:

> When she felt tired she would let her body fall and stretch out on the iron bed. She shivered under the old blanket, pulling it over her head and around her freezing feet. Her teeth chattered, making a faint sound like a baby sparrow that had fallen from its mother's nest in an arid land, trembling as its tearful eyes glowed in the dark with the frightened look of an orphan.
>
> A hot tear ran from the corner of her eye onto the pillow. She felt its wet warmth on her cheek and peeped out from under the blanket to see her mother: the long thin face like her own, the wide black[6] eyes, and the breast that offered generous warmth. She buried her head in her mother's breast, sniffing her and seeking an opening that would contain her, hoping to hide from the world and the forces threatening her. She wanted to curl up like a foetus. Her body shook with a strange violent yearning for security. She longed to curl up in her mother's womb, to feel security, silence, with no sound or movement.

Adam's yearning for paradise can only be explained in terms of the feelings of pain and guilt he experienced at the Fall. Similarly, Bahiah's longing for the safety and peace of her mother's womb can only be explained in terms of the pain and guilt she experiences outside this haven. The world into which she emerges is not only an arid land but a hostile one, or at least this is what she feels. It is a world painted in red, the colour of pain. She is a year old when she first accepts the severance from her mother's body. They are celebrating her birthday. On the table is one red candle:

> The bright red flame had seemed like part of herself. Her small, soft body crawled on the floor, sticking so close that she seemed part of it. She had been separated from the universe,[7] though her hand could not yet trace a full circle round her body. Her hand was small, her body big, vast, seeming to fill the tall space

between ceiling and floor. When she stretched out her hand to explore her legs, she could not tell whether they belonged to her or to the chair. Did the red flame come from the candle or from herself? Goaded by doubt, she decided to find out: she stretched out her finger and was burned by the flame. Now she knew the difference between the flame and her own eyes. Doubt and pain shaped the outline of her body and every part of her began to acquire its own special form.

That the world at the inception of the ego, and the 'picture of the body's evolution', take on the colour red signifies that the world for her will always burn like the candle flame. Bahiah Shaheen, who discovers her ego in this burning red, will always experience her relationship with the world in this pattern of terror: 'When she saw this deep red, her eyes widened, full of the dread of eyes before real blood.' In fact, red represents first and foremost the colour of blood. Through blood Bahiah lives all her most traumatic experiences.

First, there is the trauma of circumcision, even if this awful event is only relived in fantasy: 'The cries of her sister Fawziah still rang in her ears: there was a red pool of blood under her.' Second, there is the trauma of the onset of menstruation, the 'shame' which a woman carries branded into her flesh, reminding her every month that she belongs to the sex that 'God hates':

How did she know that the colour of blood was red?

The first spot of red blood she had ever seen was on her small, white knickers. She would draw that spot like a deep red circle in the middle of the blank sheet of paper. The young girl's eyes were large and frightened. Her body was small and thin like a sparrow's trembling behind a wall. There were also many staring eyes, like full circles. With her small, swollen fingers, she buried her knickers in a hole behind the wall. She walked out in the street without knickers. The cold wind passed between her legs, billowing her dress, but she pulled it down firmly with both hands, defying the wind. She walked along the tarmac street, her bag bulging with books.

As she neared the wooden shelter, a deep red drop of blood trickled down between her legs and onto the asphalt. It lay on the ground in a red circle that widened to grow as big as the sun. The policeman with his handlebar moustache stared at her. He poked his nose out of the shelter, sniffing the blood.[8] She threw her bag on the ground and ran home breathlessly.

Third, there is the traumatic experience of rape, imaginary though it may be. This is probably linked, through what in psychoanalysis is called the 'primal scene',[9] to the sadistic interpretation of copulation:

the painting... was black as night; the white dots looked like stars, but they were not stars, more like tiny diamonds. No, not really diamonds either, but small eyes, glittering with transparent tears. No, not eyes but a pair of small eyes in the face of the thin, pale child walking alone in the street, tiny fingers red and swollen from the sharp end of the ruler: twenty strokes on each hand for losing the bag. At the bend in the street the big man with the handlebar moustache grabbed the child by the arm. The bag fell to the ground. With puny arms and legs, the child struck at the big legs, but they were strong and gaped like destiny's jaws. The child lay between those legs, face down on the asphalt near the wall. A fine trickle of blood streamed from her nostrils down her face; it would clot before her father saw it. But her father had looked into her eyes and known from her paleness that she was still bleeding. He searched between her arms and legs for the wound. When he saw the red circle as clear as the sun, he raised his big palm and slapped the child's face.[10]

After all this, red is the colour and symbol of sexual desire, this desire being in itself a violation of narcissism. This is because it is a sign branded on the body in the form of the need for another. It is damning proof of the collapse of the narcissistic myth of self-sufficiency. Moreover, if sexual desire is coupled with feelings of guilt due to an unresolved Oedipus complex,[11] then the whole world — since it is a world of other human beings and thus of objects of sexual desire — becomes as hostile and burning as a flame. It is a world which must either be annihilated or withdrawn from, or both.

Bahiah's fear of the colour red, then, is the fear resulting from the 'painful separation' from her mother's body, the fear of discovering an objective world with all its wounding, painful experiences, the fear of sexual desire charged with forbidden feelings and, ultimately, the ego's fear of itself — the ego being formed only by the discovery of its delimitation from the objective world.

From this perspective, Bahiah is the perfect example of an ego which wants to stop developing and begin afresh in the opposite direction from which it first evolved. It is an ego which wants to vanish as an ego and (since we are still talking about the colour red) empty itself of all blood to become pale and lifeless.

Indeed, Bahiah is not content with describing herself time and time again as 'pale', but one of her most potent fantasies is when she imagines herself run over by a bus or a tram. Death in this manner is the only way she can reconcile 'the pale face which is her face' with 'the red blood which is her blood' splashed on the surface of the road.

However, inasmuch as Bahiah's ego has been formed as the result of an interface with the 'colour red', the colour of fire, blood, sex, sin, torture and narcissistic wounds, its progress in the opposite direction will be towards the colour black. Black, the colour of darkness, invisibility, eternal tranquillity, security, the totality of narcissistic capacity, the mother's womb, the earth and death: 'She knew full well that black is stronger... Black is the origin, the root that reaches back into the depths of the earth.'

Leaving aside the metaphorical use of colour, we have seen that Bahiah's regressive journey is an attempt to dismantle all that has been erected by the ego. Her frame of reference here is negativism, even at the level of identity. Bahiah does not define herself in terms of who she actually is or even what she would like to be, but in terms of what she does not want to be:

> She had no clear purpose. She had never known exactly what she wanted from life. All she knew was that she did not want to be Bahiah Shaheen, nor be her mother and father's daughter; she did not want to go home or to college, and she did not want to be a doctor. She was not interested in money, nor did she long for a respectable husband, children, a house, a palace or anything like that.

If a name is the mark of identity, the awareness of egoism is, of itself, an indication of the ego's independence, individuality and supremacy. Bahiah, however, unlike her counterpart the heroine of *Memoirs...*, sees her name as a burden. She must break this chain because, once pronounced, the name will imprison her within the confines of an independent and specific being:

'Bahiah'.

The name sounded as if it belonged to someone else. She leapt up from her stool. As she did, she realized that she had a body of her own, one she could move and shake without other bodies moving and shaking. She also had a name of her own, and when that name was called she would look up in surprise. She might even ask, 'Who's that?' She got a shock every time she heard her name and a hidden feeling would tell her that someone was calling her own name, selecting her from among millions of other bodies, singling her out among the billions of other creatures floating in the universe.

The blood drained from her face. She became deathly pale... She knew she was trembling, and she wanted to escape the voice that called her, that summons issued directly and specifically to her, that miraculous power that was able to pick her out among all the others.

Bahiah also differs from the heroine of *Memoirs...* in that when she is married off against her will, she does not care whether she takes her husband's name. So long as she is not Bahiah Shaheen, what difference does it make if people call her Bahiah Yaseen?

At the door to the new flat, the father handed over his property to the bridegroom: Bahiah Shaheen passed from the hands of Muhammad Shaheen into the hands of Muhammad Yaseen. But neither of the two men yet realized that she was not Bahiah Shaheen, and consequently could not be Bahiah Yaseen.

The heroine of *Memoirs...* reacts very differently. Her father-oriented view saves her from the 'miserable world of women', and her professional life reflects a desire to distance herself from her mother and her mother's world, to move closer to that of her father. Indeed, she wants a distinct place in the sun within patriarchal society. Thus she is bound to stand up for the surname passed on to her by her father. Bahiah, on the other hand, expresses her regression towards her mother by being ungrateful for her father's name.

In her destructive regressive journey, Bahiah Shaheen also rejects not only her name and surname but her ancestry too. By refusing to accept a position in the family tree, she is demolishing one of the strongest foundations of the ego. An ego without a father or mother can only be likened to a non-ego, a baby at its mother's breast who begins to perceive its own ego only as far as it enables it to distinguish between its father and mother:

> Now she was sure that she did not belong to this family. The blood in her veins was not theirs. If blood was all that connected her to them, then she had to question that bond. She had to question the very blood that ran in her veins and theirs. Her mother had not given birth to her. Maybe she was a foundling, discovered outside the mosque. Even if her mother had conceived her — and whether or not her father had played a part in this — it did not mean that she belonged to them. Blood ties, she felt, were no bond at all, since they were no one's choice.

Language is one of the ego's more important acquisitions. Through language, the ego develops both a sense of its own individuality and a sense of belonging. 'Real life' to Bahiah Shaheen (or in the final analysis, life in the mother's womb), on the other hand, is a life without language: 'people invent words to justify their unreal lives'. It is like a foetus: 'Only silence could express what she really felt, because silence could convey something momentous.' Silence can uncover 'the moment of eternal contact when the body would no longer feel separated from the world but would become one with it'.

Language aside, 'real life is timeless'. Time is one of the ego's basic dimensions, a yardstick for its development. So long as Bahiah hates the idea of growing older, indeed so long as she wants to curl up as a foetus in her mother's womb again, her negativistic doctrine hits out most strongly at the law of time and that of 'being' in time:

She had never used a diary. Nor did she look at the calendar hanging in her father's room... [When] every morning he would tear off a day in the same way and with the same motion, scrunching it into a ball between his fingers, she wished with her whole being that she could pull it out of his hand, shouting 'Stop! Leave it alone!'

From this point of view, it is little wonder that Bahiah should choose to open the story of her life with the occasion of her eighteenth birthday. She denies being 'eighteen', asking, before she even knows how to pose the question, 'Had the earth really revolved eighteen times around the sun?'

The fact is that the 'fourth of September' (her birthday) marks the beginning of the 'tragedy' of Bahiah Shaheen, the tragedy she feels branded into her body, 'carrying it with her at every step and every cell'. 'It was the fourth of September'[12] when humanity witnessed a 'momentous' event, that of 'the eternal separation [which] took place and the moment [which] passed, never to return'. What happened was her birth, or rather the trauma of her birth.[13]

Ever since the day 'she became aware that she had a body of her own, separate from her mother's', her whole existence revolves around a burning 'desire to return to where she had come from'. This regressive desire lies behind her refusal to eat, as she sees food as a factor in growth: 'Her mother had never understood what Bahiah wanted. She used to stuff her with food. When she wasn't looking, Bahiah would spit the food out.'

It is this very desire to regress which is behind Bahiah's rejection of her mother's affection, seeing it as something which sanctifies the severance between two previously connected bodies:

Her mother would look at her with eyes as black as her own and murmur affectionately, 'Go back to bed, Bahiah. You're a big girl now.'

The voice was affectionate. She felt its affection, like soft fingers caressing her body, turning in a circle, as if the fingers were defining her body, demarcating its boundaries with the outside world. Back in her own bed, this affection, which filled her with tenderness and reaffirmed her independent existence and separate private being, made her cry her heart out in silence, her body racked by sobs, the bed rocking under her. She would be swept by an uncontrollable desire for those fingers to abandon their false affection and to crush her, to free her from her own body for ever and to weld her mother and herself into one.

The same regressive desire is also one of the reasons for hating her father, and for her always picturing him as a policeman. With his huge size (and sexual appetite), he stands as a barrier between her and her mother's body: 'At night she would sometimes waken with a start, creep into her parents' bed and slip her small body between their naked bodies. Her father's big arms would push her roughly away.'

Not only do his arms push her away. His eyes transfix her and shut her out both from her mother's bed and from all its extensions and alternatives:

The alarm woke her in the morning. Her father's great eyes loomed over her bed, drawing her up, out of her room and out of the house. They followed her to the tram and the college. Then his thick palms shoved her into the dissecting room.

On Bahiah's birthday, her sense of tragedy is branded into her body. So also is her desire to wipe off the face of the earth whatever it is that dwells in her body under the name of Bahiah Shaheen. These two feelings grow in magnitude until they reach a climax: 'She longed to confide in somebody about that strange sensation building up inside her, like a foetus growing day by day to reach maturation on the fourth of September every year, confirming to her that she was definitely not Bahiah Shaheen.'

If the fourth of September sees something momentous, it is precisely on the fourth of September that she expects something even more critical than her birth to occur. This is her return, as if through the process of a second birth, to link up with the person from whom she has been separated. It is the moment when she will feel crushed by the universe and annihilated as a body and an independent entity:

She burned with desire to return to where she had come from, to escape the field of gravity and free herself of that body whose own weight, surface and boundaries divided it from its surroundings: a consuming desire to dissolve like particles of air in the universe, to reach a final, total vanishing-point.

Her body had felt a hidden desire since childhood, since she developed a body of her own separate from the world. It was a persistent desire to return to the world, to dissolve to the last atom so that she would be liberated and disembodied and weightless, like a free spirit hovering without constraints of time or place and with no chains to tie her to earth.

This sophist bond with the universe is clearly a narcissistic union with the mother. Indeed it is Bahiah herself who leads us to this conclusion, telling us that the universe is a womb and the womb is a universe. Her mother's womb and the universe are one and the same thing. Even their heartbeats and movements are as one:

Her mother had never understood her. But she understood her mother. If she stared at her long enough she could see her coiled womb crouching at the base of her stomach. She could see its muscles clenching and unclenching in a quick, continuous pulse, like the pulse of the world in the night silence, its motion invisible and imperceptible, like the motion of the earth.

But in the final analysis, the desire to reunite with the universe or return to the womb is surely nothing other than a desire for death. Here again, Bahiah herself confirms this interpretation by inviting us to view the desire for annihilation as real and not metaphorical. Her whole being is tied as though by 'invisible silken threads' to 'the end of ends', as if she was created only to die, as if life seeps into her veins only to lead her to her deadly fate, pushed 'irresistibly' and:

with all the speed she could muster, in harmony with the blood coursing through her veins. The heat and warmth of her blood drove her on inexorably to her destiny, whatever it might be, even if it meant death and extinction.

Bahiah has been given ears only in order to hear the call of the 'bottomless abyss'. She has been created with two hands only so that she can hold onto the ends of the threads and walk 'towards that very danger, to the brink of the bottomless abyss'. All the desires that Bahiah denies — all the desires she has stifled with her pillow, repressed in her body and spat out like her mother's food — have been replaced by one desire 'buried deep down', the desire that the heart be 'rent apart', and that the blood be 'arrested in its absurd cycle' and congeal in the veins. She is desperately wishing that 'her heartbeats would stop and die'. 'She had a strong and persistent desire to... kill her own body, while conscious and with full intent.' In a word, it is a crushing desire for 'death, both feared and desired; sought after, evaded and imagined everywhere, anywhere, in the mortuary'.

This is the only 'real' desire, the only 'heartfelt' one. As such, it is the most taboo of all desires. The others are 'weak' and 'unreal'; they 'need no laws to keep them in check'. This is originally the tragedy of 'ordinary' man, of whom St Paul said, 'Because you are neither hot nor cold, I myself have cast you out.' According to Bahiah, 'Human beings hide their real desires: because they are strong enough to be destructive; and since people do not want to be destroyed, they opt for a passive life with no real desires.'

Narcissism, which we have not heard of for some time, all of a sudden rears its head through an unexpected twist in the paradox. Frightened to death of always living 'in the middle of the road', of being unable to 'attain any goal' and of falling into 'the trap of the mundane, like countless millions of others', Bahiah has chosen to deny all her desires and replace them with a death wish, for this is the one desire which distinguishes her from among millions of passive, ordinary people.

There are two types of death, however: a lifeless death and a living death; a death which kills and a death which forces one to live; a cold death like that of the corpses in the dissecting room and a warm death 'which only has life in a living mind vibrating with life'. The difference between life and death is not the fact of living itself but the quality of life. The world of others, the world of the ordinary, of the countless millions, is a kind of world of the living dead. It is a world both ruled by the crushing similarity of the dead and ignorant of the uniqueness of the living. It has the appearance but not the essence of life, and is filled not with real people but with animated corpses.

If money is the clearest expression of a world which has lost its individuality, a world which is repressed, monotonous, repetitive and pre-programmed, no wonder that the world of ordinary human beings seems to Bahiah (who worships uniqueness) to be a universe of seriographically minted humanity:

> On the tram she sat with her back to one man, facing another. There was a man to her left and a man to her right. Rows and rows of men sat shoulder to shoulder in silence in front of her. Their lower bodies were immobile, fixed to their seats, while from the waist up they shook slowly and rhythmically with the motion of the tram...
>
> They were government employees. Their bodies were all the same shape, their features and suits, fingers and shoes identical, as if the government had stamped them from a mould, minted them like coins in the same conical shape.[14]

The 'deadly similarity' does not only apply to the category of people 'minted like coins' by the government, but includes all members of the human race without exception, men and women, old people and children, wherever and whenever they happen to meet, congregate and form 'herds':

> The usual crowd had gathered at the hospital gates. Animals pulled carts laden with oranges. There were people with skinny faces and bodies like skeletons, women carrying children with the faces of old people, and old people with the bodies of children. There were women with men's features and men with women's features. On the asphalt was blood, spittle and children's excrement; scabrous, hungry dogs rummaged in the garbage scattered here and there.

Even university students, specifically those from the college of medicine, who are presumed to form some sort of elite, seem to Bahiah to embody the real 'meaning of death' through their similarity:

Their faces, movements and voices were all similar. When you looked into their eyes you would not even see them. She was drowning in a sea of humanity, seen or recognized by no one. Her face became like those of the other female students: Bahiah, Aliah, Zakiah and Yvonne, it made no difference.

At that moment she grasped the meaning of death... She found herself running aimlessly, fleeing the college grounds, fleeing the deadly sameness within and without, inside her body and in the outside world.

By denying the value of the worlds of others — the objective world, to use the terminology of psychoanalysis — the value of the world of His Majesty the Ego is inevitably enhanced.[15] Here we come full circle: everything which has been withdrawn from the external world is re-employed by the ego, sitting comfortably on the throne of the internal world.

The world of others, all others, appears 'dead' to Bahiah, and the people in it 'dead or living a passive existence, with no warmth and no heartbeats'. She finds all human beings 'transformed by some potent power, by some terrible non-human force that had turned them into other, inhuman beings', and she finally allows herself to 'clench her teeth in anger' and 'to stamp on the ground with her feet', shouting 'How ugly ordinary life is!'[16] At the same time, she has in effect moved from the objective to the subjective world, from derision to praise, conferring on the 'real' human beings all she has denied the 'false' ones. The real person finds it 'impossible to communicate with other people' because:

> People don't want a real person... when they see a real person they panic and may even try to kill him. That's why such a person will always be hunted down, killed, condemned to death, imprisoned or isolated somewhere far from other people.

But in return for all the oppression which the 'real' human beings are destined to face, they are entitled to enjoy a greater distinction. This distinction is theirs and theirs alone; it is as full as existence itself in confronting the millions whose existence is empty, a distinction as intense as existence itself in the face of the millions whose existence is shaky.[17]

In contrast to the male students whose 'thick glasses' and 'straining eyes' prevent them from seeing things as they are, and the female students with their 'defeated eyes', Bahiah sees things 'with the sharpest powers of perception'. She 'focused on life, her dark eyes wide, sharp and unblinking... and no power on earth could make her lower them'. Once she transfixes someone with her glare, even if it is a policeman, that person can only 'reach to the ground in submission'.

The male students have 'bowed backs' and 'reddened noses', 'their heads bowed over their lecture notes', whereas Bahiah 'raised her two black eyes high, stiffened her lips in an anger which challenged fate', 'extended her tall, graceful body', and 'swept her nose round in a way which was sharp and strange, like a sword's edge, rending the universe apart'.[18] The male students have 'bowed thighs and [an] ordinary posture', but Bahiah 'stood on one foot alongside the marble table, lifting the other high as if to kick someone, then put it down with all its weight on the table's edge. A forbidden posture for man or woman.'

Finally, in contrast to the other female students with their 'fat, closely-bound legs' and their skirts which 'wound tightly round the thighs and narrowed at the knees, so that their legs remained bound together whether they were sitting, standing or walking', Bahiah wears trousers rather than a skirt, 'swinging her legs freely and striding out confidently'.

The exaggerated importance given to the body, though intolerably embellished by elitist ideology, is not based on ideological grounds alone. First, we sense a phallic use of the body in its perfection, or rather an identification with the lost phallus. Whoever loses something, and feels that loss deeply, will cause it to transmigrate and be assimilated into the body.

Second, we can detect a narcissistic use and shielding of the ego in a defensive reaction against this schizophrenic desire to rid oneself of the body in that it harbours the ego: much as she wants to destroy her body, Bahiah also wants to bring it to life.

Bahiah lives the fullness of existence not only on the physical level but also, quite naturally, on the spiritual level. Her five senses are not only more capable of perception than those of others, but, unlike ordinary beings, she is not restricted to five senses alone but probably possesses six or seven or even more!

What she felt for him went beyond the ability of her ears to hear, of her eyes to see, her nose to smell, and her fingers to touch. She realized that people have other senses, as yet undiscovered, that they lie latent in the inner self. But these other senses are more capable of feeling than the senses that are known to us. They are the real, natural senses, but they have never been developed by our upbringing, or by education, regulations, laws, traditions or indeed by anything at all. They are like a river flowing free without dams, or the rain pouring down from the sky, facing no barrier or obstacle.[19]

Once we become aware of the world with more than our five senses, with more than the mind or mere consciousness, it is clear that it is no longer the world, and thus no longer subject to the laws which normally make it the world. Its colours and shapes will no longer be the usual ones. Temporal and spatial laws will no longer apply. In other words, qualitative man can only live in a qualitative world. Someone who refuses to be like others cannot live in the world of others. A person who believes he can change the qualitativeness of his existence is content with nothing less than a world whose qualitativeness has also changed. If such a world does not exist, let us invent it schizophrenically. It is not existence which determines our consciousness:

It is our consciousness that determines the shape of the world around us — its size, motion and meaning.

The street on her left was no longer a street. For streets, like everything else, change minute by minute according to our view of the world, the pulse in our veins...

Her home, her room and her bed were now no longer her own.

Everything took on a new form and new colours. She had discovered the true colour of things. Her eyes saw that the leaves of the trees were not green, the sky not blue, the wall not grey — indeed, it was as transparent as a silk curtain. Her body could penetrate it easily. She felt a strange power... [with which she perceived that] the past merged with the present and future. Yesterday was today and the day after. Time ceased to exist...

This discovery was the real reason behind the strange ecstasy that now appeared in her black eyes, and which made her bleeding body dance with a rare agility and toy with the hordes of bedbugs swarming over the straw mat. The body acquires this extraordinary ability when it rids itself of its false human consciousness and achieves true awareness.

But what is necessary in order for the 'real' human being to live through this ecstasy, to experience in half a minute what others experience in half a century, to absorb the real colours of things, to be liberated from the tepidity of life and sample its 'biting hot taste', to have 'the pulsing of real life' seep into one, to lose 'the sense of time and place' and acquire 'the marvellous capacity for sensing time and place', indeed 'to lose feeling yet not lose it', 'as though his body vanished while he was still there, and as though the world around him had been obliterated while he remained alive, as if the sky had become the earth and the earth the sky', to see 'momentous events happen in seconds ...when you can fly, arms, legs and all, or sink to the bottom of the sea without drowning, or walk a tightrope without falling, or see a house destroyed and rebuilt in seconds, and suddenly everything becomes possible in the twinkling of an eye', in a word, to live a magical life free from the laws of gravity and all other physical laws? In order to achieve all these things, the 'real' human being must always be on the brink of the abyss, 'suspended between heaven and earth', on 'the high frightening summit, the point suspended in space with nothing before or behind it'.

He must abolish the distance between life and death, even if it is only 'a very thin thread'. He must be at the heart of danger, indeed at the heart of fear, not the kind of fear that 'takes us away from danger' but that which 'carries us closer to danger rather than further from it... a violent consuming desire to experience the peak of danger to its very end, that we might be rid of it for ever'. In short, he must 'sever the hair's breadth which separates life from death' and no longer 'fear death' because only 'when man breaks the fear of death can he become capable of doing everything in life, including dying itself'.

This is how Bahiah herself has chosen to answer Hamlet's question. The question is not 'to be or not to be', but rather 'not to be in order to be', to die in order to live, to die in order to die in order to live, to die in order to be reborn: 'It was a dreadfully momentous time, which seemed like death. No, it *was* a kind of death — one person was dying and another being born... '

This paradox, despite its obvious flaw, is susceptible to logic. Thus it is sufficient for Bahiah to maintain that her 'ordinary' existence is not life, but death personified. Building on this powerful premise, the syllogism may then be formulated as follows. Every passive ordinary life is death. Danger holds off death. Therefore, danger brings us closer to life.

As long as 'the point of total stillness and complete unthreatened security' is 'the point of death', this must mean that the 'ordinary' Bahiah stands 'on the brink of death itself and could not escape it'. It follows then that her escape route to safety is not through 'avoiding danger, by steering clear of any dangerous situations' but exactly the opposite: so long as she is 'on the brink of death itself', any move is 'a step towards safety, towards life'.

The major question this poses is the following: is Bahiah capable of moving from theory to practice? Can she actually live this intertwined paradox? Now that she has seen the light of a new formulation of Hamlet's dilemma, is she capable, not only in words but in practice, of going to the limits to which the Danish prince went?

Bahiah Shaheen was hesitant. She would stop half-way, for she was afraid of ends. The end, she felt, was final. It was the high frightening summit, the point suspended in space with nothing before or behind it, the destructive summit, after which there is only extinction.

The word 'hesitant' does not apply here, however. For in fact she did not hesitate for a moment. She was drawn by a mysterious desire to press ahead and not to stop until she had reached the dangerous end. She was aware that she was heading there inevitably: it was her destiny.

But as much as 'she was drawn by the strength of her desire to know her own destiny', so too is she driven by a similar force, 'by the intensity of her fear of that knowledge, a fear so great that it helped to drive her' in the opposite direction.

Only once does she attempt to put her theoretical option into practice. She stands at the summit of Jebel al-Muqattam gazing at the 'bottomless abyss' and wanting to respond to its call. But the moment she 'stretched out one foot and nearly followed it with the other' she finds herself pulled back by 'some mysterious force'.

This alternating movement, which brings to mind the swing between the necrophilia and the biophilia of the heroine of *Memoirs...*, is not voluntary. It is, rather, akin to a biological necessity pre-programmed into her body, like her heartbeats which come and go, continue and are interrupted, in an endless oscillation:

> She gazed at the blue veins under her skin and felt the regular pulse in her wrist, one beat after the other. Some mysterious hidden feeling told her that the next beat would be the last and that the sound would stop, that she would breathe no more. She strained to listen. The final moment was still far off, but her ears could already detect it — faint and drawing nearer, just like the beat before and the next one, a continuous buzz that she fervently wished would cease. She strained to hear, waiting for the next beat and fearing that it would never come.

This swinging between the desire to reach an end and the fear of reaching it is in fact a reflection of a split in the ego: an ego which demands on the one hand its own destruction and on the other its reconstitution. Every move towards destruction is inevitably counteracted by a move towards reconstruction, like the heartbeats which come and go. But this alternating pattern, even if successful in saving the ego's existence, does so at the expense of its unity. It is as though half the ego wants to drive the entire ego to destruction while the other half struggles to pull it to safety. Precisely because of this, there is in Bahiah 'that other self dwelling within her'. This explains the title of the novel, which provides a succinct description of the personality of its heroine: *Two Women in One*.

First, there is the Bahiah Shaheen who is 'always surrounded by girls — she went to girls' schools with classes for girls only. Her name always appeared among those of other girls. Bahiah Shaheen: the feminine ending of her name bound it like a link in a chain into lists of girls' names.' 'Bahiah Shaheen, the hard-working, well-behaved medical student', who has a 'polite, obedient voice' and a 'placid look which did not see things, but allowed them to be reflected from her, like a watery surface', and who has eyes which are 'less dark' and a nose which is 'less prominent', the one who stands at 'point zero', 'the point of death'. She is 'afraid of the end of ends', of falling back into 'the whirlpool of everyday life and everyday faces' and becoming atomized and indistinguishable from the other 'millions of atoms swimming in the universe', lost in the sea of 'deadly similitude', till her face becomes 'just like her fellow students, so that there was no difference between Bahiah, Aliah, Suad and Yvonne'.

Then there is the other Bahiah Shaheen, 'her real self', 'that other self dwelling within her', 'another diabolical being, born of neither her mother nor her father', 'that devil who moved and saw things with the sharpest powers of perception'. Her 'features resembled those she saw in the mirror, but they were more intense. Her eyes were darker, the tilt of her nose more pronounced', 'dividing the world into two, passing unhesitatingly through the middle, never fearing to reach the end, the end of the end'. It is a different person from Bahiah Shaheen, the 'hard-working, well-behaved medical student, daughter of Muhammad Shaheen, superintendent of the Ministry of Health', 'some other person. She had no connection with the world she had lived in, with the people she had known', nothing, not even her name which 'sounded as if it belonged to someone else', seeming 'stranger every time'. When someone calls her name she does not reply for she knows that the caller is 'calling someone else... She looked around, searching among the faces for someone called Bahiah Shaheen,' someone else with a 'desire to be her real self and... to tear her birth certificate to pieces, to change her name, to change her father and mother'. She looks for someone else who recognizes 'the futility of life and the futility of the universe around her', someone who, in spite of her name being on female lists, refuses to belong to the class of those who have 'bowed heads and defeated eyes', 'tightly-bound legs' and a 'worm-like crawl', someone who is fully aware that her day is inevitably coming and that 'in some magical way, she could become another person, someone other than Bahiah Shaheen'.

This split does not remain a prisoner of the theoretical conscious. Here we have Bahiah on the tram:

When she heard a cry and leaned her head out of the tram window to see a body torn to shreds on the rails, she felt that the body was hers, the pale face hers, the red blood spattered over the tar her own. But the tram moved on again and she found her body where it had always been, intact on the seat. Her blood still flowed through her veins: it had not gushed out. A hidden certainty told her that the day had not yet come, that she was still Bahiah Shaheen, hard-working, well-behaved medical student...

On the tram she felt someone riding behind her, following her. When she got out... she imagined she heard his steps. As she went in through the college gate, so did he.

Walking along Qasr al-Aini street, she wants in her conscious to turn left towards the road leading up to al-Muqattam:

But her body held fast and she was unable to lift her foot from the ground. She shuddered in panic and her satchel fell, the anatomy books scattering all over the road.

From the corner of her eye she saw the white label on the cover: Bahiah Shaheen, 1st Year Anatomy. Her arms seemed to shrink. They refused to pick up the books, but with her body still bent over the pavement she managed to gather them up and put them in her bag. Stooping over was enough to bring back Bahiah Shaheen full force. That other person disappeared down the long corridor...

Under the pressure of this split, existence itself becomes suspect. As in dreams, a large question mark hangs over it. Just as someone who has been asleep touches his own body to reassure himself that he is awake, Bahiah feels an urgent need to 'run her hand over her body' and to 'feel its external boundaries', to reassure herself that she still exists. But as the body is no longer proof of existence in the light of this split: 'any attempt to make certain would only add to her doubts'.

Faced with this escalating doubt, her need to be fully aware sometimes becomes so acute that it turns into 'an overwhelming desire... to plunge a kitchen knife into her chest so that she would cry and hear her cries with her own ears and know for certain that she was alive and not dead'.

This exhausting search for the meaning of existence may explain Bahiah's love of drawing. Even though existence is fleeing from her consciousness, and indeed her body, it can at least be made more permanent on paper. This is why she continually draws self-portraits. When she draws, 'she would make her eyes blacker, her nose more upturned and her lips pursed in ever greater anger and determination'. It is only by using the comparative that she can establish that the features drawn on the paper are her own, that she 'knew them as she knew her own face', that she 'could distinguish her face... never confusing it with other faces'.

Searching for the meaning of life may also explain Bahiah's love of scandal:

> for scandal alone could save her now, could make everyone cast her out. She wanted to be cast out, to have no mother or father, and no family to protect her. For protection itself was the real danger: it was an assault on her reality, the usurpation of her will and of her very existence.

Bahiah's first experience of scandal comes on her wedding night, when she summarily ejects the husband chosen for her by her father, throwing him out of bed and refusing to yield up her supposed maidenhead, kicking him in the stomach instead.[20] Scandal will from now on be her daily bread: she is determined that the stance she has adopted in college will be extended unaltered to the neighbourhood where she lives. She lifts up her black eyes, stiffens her lips in an anger which challenges fate, and makes her way with:

> her tall slim body, her straight legs enveloped by her trousers. One foot trod firmly on the ground before the other, and her

legs parted noticeably. The men of the neighbourhood gazed at her from the shops; the women stared through keyholes and cracks in the windows. Was she woman or man? Had it not been for the two small breasts showing through the blouse, they would have sworn she was a man. But since she was a woman, it was legitimate to stare. Her body was the victim of hungry, deprived eyes. They stared at her and whispered. One dared to laugh obscenely, another made a dirty crack. Street urchins were encouraged to follow her... Teenage boys would expose themselves to her. One threw a stone, another let out a long cat-call. Men sitting in the cafe laughed hoarsely, slapping their thighs... Women would strike their breasts and heave that ever-suppressed feminine sigh, saying, 'Just look at what Western women are like!'

Here Bahiah seems to be as much a martyr to the cause as the victim of scandal. The scandal lies in denying any anatomical difference between the sexes. The cause is the confirmation of the qualitative distinction between human beings. The paradox is the bridge which links the scandal to the cause. The creature who is neither male nor female cannot exist unless it was originally neither of these beings. Its non-existence *vis-à-vis* others is the primary proof of its existence *vis-à-vis* itself.

The paradox can be summed up in the following phrase: 'what Western women are like'. This is a vivid reference to a being whose non-existence is the proof of its existence, to a being derided by others because it is unlike them. But it is only other people's scorn which brings it to life and enables it to declare itself. Had it not been for this scorn, such a being would have been relegated to a place in pre-history.

For Bahiah, the paradox is a question of life and death. To her, absence is the proof of presence, negation is the proof of existence, and extreme negativity is the way to maximum positivity. The acrobat's skill is measured in direct proportion to the amount of danger to which he is exposed. For the pilot, the dangerously nearer the ground he ventures, the greater the ecstasy in taking off again: 'We feel alive only when we face death. It is like the colour white that becomes white only when contrasted with black.'

As the only alternatives are suicide or madness, Bahiah's route to salvation can only be a series of paradoxes. The first of these is a geographical paradox: all Cairo's 'usual flat streets... stretched on and could be seen right to the end' except the road leading up to Saleem's flat in al-Muqattam. 'This street was not horizontal. It rose, like a road climbing a high mountain.'

Obviously the reference lends itself to a symbolic interpretation, but the symbolism itself was chosen only because it allows the paradox to take shape in the geometric space:

> She had never been there before. She had never walked up a mountain road, as she was doing now. Her life had always run on flat, horizontal lines. Her home was on the ground floor... The tram took one or two steps. The dissecting room was on the ground floor, and the lecture hall was just three steps above the college grounds. The six steps leading to the laboratory were as high as she had ever climbed.

To this spatial paradox is then added the paradox of physiognomy. Saleem's face, like his flat, is the very exception at the heart of the rule, an embodiment of the extraordinary in the midst of the banal:

> When she looked up... she realized that someone was standing in front of her. Not just anyone. He was the sort of person you have to look at, even if only for a few seconds... When the first moment had passed, she managed to stifle her surprise and return the stare. With her natural inquisitiveness, she scrutinized the unusual features, trying to understand what made them so extraordinary. The forehead was commonplace, the eyes ordinary; she wondered how such ordinary features could make up such a strange, extraordinary face.

Any paradox implies discontinuity, but discontinuity of the kind which creates existence, cancels out similarity and engenders individuality. It makes the non-existent exist, what is absent present, what is invisible visible, and what is lost found:

> Her black eyes continued... staring into space as if seeking something. They released millions of floating particles into the

atmosphere. They probed the minute organisms drifting through the world, searching among the thousands of similar beings for the extraordinary face, for the eyes that would see her and make her visible — the black eyes that would pick her face out from among the others, and extricate her body from among the millions of bodies lost in the world.

Paradox therefore is a conjuror's cloak, but it has the reverse effect to that in *The Thousand and One Nights*. It is not the wearer who disappears from view while all the others can be seen; on the contrary, he is the only one visible while the others disappear. It is a factor which engenders individuality and abolishes ordinariness. Here, precisely, lies the miracle of the name. The borrowed name with its feminine ending links Bahiah with the 'lists of girls' names', drowns her in a sea of 'similar faces, movements and voices' and fails to distinguish her from those called by other names, 'something like Kufiah, Najiah, Aliah or Zakiah'.

Her name loses its ordinariness on Saleem's lips, however:

The name Bahiah had become very special. It was not like the name Bahiah — any Bahiah — but referred to her in particular, her and nobody else, her to the exclusion of all others, that particular being of hers now standing beside him, the borders of her body sharp, separate from the space outside.

After the miracle of the name, can we next talk in terms of the miracle of love? Bahiah has now begun to be 'seen by eyes other than her own', after all other eyes 'in the street, on the tram or at college' were 'incapable of seeing her or distinguishing her from thousands of others', incapable of saving her from being 'lost among the sameness of bodies'. She has fallen in love with the militant nationalist Saleem Ibraheem and the class-militant Saleem Ibraheem has fallen in love with her. The big question is whether, after all this, she is now content with the phenomenon of 'eternal severance'. Does she accept that she has 'an independent existence', 'a personality of her own', 'a name of her own', 'a body of her own separate from her mother's' which is not destined to be crushed and submerged into the body of the mother to become 'one and the same thing'?

Are we to believe that love has transformed Bahiah from someone who demands annihilation to someone who demands the opposite — existence? Can we believe that, now that love has shown her the way to an awareness of her 'real self', she no longer feels the need to destroy her false self? She is in love and has found someone who understands her and can penetrate 'long narrow corridors leading to her very depths'. Her existence has melted in the arms of one she loves so deeply that it has become difficult to 'distinguish her body from his' and both have become as if 'one body'. After all this, are we to believe that she is no longer in need of the 'instinctive knowledge' that 'her mother's body was the only thing that understood her', and that her loss of contact with the field of gravity will turn her into an atom lost and whirling amongst the millions in the universe, an atom destined to 'spin madly and helplessly in its orbit until the revolutions destroyed her'?

In fact it is precisely at this level that Bahiah, 'who is searching for her own annihilation', prepares us for her greatest paradox, indeed her biggest surprise. In Saleem's flat on al-Muqattam, as we have seen, she experiences a tremendous urge to move from theory to practice, to leap into space and be swallowed up by 'the enormity of the universe'. With Saleem, her belief grows ever stronger that 'the time would come and the pulse would stop. So sure was she that she longed for that moment, for the pulse to stop, relieving her of the burden'.

When Bahiah first asks Saleem to take her in his arms to protect her from 'her fear of death' and 'her fear of life':

She said faintly, 'Hold me with all your strength until...'

She stopped before she had finished the sentence. She had wanted to say 'until my pulse stops', but her secret death wish, once out in the open, would have seemed taboo and she understood why, for most people, the forbidden wishes are the real ones and the licit wishes unreal.

This death wish lies behind her compulsive drive to visit Saleem's flat again. Her companion on the road up is the image of the mythical god from the stories and legends she listened to as a child: 'a terrible god worshipped by the people of an enchanted

city... could grasp any solid object and clench his fist, and when
he opened his hand it would be gone'.

It is the anticipated ecstasy caused by this sense of impending
annihilation which beckons to Bahiah and pushes her onwards and
upwards, not the imagined ecstasy of meeting Saleem:

> The street lengthened and protruded from the belly of the
> mountain like an outstretched arm. Above it, caught between
> the mountains and the buildings, a strip of sky formed a second
> arm. The two huge arms, like those of the mythical god,
> stretched out before her like the gaping jaws of fate, extending
> toward the horizon, lying in wait for her, willing her body to
> turn to them.
> She longed to throw herself into those outstretched arms.
>
> She was sure that someday the jaws would inevitably close.

Even when she has experienced the joys of physical love with
Saleem, the main image she is left with is of death and annihilation:

> Like the force of gravity that attracts the body to the earth, his
> arms moved round her. They embraced with a violent desire
> to dissolve into the world, to lose all consciousness of the body
> and its weight, and to be annihilated and vanish in the air, like
> death, if you could manage to die and then come back to life
> and describe it...
> ...the key to the moment of eternal contact when the body
> would no longer feel separated from the world but would
> become one with it, an enormous entity filling the space between
> sky and earth. [21]

After the miracle of love, Bahiah discovers the miracle of
political struggle. When she first takes part in a student
demonstration, her ecstatic response to the screams of this
'immense body' of people demonstrating for the freedom of the
greatest mother of all, Egypt, is to submerge herself in it. It
becomes a recurrent regression, in the full sense of the word, back
to the ecstasy of the union with her mother's body:

She had the strange sensation of blending into the larger world, of becoming part of the infinite extended body of humanity, of dissolving like a drop of water in the sea or a particle of air in the atmosphere. It was a delicious, wonderful feeling, an overwhelming happiness as intoxicating for her body as the ecstasy she had experienced yesterday in that far-away place in the bosom of the mountain, or as a child when she saw the mythical god crushing something in his grip, then opening it and it was gone, or her childish laugh when her mother embraced her with all her might and their bodies would almost melt into one.

Her body had felt a hidden desire since childhood, since she developed a body of her own separate from the world. It was a persistent desire to return to the world, to dissolve to the last atom so that she would be liberated and disembodied...

It was a desire for the limitless, overwhelming freedom that comes only when you opt for salvation and destroy the hair's breadth that separates life from death.

Up to now, we cannot be certain that freedom is the result of the sophist reunion with the mother. What we are sure of, however, is that the totality of the narcissistic capacity — a capacity that man imagines he enjoyed in the womb before 'falling' into the outside world — contributes to a meteoric outburst of a feeling of ecstasy. After all, it is Bahiah who tells us that:

At that moment she felt she could pierce iron with her body, take bullets and poisoned daggers in her chest, and that no power on earth could make her body fall, stop her legs from moving on, or prevent her voice from calling out for freedom.

Has not this sense of omnipotence, derived from her union with the collective body, taken on a sense of immunity from death itself? When she:

awoke to the sound of gunfire... she saw some students fall to the ground. Others advanced, facing the bullets head on, while still others sought protection in the doorways of houses and shops.

She stood still as a statue, her black eyes gazing up. Had a bullet been aimed at her body, she would have been killed immediately, but she knew she could not die against her will. She did not want to die yet.

The narcissistic use of political struggle does not stop with Bahiah, but goes beyond it to reverse the very equation of struggle itself. It is not the ego which works in conjunction with other people's desire to change the world: it is the world which operates to change the sensations of the ego. It cannot be denied that the status of 'struggle' spawns egotistical feelings and is an important means of enriching them. Thus it is both legitimate and natural for Bahiah to experience all the feelings of a struggling militant and to know:

the true taste of life: hot and biting... the tremor of real life [and] a mixture of fear and bravery, a sense of both danger and safety, a loss of time and place and yet the acquisition of a remarkable ability to experience them both. It was a heady mixture of contradictory feelings, melting in complete harmony like the colours of a rainbow.

But the joy of the struggle is one thing: interpreting it subjectively is another. In other words, the stream of the ego flowing into the river of 'the cause' is entirely different from the river of 'the cause' flowing into the stream of the ego:

She thought that the entire world must be in motion to provoke this strange mixture of feelings in her body: the strike, the demonstration, the chanted slogans, the anthem, the bullets, the falling bodies, the red blood flowing on the ground... it was all this that created that contradictory mixture of sensations in her body.

Thus the moment of ego-assertion takes precedence over that of changing the world through political struggle. This in turn changes the struggle from a theoretical comradely revolutionary cause into an individual adventure and an exercise in risk-worship and brinkmanship:

that frantic movement of people who feel threatened, with known or unknown forces lying in wait to destroy them... The head jerks continuously: every cell is alert, thinking: how can I save myself from the impending danger? ... [a] rapid, regular pulse: it is the throb of anxiety, bringing with it the sensation of life... the only movement through which the difference between life and death becomes clear.

It was a frightening moment. She feared it as much as she desired it. She longed to escape from it and yearned to pursue it. It was the only time she saw that she was real and alive...

This moment was her goal. She had wanted it from the very beginning and had marched toward it firmly and with determination. She knew that she was heading only toward danger, and at its brink was that small place, just a foot wide suspended in air; above was sky and below the abyss. It was a moment ruled by two powerful forces: one pulling down to the abyss, the other urging soaring flight.

When political struggle is thus turned into a game of Russian roulette, though not quite so chancy, it necessarily acquires an elitist bent, in spite of the class struggle proclaimed in the secret pamphlets distributed by the militant Bahiah ('People of Egypt! Awake! Throw open your windows, open your eyes... the sweat of your brows is being plundered. Your crops are stolen, your flesh devoured until you are left only skin and bone...').

It is rare in revolutionary literature (the literature of 'going to the people on a pilgrimage', as the Russian Alexander Herzen put it, or 'studying at the school of the people', as the Chinese Marxists put it) to find anything comparable to the message contained in *Two Women in One*. The novel endorses and confirms the wide gulf between the individual militant and those in whose name he campaigns. The world of others, the 'world of transmuted human beings', of 'identical heads and necks hanged by their ties', of 'bulging... eyes', in a word, the world of people 'on the treadmill of their daily lives', is despised and scorned.

At the end of her story, Bahiah presents us with the strange case of a class-militant whose militancy alienates rather than brings her closer to those in whose name she struggles. As long as the moment of danger in the struggle is more important than the struggle itself, then it goes without saying that the gap caused by this separation widens in direct proportion to the momentum of the struggle, until it becomes a total separation.

When Bahiah is first arrested, she does not hesitate to deprive all ordinary human beings of any sense of existence. In the car taking her and Saleem to the police station, she appropriates this existence to herself:

The churning in the streets and the people's actions seemed odd to her, divorced from the world she now inhabited, a world that seemed to know nothing of food, drink, sleep, homes, fathers, mothers, shops, shoppers, new-born children, dying old people, and streets for people to walk on... People's movements as they walked seemed absurd and meaningless. She imagined that they were dead or lived in a passive world without warmth or pulse. The world of other people appeared dead to her. Her whole life was focused on that car like a closed box, or more specifically on the seat occupied by that slim body, with its exhausted head and... its deep eyes with their strange ability to see and penetrate to the reality of things.

And when Saleem is transferred to Torrah prison to spend 'long years, no one knows how many', her only recourse is to pour out all her pain, anger and frustration on the 'ordinary' people:

She saw people going to work or going home as if nothing important had happened. The most momentous possible thing had happened and no one knew or cared... She growled in anger and stamped the ground. How ugly ordinary life was after a great event!

...The sky remained suspended on high, the earth stretched out below... and people walked in the streets with their usual indifference. Would such frivolity never cease? Again she stamped her foot. Why wouldn't this indifferent motion stop its grinding cycle?

When her turn comes to be arrested, she directs a last scathing, satirical farewell to members of her own sex, whom she describes as having 'a brain soft like a rabbit's, knowing nothing of life except eating and reproduction'. While she is being followed by the secret police, women and girls are strolling down al-Moski street with:

> their closely-bound fat legs... [and] their bottoms visible under their glossy dresses. Their made-up eyes devoured the shop windows: they lusted after clothes, transparent nightdresses, slippers, make-up, perfume and body lotions. Their sharp, penetrating voices mingled with the popping of chewing gum and the clacking of pointed high heels bearing bodies laden with shopping.

When she is finally arrested by the detectives, and she is convinced that the 'frightening moment' she 'feared as much as she desired' has come, 'her lips parted in a smile and her eyes shone', as she knows that from now on 'she would not be Bahiah Shaheen, would not return to the ordinary faces, would not sink into the sea of similar bodies or tumble into the grave of ordinary life'.

Thus political struggle changes from the smelter to the generator. The person who is 'generated' is a higher evolutionary being, genderless and unique, neither female nor male. It is not a human being, but a mythological being, which takes its very mythology as proof of its existence.

The elitist solution with which Bahiah concludes her life story is imposed on her not by her conscious will but by the vicious circle in which she imprisons herself. Bahiah Shaheen wants to rid herself of Bahiah Shaheen, tied by the feminine case ending to the 'lists of girls' names' and the lists of human beings. But she cannot do this any more than the body can consume itself or the stomach digest itself. Thus the only alternative is for the world to be devoured. In a world which is deadened by similarity, difference lives only in Bahiah Shaheen. In a world drained of its existence, nothing but Bahiah's existence can refill it. In a world which has turned into a non-world, Bahiah has become *the* world. As the saying goes, 'I am the world and the world is me.'

At the end of our journey with Bahiah, and after all the criticism directed at her elitist vision of the world, perhaps a word of self-criticism is called for. To hand it to her, Bahiah pushes us ordinary human beings into a totally unfamiliar world. With her and through her, we experience completely new sensations. We also see the world through new eyes. The 'brinkmanship' strategy has been described as one of madness, yet it undeniably generates the most unexpected streams of beauty and imagination, and the highest degree of truth and authenticity.

In the one hundred or so pages of the story of her life, Bahiah tells us as much as one thousand pages of ordinary history. In spite of and perhaps because of the exaggeration, she plumbs the abysmal depths of the human psyche, revealing facets not normally seen by the average human being. If we are to criticize our own criticism of the way in which she perceives the world, nothing seems more apt than to quote Wilhelm Reich's words in defence of the 'madness' of the schizophrenic as opposed to the alleged 'sanity' of the normal man. As the defender of 'the small human being' whose integrity is beyond doubt, Reich says:

The schizophrenic world mingles into one experience what is kept painstakingly separated in the homo normalis... The fact is that the schizophrenic is, on the average, much more honest than homo normalis, if one accepts directness of expression as an indication of honesty... He is also what is commonly called 'deep', i.e. in contact with happenings. The schizoid person looks through hypocrisy and does not hide it... This is so because the schizophrenic tells us frankly what he thinks and how he feels, whereas homo normalis tells us nothing at all and keeps us digging for years before he feels ready to show his inner structure...

One must learn to read his language. What is never admitted by homo normalis, what is lived out only clandestinely or laughed off in a silly manner, are the severely distorted forces of nature; exactly the same forces which imbue the great sages, philosophers, musicians, geniuses of science, in the wide realm beyond the conceptions of homo normalis and his everyday political clamour. I venture the statement that in our mental institutions many potentially great artists, musicians, scientists and philosophers are rotting away their lives because homo normalis refuses to look beyond the iron curtain which he drew in front of his real life, because he dare not look at living realities.

These great souls, broken down and wrecked as 'schizo-phrenics', know and perceive what no homo normalis dares to touch... I claim... that they look through our hypocrisy, our cruelty and stupidity, our fake culture, our evasiveness and our fear of the truth. They had the courage to approach what is commonly evaded, and they were wrecked because they went through the inferno without any help.[22]

4
The Absentee

The preceding chapter sought to show that the meeting between Bahiah Shaheen and Saleem Ibraheem[1] is that of a female individualist and a male individualist, and that their relationship is elitist in the extreme. Nevertheless it cannot be denied that Bahiah's relationship with Saleem allows her to discover the objective world and its joys; her inner world is suffused with a vitality and splendour such as this 'seeker of her own annihilation' has never known before. For this we rely on one piece of evidence. After their first meeting, and so that she can have complete freedom of choice in deciding on future encounters, Saleem takes a small key from his pocket and hands it to her, saying, 'This is the key to my flat in al-Muqattam... Come any time after three. I'll be waiting for you.'

It is as if he has given her the key to the gates of paradise, as if thousands upon thousands of flares have driven away the darkness of existence:

He vanished behind the college building. As she stood there, her fingers coiled around a small metal object with a rounded top and a hole in the middle. Its tail had small pointed teeth. As she ran her fingers over it, a shiver swept through her like particles of soft hot sand tingling in her hands, down through her legs, up through her head, along her neck and arms, and accumulating in the hand that gripped the small object.

It looked like the key to any other door. But she knew that objects change when feelings do. A little metal key can suddenly become magic, radiating heat that surges through the body like a burst of air and swells in the palm of the hand, filling it to overflowing. She felt drops of sweat in her hot hand under the solid object... Wrapping it in her handkerchief, she put it in her pocket and slipped through the crowded grounds, moving with a panther's long strides. She felt eyes staring at her, and slid her hand into her pocket to hide the key, as if, magical as it was, it might tear through handkerchief and pocket, leaping into view, as visible as the sun.[2]

It is this glow that is the great 'absentee' in the novel of the same title.[3] This absence is in turn connected with another form of absenteeism. Saleem Ibraheem (who has now become Fareed) is in a prison for political detainees. Bahiah Shaheen (in this novel renamed Fuaadah Khaleel Saleem) is free but, because of the absence of her beloved, she is similarly absent from both herself and the world. In *The Absentee*, Fuaadah is the epitome of the non-existent in the heart of non-existence. Thus she goes one step further than Bahiah who, in *Two Women in One*, monopolizes the distinction of existence in the heart of non-existence.

In *Two Women in One*, fluidity is the stuff the world is made of and the form of its non-existence. Saleem's key represents the only solid thing in this amorphous, non-existent world.[4] By identifying with the key, Bahiah is able to give her existence — and the body which harbours this existence — a stiff shielded woodenness, both while walking and at rest. It is this rigid shield which, as we have seen, provokes such scandal in the neighbourhood. Fuaadah, on the other hand, in the absence of Fareed, has lost all the solidity which Saleem gave Bahiah. She moves or rather sinks from a state of solidity to one of liquefaction. She changes from wood to wax.

The fact that Fuaadah, like Bahiah, remains unbreakable has nothing to do with her solidity. Rather, it can be ascribed to her amorphousness and ability to take on all or any of the shapes she is supposed to repress. It is as though she has regressed into a purely shapeless creature, a bitter and contentious entity. From among all the various forms of existence, all she is destined to achieve is formlessness.

Bahiah will 'spring like a panther', 'pound the ground' as she walks, rending the universe with her strides, 'challenging destiny' and destroying 'all other wills' with the voluntary, liberated movements of her legs. In the case of Fuaadah, however, the movement of the legs is involuntary and has no distinctive rhythm of its own. In a sense, it isn't Fuaadah who walks, but her feet which carry her along 'without her being aware of it' and 'without the control of her mind'. It isn't her will that controls her feet but her feet that control her will: 'She turned round to go back, but her feet moved forwards, and walked to the end of the corridor and turned left.' This is why Fuaadah wonders from time to time, 'Why isn't the brain between the legs?'

In fact, she never walks; she allows 'her feet to walk on their own'. Action is theirs, not hers. The reader of *The Absentee* cannot help noticing the many instances where it is the feet that instigate the action: 'Her feet stopped at the bus stop' or 'Her feet continued walking along the street.' Moreover, it is often the 'self' that is the object or 'sufferer' of the action: 'Fuaadah found herself walking along Nile Street...', 'After a few steps she found herself in front of the iron fence... ', 'She found herself in the wide avenue of Duqqi Street...', and so on. This abdicating of command to her feet brings to mind the image of a donkey:

She found herself in front of the rusty fence around the ministry, and came to with a start as if a jug of cold water had been flung over her to wake her up, remembering that she hadn't intended to come here at all but that her feet had carried her here unconsciously, following her usual daily trek, like a donkey who makes for the fields as soon as the stable door is opened...

She didn't know how her feet had managed to carry her all this way, how they had climbed onto a bus, alighted at the right stop, walked from the bus-stop to the house, done all these things on her own without her realizing. She didn't ponder this trivial matter for long, being quite incapable of imagining that this was a trait of some uniqueness or distinction with which her feet were endowed, as the feet of a donkey plod on the same way silently and without fuss.

In pausing, in walking and consequently in existing, Bahiah is particularly concerned to have a special rhythm that distinguishes her and makes her unique. Fuaadah, on the other hand, lacks precisely that rhythm. Her personal rhythm comes not from herself but from her feet. And the rhythm of her feet is picked up in turn from that of other people's feet. It is the rhythm of 'contagion':

> She allowed her feet to stroll, but the fast pace in the street was contagious. She found herself quickening her pace as if she was going somewhere for an important date. There was no date, important or unimportant. There was nothing. She didn't know where she was going in such a hurry.

Bahiah has a 'herd phobia'. Whenever she finds herself in a crowd of people, she reacts by adopting a stiff wooden attitude which allows her to put up barriers of opposition, enabling her to be as distinct and visible as a black dot on a white page. But Fuaadah seems to live by a principle of 'amenability': she does not swim against the tide, or even with it, but allows the current to carry her, buffet her and wash her away as its eddies dictate:

> It was very crowded. Bodies were crammed together. Someone trod on her foot and almost squashed it, but she only felt a light pressure on her shoe. She only knew that she was inside a bus by the familiar trembling shaking her body and by the strange smell which she could never quite pinpoint. She was suddenly aware of something sharp pressing into her shoulder. She had sensed it before but hadn't paid any attention to it. After all, all sorts of things were pressed against parts of her body from all over, so why should she pay special attention to her shoulder?
> She did not brace her feet but allowed her body to move with the current flowing in the direction of the door. She was caught up in a moment of unidentified violent pressure. She felt like a leaf or a butterfly pressed in a book. Then she felt the pressure suddenly relieved, leaving her body to whirl through the air like a pigeon's feather, eventually hitting the ground like a brick.

She gets on and off the bus in this same mechanical way, just like a silent movie where a scene is played backwards:

She saw a bus about to move off. She jumped on without knowing its number. She put one foot on the step but the other was left dangling in the air. Hands were extended to help her haul herself up and she was able to find space for her other foot among those already on the steps. A long, strong arm wound round her to prevent her falling and she found herself pushing with the other bodies into the interior of the bus.

An existence governed by the principle of 'amenability' rather than that of opposition, and consequently by similarity rather than difference, is, in the nature of things, quantitative rather than qualitative. This 'quantification' which Bahiah shuns like the plague seems here to be the distinctive feature for that 'drop in the ocean'. Fuaadah is:

One among millions. One body among all the human masses which crowd the streets, the buses and trains and the houses. She is one among millions indeed. Indeed, one of the bodies crammed into the bus... One among millions and millions and millions.

Does this mean that Fuaadah has not inherited from her counterpart Bahiah 'the worship of the unique'? Far from it: uniqueness is the pivot around which the life of the heroine of *The Absentee* revolves, in the same way as that of the heroine of *Two Women in One* did before her. In the case of *The Absentee*, however, what was reality has become legend. Fuaadah does not experience moments of illusion but a life of dispelled illusions. Bahiah has wants and manages to satisfy them, whereas Fuaadah has wants but is unable to satisfy them.

Uniqueness is always before Bahiah: it's the horizon of her future. Fuaadah has left uniqueness behind her; it's the horizon of her past. Bahiah is eighteen years old; Fuaadah is thirty.[5] The difference in age between them reflects the gap that separates adolescence from maturity, illusion from reality, hope from disappointment and aspirations from failure.

Like Bahiah, Fuaadah wants to experience the two negations simultaneously: she is neither of the 'female' sex, nor of 'the other' type. She is confident that she is 'not like other women' and although she is actually a woman, since her name has a feminine ending and she has the 'fingers and complexion of a woman', she nevertheless does not want 'what other women want'.

Not only is she certain that 'in her there is something admirable'. She also feels that 'in her depths there is something which confirms that she is not just one of the millions', that 'she has what others don't' and that 'people are creatures of a kind other than herself; she is something else'. But what existential or even material evidence does she have to support her claim?

All she has are a handful of memories from a distant past that will never return, the echoes of a few voices 'which once or a number of times had resounded, created vibrations and ceased'. There is the voice of her mother when she said to her as a child long ago, 'You will become someone famous like Mme Curie.' Or the voice of the chemistry teacher when she uttered, on 'that historic day' many years ago, 'in front of the whole class and the inspector too' the sentence which is engraved on her mind: 'Fuaadah is different from all the other girls in the class.' Or again, Fareed's voice when he said, 'There is something within you which is not found in others.' But can memories replace evidence? Where are the witnesses? Where is her mother? Where is the chemistry teacher? Indeed where is Fareed himself? Hasn't 'his voice been swallowed in space and he himself vanished as though he had never existed'?

The myth of superiority which has been spun in adolescence is to disintegrate in maturity. The girl whose mother was convinced from the day of her birth that she is 'better than any other girl', and will become 'a great woman' and make 'a great discovery in chemistry', has ended up as an underemployed clerk at the Ministry of Organic Chemistry. For the last six years she has spent six hours a day in the gloomy ministry building which is like 'a foul-smelling tomb reeking with the stink of toilets', in a 'room with battered doors and windows' that has 'a strange smell like that which lingers in a tightly shut bedroom'. Before 'a scabrous, mean desk' she sits 'inactive for six hours at a time', stared at by the male clerks with their mummified heads 'while she in turn gazed at an empty file carrying the title "organic chemical research" and in which she had never scratched one word in six years'.

After office hours she leaves the embalmed world of the ministry, where her work and her very existence never go beyond signing in and out in the 'book of attendance', and heads for what she calls the Fuaadah Laboratory for Chemical Analysis. Here she faces total emptiness: no customers ever patronize the laboratory and the test-tubes are empty. Every time she puts on her white apron, prepares the test-tubes, lights the Bunsen burner and embarks on the research which will come up with 'that great discovery', she is astonished to find that the test-tube is empty and the subject of the research has evaporated from her head. It has left behind only 'cold sweat dripping from her forehead' and 'every time she thought and thought' it recedes 'further and further away'.

In fact, before settling in the file on her desk or into her private lab, this emptiness has dwelt in her head. The emptiness of the outside world is merely a projection of her internal world. Describing the other clerks as 'wooden statues', comparing the telephone to a 'dead black cat' and generalizing the concept of embalming to include the Nile lying lazily with its long 'wrinkled' body like that of 'an old prostitute' implies once again a disinvestment from the objective world. There is a major difference here, however, between the heroines of *The Absentee* and *Two Women in One*, and even that of *Memoirs of a Woman Doctor*:[6] Fuaadah does not reinvest the withdrawn libido in herself, nor does she grant the world of her ego a full life at the expense of withdrawing from the world of others. On the contrary, the death of the world reflects her own death from herself, and the emptiness of the outside world reflects the emptiness within.

Fareed used to say that he saw in her eyes something he had never found in the eyes of others, something which distinguished her from other women: 'She stood up, walked over to the mirror and gazed into her own eyes. She looked closely for "that something". Where was this thing that Fareed had seen? That something wasn't there. Fareed had lied.'

If this something isn't to be seen in her eyes, could it be inside herself? But here is Fuaadah putting:

her hand into the pocket of her coat, and poking her fingers into the holes in the silk lining as if she was searching for something important within herself, suddenly discovering that her self owned nothing of importance. It was not a discovery, nor was it sudden, but a slow, gradual, ambiguous feeling which had started some time ago, she knew not when.[7] She swallowed bile and moved her dry tongue, saying to herself in a barely audible voice, 'Yes, I am nothing.'

So is this 'something' perhaps in her head? But her head is empty and vacant. A 'sort of paralysis' has crept into it, 'the sort of numbness caused by a drug's action on the brain cells'. It has become 'heavy; within it a solid mass shook and reverberated against the bones of the skull, as though her brain had solidified and turned into a lump of metal' or 'turned into stone, or become like a brick wall'. Is it something else, then? Is it anything other than a 'soundproof wall repeating the echo'?

We are repeatedly confronted with this image: 'a soundproof stone head, a head of solid matter which knows nothing... ignorant, knowing nothing, and capable of nothing but repeating the empty echo like any wall'. Or: 'a soundproof wall containing nothing but silence and emptiness', 'everything inside it reduced to a dumb humming', 'changing to a continuous, piercing whistling' which it produces 'when everything else goes silent'.

The contagious nature of this silence, this empty echo, this desolation, this nothingness, moves from the soundproof head to the entire body. The woman who cries from the depths of her desert, 'I don't know the secret or meaning of my life', and who sees her own emptiness reflected in the test-tube whose transparent sides reveal that it 'exists without contents', is bound to feel an absolute strangeness about her body: so long as the body encapsulates existence, and as long as her existence has no content, what need is there for the body?

She kicked away the covers from her body. She wanted to kick off her arms and legs too. She wanted to kick off her whole body, but it remained attached to her, tethered to her, lying on top of her with its depressing weight and abominable wetness,[8] like a stranger to her, the strangeness of a stranger who might accidentally bump into her on the street, the strangeness of the concierge of the building, the strangeness of Saati. She trembled; yes, quite as strange as all these things.

When the frontiers of existence contract to become 'the frontiers of the body' and nothing else and when the body itself becomes a mere empty vessel, 'of silence and nothing but silence', then what use is it? What is the point in 'eating, drinking, urinating, sleeping and sweating'? 'Why should it remain if it is empty of everything?' Isn't total emptiness preferable in this case?

She spread her arms wide and embraced emptiness. Yes, emptiness is best. Nothingness is better. But how can she become as nothing? How can her body vanish? She stamped the ground with her foot: why don't I just vanish? She held her breath to prevent the air entering and leaving her lungs. With her hand she pressed on her heart to stop it beating. She imagined that air was no longer being inhaled and that her chest no longer rose and fell, and that her heartbeats were no longer audible to her ears, and she smiled contentedly. She was vanishing.

We have already come across this desire for annihilation in the heroine of *Two Women in One*. But what a difference between the two cases! In the case of Bahiah Shaheen, this desire is an expression of the excessive richness of the ego. In the case of Fuaadah, on the other hand, it is an expression of the impoverishment of the ego. For Bahiah it is the result of overcharging the battery of egoistic existence beyond its capacity. For Fuaadah, however, it is the result of using, depleting and consequently emptying this capacity. For Bahiah the desire translates itself into what might be called the 'wedding' of the ego. For Fuaadah, by contrast, it turns into the 'mourning' of the ego. It is as though the river which strays from its course because of flooding in Bahiah's case, now, with Fuaadah, loses its way because it has evaporated and dried up.

But why this transformation? Why this reversal from euphoria to depression? Why this transfer from positive to negative narcissism? Here we must return to the 'magic key', the theme with which our analysis of *The Absentee* began. Bahiah's fantasizing around Saleem's key is a source of richness and ecstasy in that it represents identification with 'the good object'. Fuaadah, on the other hand, now that her lover Fareed is absent, is left only with an identification with 'the bad object'.[9] It is here that we can detect the 'mourning' and the loss of her self-esteem. On the one hand, she is mourning the loss of 'the good object' (Fareed). On the other, she feels diminished in value as a function of her integration and identification with 'the bad object'.

It should be pointed out here that, contrary to what the title may suggest, *The Absentee* is not a story of absence alone but also one of presence. The entire area of existence (occupied by the absence of Fareed) is invaded inch by inch, and with ineluctable will, by the shifty, pestering leech Muhammad el-Saati. President of the Higher Commission for Building and Construction, Saati owns the building in which Fuaadah has rented a flat to use as a laboratory.

Let us begin with the physical image. The repellent Saati immediately brings to mind Sheikh Mahmoud to whom Firdaus is married off in *Woman at Point Zero*. Saati is 'huge-bodied and wide-shouldered', with 'a thick fleshy neck like the trunk of an ancient tree from which sprouted a small black growth which instead of living and growing had rather died and rotted'. He has 'a fat hairless soft chest, and a high prominent belly from which dangled two hairless crooked legs'.

With 'his round upper half' and his crooked legs which dangle like those of an ostrich, he looks like 'a strange kind of wild reptile'. His face is 'large and fleshy' with a thin upper lip that curls to reveal 'large yellow teeth' from between which issue 'quick swallowed words'. The ugliest part of his face are two protruding eyes which rotate 'constantly and involuntarily' beneath 'his thick white glasses like the eyes of a big, deep-sea fish', quivering 'like the eyes of a frog stealthily peering up through stagnant water'. His gross body gives off 'a strange disgusting smell', 'a strong pervasive rusty smell which blocked up the nose'.

He has the type of 'huge fat face padded all over with flesh' that 'from the moment we see [it] makes us lose confidence in whoever [it] belong[s] to'. There is something about the movement of the eyes, or some other undefinable 'something', which suggests that a person is 'telling a lie or... simply cannot tell the truth'.

In his capacity as a 'respectable' personage, president of both the Higher Commission for Building and Construction and the Political Council, someone 'newspapers write about and who speaks on radio and television, giving people advice', he not only tells lies but also believes in them. His entire fund of political knowledge consists of 'a few slogans' repeated with 'elegant enunciation'. In short, this 'great master', with his boundless political ambition, is a 'common thief'. In fact, he has the eyes of a thief.

It is with precisely these eyes that he looks covetously at Fuaadah. The meaning of these looks is not lost on her. He could have rented the flat in his building for 1,000 Egyptian pounds; for her, he has settled for a mere 200. He signs the contract 'with his glassy eyes eying her thighs and casting lascivious glances over her breasts'. As she signs the contract she pulls her skirt 'down over her knees' and crosses her arms over her chest to protect it from his greedy looks. Although she senses 'those beady eyes looking at her hungrily and greedily as if she was a piece of meat', this does not prevent her signing the contract.

From the day she takes the flat at such a low rent, he besieges her with his clinging, leech-like existence. He devours her with his shifty looks. She feels 'the impact of his gaze on her body'. His looks frighten her, but she never tries to shut the door in his face. When he touches her for the first time with his 'fat flabby hand', she jumps in disgust, but she does not throw him out of the flat. Then he insults her — unforgivably in her opinion — by commenting on her playing hard to get and standing him up, saying, 'This is the nature of all women.' The phrase 'all women' resounds in her ears and she retorts angrily, 'I am not like all women.' But she still does not throw him out or shut the door in his face. Nor does she refuse his offer of a drive round Cairo's dark streets by night. As she watches his protruding eyes in the pitch dark, she remembers 'a story she had read about a pervert who used to hunt women, taking them somewhere dark and distant to kill them'.

Despite the terror in her head, the claustrophobia in her heart and the disgust in every pore of her skin, the next day she allows Saati to drive her to 'a quiet spot near the Pyramids'. Instead of summoning up all her will-power and capacities of resistance to protect her existence from this parasite who has forced himself into her life-space, to keep off this blood-sucking leech who has attached himself to her skin, it seems as if she has resigned herself to the philosophy of 'what must be must be'. Instead of the exaggeratedly strong will that distinguishes her counterparts (Firdaus in *Woman at Point Zero*, the doctor in *Memoirs of a Woman*

Doctor and Bahiah Shaheen in *Two Women in One*), Fuaadah gives in to a fatalism that cancels out any exercise of will and negates any ability to interfere with the preordained nature of things.

Where to go? Everywhere has become like the lab, a trap for impotence, silence and the howling of the wind in the desert. No way out, no escape route. The trap opens its jaws and she enters between them. Saati will come after a while. He will inevitably come to the lab or somewhere else. He knows the place. He knows the telephone, the house, the ministry and the lab. He will arrive in his long blue car with his protruding eyes and fleshy neck. He will inevitably arrive.

Her succumbing to this fatalism reaches the point where she begins to fear not what must happen not actually taking place, but what must not happen actually taking place!

She entered the lab, put on the white apron and stood behind the window overlooking the street, watching the cars as if she was waiting for him. She was actually waiting for him. She saw the long blue car park in front of the building and the huge upper half of Saati and his skinny legs emerging. With heavy steps she walked towards the door.

Like a prey mesmerized by the trap, she opens the door instead of shutting it in his face:

He rang the door-bell. She struck out at the air with her fist, saying, 'I won't open it' and stood there frozen like a statue. He rang the bell again. She began to breathe faster, her chest heaving as if she was out of breath. She looked around eying the aperture as if it was a trap, then walked to the door and opened it.

When Saati buys her a fine diamond ring as a present, her only reaction to this prostitute–client type of relationship is to think, 'He is trying to acquire the right to order me around. Now he has paid the price for this right, he is entitled to use it.'

At a quiet spot near the Pyramids he tells her that he is a thief, as he has stolen seventy-three research papers from a poor, needy student in order to surround himself with the aura of a great university professor. Yet she still relinquishes her lips for him to kiss. True, she does not give herself completely at that moment; she simply allows him to come up close behind and put his arms around her waist while 'his eyes widened and bulged out even further', his cold lips close in on hers, 'his large teeth clattered against hers', and his 'strange disgusting smell filled up her nose', 'a metallic smell like rusty iron', and 'a burning bile which scorched her throat'.[10]

The minute she feels his cold lips on hers, she tries 'to raise her hand to slap him but her arm wouldn't lift'. Similarly, the first thing she does on getting up next day is:

> take the handkerchief from under her pillow, spitting into it repeatedly but finding the bitterness stuck in her throat. She thought she was about to be sick so she threw off the cover and headed for the bathroom. But the urge to vomit was not to materialize. She brushed her teeth hard with toothpaste and gargled in her mouth. The bitterness stayed in her throat, descending gradually inside her.

The picture we are given in the last few pages of the novel is of someone determined to drain her cup to the dregs. She has convinced herself that what must come 'will inevitably come, unimpaired and unfalteringly. Its bitterness will scorch her throat and its rusty smell will fill her nose.' She decides to go ahead with the experiment of internalizing 'the bad object' to its ultimate extreme and so, in this quiet spot near the Pyramids, she offers Saati a cold body, cold as a corpse, for him to have sex with. At the same time all her senses are on full alert, 'to see, hear, feel, taste and smell': to see his swollen, bulging belly 'going up and down' on top of her; to hear 'a strange strangled groan like the groan of a wounded ox' emanating from 'this huge mass' which 'panted and shook' on top of her; to feel 'the damp fat hand on her breast'; to inhale 'the smell of rusty iron stopping up her nose'; and to taste 'the bitter burning bile collecting in her guts'.

The first thing she does the next morning is creep into the bathroom and spit into his sink:

But the bitterness churned in her guts and she threw up. The despised rusty smell exuded from her mouth, her nose and her clothes. She took off her clothes and immersed her body in running water, washing it with soap and a sponge, but the smell lingered on. It had penetrated into her guts and the cells of her body and mixed with her blood.

She then feels 'some relief' as though secure in the knowledge that internalizing the bad object is irreversible and that Saati has occupied within her very flesh the entire area once occupied by Fareed. There is 'no longer anyone else' and 'the only thing left to her is to swallow the poison day after day, to fill her guts with this bitter burning bile and soak her body in the essence of rusty bitterness'.

The main question which arises is the following: why does Fuaadah (who can be seen as an extension of those daring heroines of the first three novels[11] whose fighting spirit knows no bounds in protecting their bodies and an independent existence) agree to be an object, indeed a sex object (with all its servile connotations), for Muhammad el-Saati, a man who is physically as well as spiritually deformed? Why does she agree to receive in the flesh of her flesh a transmutation which repels every cell in her body and soul? In fact, Fuaadah could have been described as throwing herself into the path of 'exaltation of her sexuality', and to be killing three birds with one stone — were it not more correct to say that she strikes herself three times with one stone, as will be explained below.

First, by moving into the stage of depressive descent to earth after she has lived the phase of ecstatic flying (in the persona of Bahiah Shaheen), Fuaadah does not seem to have freed herself of Bahiah's schizophrenia. She merely experiences this schizophrenia at the level of the object and not of the self. Here we are faced not with 'two women in one' but 'two love objects in one'. It is as though Bahiah/Fuaadah has projected the 'cleft' she despises in herself onto Saati, while with her other self — the self she loves and wants to be — she has identified with Saleem/Fareed.

In doing so she is reiterating or resurrecting the child's schizophrenic stance towards its first love object, the mother figure: two breasts in one, a bad and a good one, a saintly and an evil one, a lovely and a despicable one. It is largely a 'projective' breast: it is not sweet or bitter *per se*, but sweet (jasmine sweet, as Firdaus says) in so far as the child projects its love onto it, and bitter (bile bitter, as Fuaadah says) in so far as the child projects its hatred and hostility onto it. The duality of the object derives from the duality of the self. The duality of the object determines the particular rhythm of *The Absentee*, just as the duality of the self determines the rhythm of *Two Women in One*. Similarly, the duality of the biophilia and necrophilia is what determines the rhythm of *Memoirs of a Woman Doctor*.

Second, the mechanism underlying this process of projection and internalization in adults is to banish to the outside the disturbing, loathsome object and admit the pleasurable, lovely one. However, Fuaadah seems to be doing the opposite. While Fareed is absent, his place is taken by Saati. This reversal of both the internalization and the projection process seems to be a kind of self-punishment. Fuaadah's insistence on admitting the loathsome object personified by Saati, with his rusty, metallic smell and burning bitter taste, is reminiscent of the masochist's insistence on punishing himself.

It is as if Fuaadah is using Saati as a means of punishing herself for all the pleasure she has experienced with Fareed. Saati's hell is the other face of Fareed's paradise. Since the pleasure she experienced with Fareed was on a sexual level, she must experience her painful self-punishment at the same level. An eye for an eye, a tooth for a tooth and an organ for an organ, but with one difference: this law of revenge governs the relationship with the self and not with the 'other'.

Third, paradoxical as it may seem, the self-punishment actually represents a defensive measure, a protective act to preserve the ego from worse evils and save it from more savage punishment, reducing its expectations of something even worse. With Saati, Fuaadah has experienced the highest possible degree of humiliation and self-degradation, so that she now seems to have become immune to further punishment. The defensive, anti-restrictive nature of this mechanism is clear: the ego which has lost everything no longer has anything to fear. Moreover, as long as it is the ego which assumes the responsibility of punishing itself, why should it be punished further or fear punishment from any outside agency?

But who is Fuaadah afraid of? Why does she consider herself worthy of punishment to this extent? To whom does she want to prove that she has had enough punishment? What or who is the one object she loves as much as Fareed and loathes as much as Saati? Who or what is the one object she fears losing like Fareed, the good half, if she doesn't internalize the other ugly half? And who or what is the one object which can be the focus of an overwhelming schizophrenia of the conscious, that is of a love which knows no bounds and a hatred which has no limits?

The very fact of posing questions such as these necessarily suggests the answer: all roads are actually grist to the mother's mill. She is the primary object of love and hatred. All subsequent adult, psychic schizophrenia will largely be a repetition of the child's psychic schizophrenia towards the mother, and the proof that she has not been completely and consistently eliminated.[12]

From this perspective, the most distinctive feature of *The Absentee* is, as we shall see, not only the large area occupied by the mother, but also the mother's simultaneous mobilization of the emotions of love and hatred. We should, in addition, note that this mobilization comes to the surface of the psychological life of the daughter (the heroine of the novel) without the constraints of the rule which stipulates that the gates of the conscious can be opened wide to love whereas hatred must remain the hostage of the subconscious.

The Absentee presents an exaggerated and flagrant love of this type: 'She loved her mother more than anything else, more than Fareed, more than chemistry, more than discovery, more than herself.'

It is this very exaggeration that suggests surreptitiously, as it were, that this overwhelming emotion is suspect. A careful reading of the rest of the text removes all further doubts:

She was never to be free of this love, despite her desire to be freed of it. It was as though she was caught in an eternal trap, entangled in its wires and bound hand and foot, unable to escape for the duration of her life.

This metaphor, which not only compares love with a trap but gives it the connotations of a net or spider's web,[13] is the clearest indication that hatred is the other subconscious side of absolute, eternal love.

Just as metaphor may express subconscious facts better than straightforward expository language (as can be seen from the images quoted above), so also slips caused by forgetfulness or memory lapses can open up a vast arena of the unconscious. Fuaadah herself recounts the following incident:

> She remembered when her colleague prophesied by reading the grounds in her coffee cup what the future held in store for her. As the colleague was interpreting the signs, she suddenly stopped and asked her, 'What's your mother's name?' Fuaadah was so taken aback by the question that she forgot her mother's name. The colleague insisted on knowing the name. The more she insisted, the more the name eluded Fuaadah's memory. The colleague finally continued the reading without knowing the name, but Fuaadah remembered it the minute the reading was over.

Forgetting an unforgettable name such as that of her mother so suddenly and unexpectedly, and its stubborn vanishing from memory despite all efforts to recall it, says unintentionally all that cannot be said deliberately. It speaks of the hatred for the mother, of the desire to deny her, to escape from her domination, to sever the hidden tie with her and to burst asunder the bounds of 'the eternal trap'. Finally, it reveals a hope for the future that the colleague reads in the cup, free at last of the mother's noose.

But why do we have to resort to the language of the subconscious and all its involuntary manifestations in tracing the effect of the hatred for the mother? Doesn't Fuaadah herself consciously and quite of her own accord tell us that she hated her mother? Isn't she the one who tells us that the day her mother refused to allow her to go and play in the street, 'she hated her mother at that moment and envied her friend Saadiah whose mother had died giving birth to her'? This might be merely a childhood memory, but Fuaadah herself tells us quite consciously that the day her mother died (when Fuaadah was thirty) was the great day of her liberation, when she escaped the crowd of mourners and sympathizers surrounding her mother's coffin and went off into the desert to the Pyramids in Saati's car?

The 'great energy' imprisoned 'in the fibre of her being' seizes on precisely this moment to burst forth. To the strains of the 'dance-music' on the radio, she abandons herself to a fast and furious dance in which she frees her muscles from 'the fist of her consciousness, her body swaying to the tune, releasing the poisons of imprisoned energy, and soaking in the pleasure of dancing unconsciously', until 'her body fell on the sand, out of breath and soaked in sweat'.

This 'dance of salvation'[14] is actually only the concluding act of triumph and an aesthetic manifestation of the desire to spit out the mother. This gives *The Absentee* its leitmotiv in the same way as the desire for union with the mother and the return to the womb does in *Two Women in One*. From the very first line of *The Absentee*, from the moment 'Fuaadah opened her eyes that morning feeling a strange dejection', we are faced with someone whose existence has shrunk to include only the area between her mouth and her stomach. She sleeps, wakes up, moves, walks, thinks, feels, only under the dictates of one supreme motivation — 'an unfulfilled desire to vomit'.

In concrete terms, this desire is linked to Fuaadah's work at the Ministry of Organic Chemistry, a job without meaning or content. It is enough to look at her watch in the morning and see the hands approaching eight o'clock, reminding her that 'the time has come for her to go to the ministry', for her desire to vomit to play havoc with her entire being:

The word 'ministry' entered her nose along with the air, like a sharp piece of gravel. She wanted to sneeze and cast it out, but the air pushed it deeper into her, allowing it to settle at the base of her chest, in that triangular trench under her ribs, more precisely at exactly the point where the oesophagus opens into the stomach. She knew it would settle there and grow in that fertile area, eating, drinking and swelling up. Yes, it was swelling up day by day, pressing on her stomach with its solid body. Her stomach often tried to get rid of it, its muscles expanding and contracting. It would empty itself of all its contents, but the sharp solid mass stayed rubbing against the wall of the stomach like a nail, stuck to it, clenching it in its teeth like a tapeworm. She went into the bathroom feeling a chronic pain beneath her ribs, accompanied by the unfulfilled desire to vomit. She rested her head against the bathroom wall. She was sick. Her sickness is real and not pretence. She cannot go to the ministry.

But she has to go to the ministry every day at eight. No matter how she deludes herself that she is not going, she finds herself willy-nilly on the way. No matter how ill she pretends to be, even if she takes to her bed, she still finds herself getting up, leaving the house and heading for the ministry. No matter how hard she tries to make her feet lose their way, they inevitably lead her to the ministry in the end. No matter how happy she feels on looking around and realizing that she is moving unwittingly 'to a place she has never seen before', her happiness does not last long for she finds herself 'after a few steps in front of that rusty iron fence' and 'the ever-present worm sinking its teeth into the walls of her stomach'.

As she approaches the ministry her desire to vomit reaches a peak:

She raised her head and saw between the iron bars the black building scattered with small yellow spots betraying its true colours. She would surely realize that there is a link between this building and the chronic desire to vomit from which she suffers, starting when she remembers it, intensifying gradually as she approaches it and reaching its peak when she finally arrives and sees it with her own eyes.

But what is this ministry building? It is clearly a foul-smelling place with locked rooms, a fossilized existence and a monotonous rhythm, where 'she swallows her days like a gulp of castor oil'. But it is more than that. It is also a symbol and, like most buildings, a maternal symbol. And if we take into account the fact that it houses the Ministry of Organic Chemistry, it then becomes a symbol for that part of the mother's body where formative chemical interactions occur and life is created. This might seem a somewhat far-fetched interpretation, but it is Fuaadah herself who, in a moment of subconscious awakening, leads us forcefully towards this very conclusion:

> She raised her eyes to the dreary building and saw that it stood in
> the courtyard, flattened like her mother's belly. On its tanned
> dark surface horizontal and vertical cracks were scattered like
> wrinkles on the skin. She began to smell the strange odour
> reminding her of maternity wards in hospitals or smelly toilets.
> She stumbled and the feeling of sickness intensified. She knew
> she was approaching her office.

Thus it is not the shape of the building or its name alone which
imposes a womblike interpretation but also its smell. The
association of this particular smell with that found in maternity
wards and toilets is far from arbitrary. Isn't it Fuaadah who
somewhere else, and in a predictable context typical of theories of
infantile sexuality, says she has never known why, but she has
always associated birth with urination, feeling they must be related?

So when Fuaadah says that she does not want the huge power
imprisoned within her to be dissipated in that 'stinking grave
smelling of toilets', this stinking grave may be seen not only as
the ministry but also as her mother's womb. It is the foul air within
the womb, not only that inside the 'dingy' office, that bears the
true responsibility for her empty, meaningless life and the loss of
the ideal of research and a great discovery:

> No, she won't go to the ministry. She will not dissipate her
> days. Will she bury her intelligence in that enclosed room with
> foul air? Yes, it is the foul air which dissipates her energy. It is
> the foul air which thwarts her schemes and kills them even
> before they have taken form. Often she had an idea for research.
> Often she would come close to a discovery. But everything
> gets lost in that room with the closed doors and windows,
> within the empty dark offices with the three mummified heads.

Thus all the aggression Fuaadah directs against the dirty black
ministry building when she wishes that 'someone would drop a
live cigarette end in the filing room' and set the whole building
alight, or that 'a bomb would drop on it from the sky' and raze
it to the ground, is at the same time directed towards the mother

and her womb. In fact, from the hostility directed towards her mother, we should not be surprised that Fuaadah tries to strip her mother of her womb immediately after her birth by Caesarian section. A mother who has a hysterectomy and thus becomes 'barren' is indeed a 'barren' mother, not only in the sense of her 'inability to give birth' but also in the sense of 'not accepting the baby' (as the Arabic etymology indicates). She is not only a mother 'without a womb' in the literal sense, but also because of her cruelty, lack of compassion and failure to strengthen the bond of motherhood.[15]

Moreover, a woman 'without a womb' is a woman who, by definition, has no womb to which one might return. How can one go back to something which no longer exists? Thus Fuaadah never experiences that 'violent, strange yearning to curl up inside the womb'. It is here that she moves in the opposite direction to Bahiah Shaheen in *Two Women in One*. Fuaadah is demanding cession not union. She is destined to 'vomit', not to 'suck', the mother's burning, bitter milk.

This regressive journey is clearly seen in a qualitative kind of discrepancy we find only in Fuaadah as distinct from the other heroines we have analysed so far. The heroine of *The Absentee* seems to enjoy the taste of failure rather than that of success. Never has she attained 'that thing which fills her with pride and pleasure' which Firdaus, the heroine of *Woman at Point Zero*, seeks so avidly. She has never won that 'astounding victory' which the heroine of *Memoirs of a Woman Doctor* yearns for in her battle with society, that success which fills her surgery with 'men, women and children' and her coffers 'with money and gold', making her name 'as famous as that of a movie star'. Nor has she achieved that uniqueness to which Bahiah devotes her life in order to be unique among countless millions, to be the only real person, to be the only one to stamp forcefully on the ground as though she is treading underfoot all 'those soft tails, all those sharply pointed heads, all the lecturers and doctors in their shining cars with their protruding bellies', as though she is 'wilfully stamping out all other wills'.

It is true that Fuaadah is another woman who finds herself swallowed up by the spider-like web of the myth of uniqueness and superiority, but the myth this time is not of her own making. It has to a large extent been initiated by her mother. Her mother is the one who prays for her, 'Fuaadah! May God grant that you make a great discovery in chemistry!' It is her mother who reads 'a story about an ordinary schoolgirl who grew up to be someone great, maybe the story of Mme Curie or of some other famous woman'. She wants to satisfy her own 'lack of ambition' through Fuaadah, toying with the dream of 'her only daughter' becoming another Marie Curie and achieving 'something great' in life, something she has been unable to do herself.

But however much the mother wants her daughter to be a successful extension of herself, to Fuaadah nothing seems 'more satisfying to herself and to the curing of her sickness' than to disappoint her mother's ambitions on her behalf, and actively to negate through her failures her mother's intention of projecting her dreams onto her. Through the medium of projection, all Fuaadah's failures are in fact those of her mother. All her catalogue of disasters are like poisoned arrows levelled at the person who wants to extend her own life through that of her daughter. Fuaadah shouts gloatingly, 'Your great expectations have been disappointed, mother, and your prayers have fallen on deaf ears.' With similar glee she repeats these mental ruminations which run counter to the overwhelming elitist ideology in the first three novels:

> Her mother sat on the edge of the bed looking at her. Why is she silent? Why doesn't she say anything? Why wasn't she born a genius? The dream is gone and the illusions lost. She hasn't given birth to a genius. Who told her she would give birth to a genius? Why her? Why her belly in particular? Millions of bellies give birth daily; who then put that notion into her head?

Thus when we recall how Fuaadah discovers that 'she wasn't anyone important' and how she screams 'I am nothing' while 'swallowing the bitter bile', it is not difficult to interpret the phrase merely by changing the subject: 'You, mother, are nothing.' The bridge for this transformation is precisely the bitter bile: 'You, mother, are nothing; your milk is sour.'

Also contrary to the heroines of the other novels, Fuaadah does not use her body, face or looks in a narcissistic way — quite the opposite. She does not feel she is beautiful, but that everything about her is ugly (except her eyes in which there is 'something which distinguished her from other women', as Fareed tells her). Every time she looks at herself in the mirror, she purses her lips and swallows 'saliva with the taste of bitter coffee'. The thing she hates most about her face is her mouth 'with its ugly involuntary opening'.

The novel opens with Fuaadah getting out of bed and walking over to the mirror with a compulsive, repetitive automatism:

> She looked into the mirror and saw the face she looked at every day. The skin is light brown, the colour of cocoa with milk. Over the wide forehead falls a lock of dark black hair. The eyes are green with a kernel of black in each centre. The nose is long and sharp, and the mouth... She instantly withdrew her gaze from the image of the mouth. She hated it. It was the one thing that spoilt her whole face, with its ugly involuntary opening, as though her lips should have grown more than they did, or that her jawbones should have grown less. Whatever the reason, her lips do not close easily and are always slightly apart, and through this opening are glimpsed protruding white teeth.

Does Fuaadah hate herself? Certainly. It is from this perspective that she undertakes her journey throughout the pages of *The Absentee*, through what we have termed 'negative narcissism'. But why does she hate the involuntary opening of her mouth more than any other feature of her face? Is it because she is ugly? She certainly feels that too, but why the mouth in particular? Because it is the one distinctive feature which she has inherited from her mother and which she recognizes every time she looks at her mother's face, as though at a mirror:

> Fuaadah was awakened by her mother's voice. She saw her standing beside her, handing her a cup of tea with her two thin sinewy hands. She raised her eyes to her and saw her face with its many wrinkles and her two open lips. *The same opening and the same teeth.*[16]

When Saati sets her up in the trap of hopelessness, silence and howling emptiness, she notices an increasing widening of her mouth:

She saw the long blue car standing in front of the building. Saati gets out with his heavy torso and spindly legs. She walked to the door with leaden steps. She caught sight of herself in the long mirror next to the door. Her face had thinned and become longer. Her eyes had sunk into their sockets and lost their gleam. The gap between her lips had widened. Her teeth are sticking out even more, just like her mother's. She closed her lips to hide her teeth, pressing the upper jaw down onto the lower as hard as she could as if to crush her teeth in the process, or to crush something else. There must be something that can be crushed.

But just as the stomach is incapable of digesting itself, so the teeth cannot crush themselves. The mother who has entered into her through her mouth seems uncrushable. This is the same as her inability to vomit — the mother cannot be spat out, as we have already seen. She is a tapeworm in every sense of the word. Parts of her may waste away, parts be expelled, but she still clings on with her teeth to the walls of the stomach or the intestines, inseparable from the host.

Even when she dies, the mother borrows her daughter's body to live on through it. It is true that the moment the mother dies, the daughter abandons herself to her triumphal dance of salvation from the 'fencing in' she has suffered from her mother, but this overwhelming sense of release only lasts a few minutes. No sooner does the music stop and her breathless body fall to the sand than she finds herself forced, now that her mother has gone, to succumb sexually to the ugly, gross, foul-smelling man known as Saati. Thus it is not her mother but herself that she has banished in the dance. She empties herself of herself, leaving an empty space to be occupied by the recently dead mother, as though the mother can only live on through her daughter's body after first dying and vacating the body.

Before her mother's death, Fuaadah watches herself gradually getting older and becoming more and more like her. She sees her long thin fingers become like her mother's wrinkled fingers, their bones sticking out like dry stalks of corn. When she looks at her mother's 'wrinkled face', she is filled with foreboding that 'her face will be covered in wrinkles too'. Even her teeth stick out more and more like 'her mother's teeth'. But the moment her mother dies, the process of transmutation is complete. Fuaadah no longer resembles her mother, she *becomes* her mother. She obliterates herself and brings her mother to life, making her dwell in her body and submit to the alternative anal father, Saati, to copulate with just as her mother was forced to with her husband. This is the most extreme punishment Fuaadah can devise for her mother because, as we shall see, there was nothing her mother hated more than her husband, Fuaadah's father, and her hatred always rose to a peak during sex.

This may seem a somewhat extreme interpretation of the extraordinary relationship between Fuaadah and Saati. But only if seen in this way does it cease to be so astonishing. It is Saati himself who encourages Fuaadah to cast him in the role of the anal father, not only by his shape and gross body,[17] but also by confiding in her right from the start of their relationship:

> I will tell you something. Do you know that you look just like my daughter, the same smile, the same eyes, the same way of walking, everything? When I saw you for the first time, I felt this strange similarity, and I imagined that you were related to me. This is probably why I promised myself to give you the flat.[18]

Since he looks on her as a daughter, she in turn sees in him a father, and her father is necessarily her mother's husband. Her mother had hated her husband as much as Fuaadah hates Saati. Indeed, her mother had hated Fuaadah's father from 'the first glance' in the same way that Fuaadah instantly hates Saati and suspects him of being 'a thief' because of his looks. Her father was also 'a thief' as he had robbed her mother of an independent life. Her mother 'had ambitions unlike those of ordinary women. Before she was married, she had been to school' and dreamed of studying and becoming 'something great' but:

> She opened her eyes one morning and couldn't find her school overall where she had left it on the stand the previous night. She heard her father's rough voice saying, 'You will not go to school!' She ran to her mother in tears to demand an explanation.

The explanation was 'a husband!' That was enough to make her hate him on sight and continue to hate him until he died and even after his death.

Her hatred of him intensified at night when she was forced to perform 'her conjugal duty'. We do not have a first-hand description of the frigidity with which she performed this duty, but we have a description by proxy, as it were. It is the one Fuaadah reconstructs in her imagination:

> Fuaadah didn't know what brought to mind the incredible and unimaginable scene of her mother lying on the bed next to her father. It had never occurred to her before that her mother did the same things as other women, before giving birth to children.[19] But she was certain her mother must have done these things: her own existence proved it. She tried to picture her mother in this situation and guessed she would be as she had always known her: the white scarf covering her head, wearing the long galabiyah with long black stockings and woollen slippers on her feet. Yes, she imagined her fully clothed lying on the bed in her father's arms, lips firmly closed, a serious frown wrinkling her forehead, performing her conjugal duty, moving slowly and reverently as she would do if she were at prayer.

In her relationship with Saati, Fuaadah has resuscitated the Oedipal triangle which her mother had wanted to restrict to the two of them. The father was denied access to the symbiotic relationship between Fuaadah and her mother. It was her mother who gave Fuaadah the idea that her father had rejected her at birth because she was a girl:

> You don't know how I felt when I saw you for the first time after you were born. You were lying beside me like a little angel, breathing quietly and looking around you in amazement. I picked you up in my arms and held you up for your father to see, and said, 'Look at her, Khaleel.' Your father cast a quick sorrowful glance at you and said, 'It's a girl.' Bringing you nearer to his face I said, 'She will become a great woman,

Khaleel. Look at her, kiss her!' I brought you even closer so that your face almost touched his, but he wouldn't kiss you. He turned his face away, left us and went out. I hated him that night more than any other night!

Her mother didn't stop at making her hate her father. In as much as a man, any man, is an extension of the father, her mother made her hate all men. She would say, when 'doing her soft black hair in front of the mirror, admiring her elegant pose,[20] "Your future lies in studying, daughter! Man is useless."' If we are to believe Fuaadah, or rather her feelings, things actually go as far as her obliterating her father from her life in the same way as her mother did. She feels no grief when he dies, indeed she feels 'a little happy' and:

> her happiness was for no particular reason, her father was of no significance in her life; he was merely a father. But she was happy because she felt her mother was happy. She overheard her a few days later saying, 'He wasn't much use.' She truly believed her mother's words, what use had he been?

In a bi-symbiotic relationship, any third party — even if it is the father himself — necessarily appears as an uninvited guest and a parasite. He is by definition, precisely as both the mother and the daughter define him, useless. Consequently, the joint hatred of the two parties in the dual relationship will be directed at him. It is here that he, as any hated father, takes on the role of the anal father. The picture Fuaadah paints of him is reminiscent of the portrait Firdaus paints of her father:[21]

> [Fuaadah] would see her father only on a Friday. He used to come home after she had gone to bed and leave the house before she got up. The house was clean and quiet all week except for Fridays. Her father would leave the bathroom soaking wet after his bath, allowing the water to seep down into the sitting room.[22] He would throw his clothes all over the place, raising his rough voice from time to time. He coughed a lot and spat a lot and cleared his nose with loud snorts. He had lots of handkerchiefs and they were always dirty. Her mother used to

put them in boiling water, telling her it was 'to sterilize them from germs'.

At the time Fuaadah didn't know what a germ was, but she heard the hygiene and biology teacher telling a class that germs were minute organisms harmful to man. That day the teacher asked, 'Where do we find germs, girls?' The class remained silent, no one raised their hand. Fuaadah felt she knew the answer and raised her hand confidently and proudly. The teacher smiled intelligently and said gently, 'Do you know where we find germs, Fuaadah?' Fuaadah stood up, her head held high above those of the other girls and said loudly and confidently, 'Yes, Miss. Germs are found in my father's handkerchiefs!'

This strange anal father is the one that Fuaadah resurrects and imposes on her internalized mother through her relationship with Saati. In the final analysis, it is Fuaadah who has sex with Saati; thus she will have been revenged on her mother twice — once when she has sex with him acting on her mother's behalf, and once when acting on her own behalf.[23] In the latter case we may speak of the alternative fulfilment of a subconscious desire for incest.

Not only does Saati behave incestuously with someone resembling his own daughter; Fuaadah also behaves incestuously with someone like her own father. In this relationship, it appears that it is the mother who is shut out, as the father was before her. This vengeful tactic — i.e. excluding one of the two parties in the Oedipal relationship while espousing the other — is not uncommon in Fuaadah's psychological make-up. There is at least one example.

One day while still at school, Fuaadah is punished by the history teacher who raps her hand twenty times with a ruler, twice on each finger.[24] When she gets home Fuaadah complains to her mother. But all her mother does is 'slap her face for being careless in history, and [leave] her in the house on her own as she [goes] off to the dressmakers'. For the first time ever, 'and as she [is] wandering in the house contemplating the walls as if she was in a prison', she sees the picture hanging in the hall of her mother and father on their wedding day. She suddenly realizes, 'as though a sharp knife pierced her heart', that her father's eyes are like her own and that 'she loved her father, she wanted him, and she needed him to look at her with those eyes and take her into his arms':[25]

> She buried her head in the cushions of the sofa and began
> sobbing. She was crying the tears she had never shed on his
> death. There and then she wanted her father to come back and
> die again so that she could cry for him and ease her conscience.
> She wiped away her tears on the cover of the sofa and got up
> and took down the picture. She wiped the dust from the glass
> and looked at it again. It was as though the dust had hidden
> her mother's eyes from view, because they now appeared wide
> and clear, reflecting a strange look which she had never seen
> before, a fierce, tyrannical look.

This key extract enables us to reconstruct the development of
Fuaadah's psycho-libido. Since any reconstruction of this kind is
bound to have gaps, we shall also draw on material taken from
the lives of Fuaadah's counterparts: Bahiah Shaheen, the heroine
of *Two Women in One*, and even Firdaus from *Woman at Point Zero*,
in as much as Fuaadah takes on (at least in her early life) some of
the characteristics of this hybrid personality, a sort of synthesis of
the personalities of the heroines of *Memoirs...*, *Two Women in One*
and *The Absentee*.

The libidinal path of Fuaadah Khaleel Saleem may be seen as
passing through three main 'stations', or stopping-points: 1. the
Oedipal station; 2. the regressive station (the regression not only
to the pre-Oedipal stage but to an even more primitive stage, that
of symbiosis with the mother); and 3. the restorative station
(retrogression to the Oedipal stage).

1. The Oedipal Station: Fuaadah seems to enjoy one unique trait
in her libidinal development. Usually the more recent the phases
of this development, the less likely they are to be repressed, while
the earlier and more established the phases, the deeper they sink
into the subconscious. Fuaadah, however, presents us with quite
the opposite picture. In her case, the Oedipal urges seem to be the
ones subjected to the most repression and they have consequently
sunk to the depths. On the other hand, most of the pre-Oedipal
repressions have emerged and are floating on the surface of the
subconscious.

Moving away from these abstract generalizations, let us say that Fuaadah's love for her father is the most recent thing in her memory and the last of the psychic drives to be present in her conscious mind. This can only be explained by the violence of the Oedipal drives related to the father. Weaker taboo desires do not require such rigid repression. Overwhelming taboo desires that cannot be overcome or controlled seem dangerous, on the other hand, and require the strongest defence barriers to prevent their emerging.

. The most effective preventive measure is undoubtedly to negate sexual desire itself. Sexual desire overwhelmingly takes on the unmentionable taboos, necessarily leaving behind an unbearable burden of guilt. Since sexual desire cannot be separated from its taboo foundations, the only alternative is to negate the desire *per se*. In other words, since it is impossible to dispense with the taboo object — here, the father object — in sexuality, only one solution remains: to dispense with sexuality itself, at least in the early stages.

We can now understand why Fuaadah wants to appear both to herself and to us as a creature without sex organs. After everything we have seen in Bahiah Shaheen, and before her in the heroine of *Memoirs of a Woman Doctor*, the following quotation speaks for itself:

What is the meaning of love? She used to hear this frequently. And because she heard it so often, she lost track of what it meant, like her sex organs which she saw continually, as part of her body, washing them daily with soap and water without actually knowing them.

With such ignorance of her sex organs, the physiological phenomenon of menstruation appears scandalous. Once a woman has menstruated, the myth of a creature without sex organs can no longer be sustained. To deny the sexual function would be like trying to turn a circle into a square. Fuaadah thinks:

She was the only one amongst all the girls to have contracted a malignant disease. She hid the catastrophe of her body from her mother's eyes. But her mother caught her once washing the sheet from her bed in the sink. The earth spun round her in shame. She crumpled the sheet up in her hand and saw her mother's eyes looking at her with a strange opacity that she had never seen before. She put out her hand and spread the sheet, discovering a blotchy wavy red mark staining the white cloth, lying there outstretched like a dead cockroach.

She tried to deny her awful crime but her mother seemed as though she was an accomplice to it. She was not alarmed or angry. In fact she was not surprised at all. It was as if she had been expecting this catastrophe which had befallen her and that she would accept it as calmly as possible. Fuaadah was ill at ease in the face of this calm. In fact it frightened her so much that her body began to tremble. It is not a catastrophe then. It is not some temporary abnormal disease. It is something ordinary, very ordinary. Her fear increased in proportion to the realization of the normality of the event. She wished it was something abnormal, as abnormal things are more likely because they are unusual and temporary.

We need only pause at one stray point in this sensitive psychological analysis. Menstruation appears in the text as a sign of shame and ignominy, a malignant disease, a catastrophe, a disaster, an abominable crime — in a word, a scandal and a punishment at one and the same time. So what is it that has been revealed and at the same time deserves punishment? As the literature of psychoanalysis has revealed, it can only be masturbation, a secret, subjective, erotic activity — something that adolescents and those on the threshold of puberty try to hide, and for which they expect to be punished.[26]

By its very nature, this activity is 'wetting'. It is in this light that we can understand Fuaadah's fear of what she terms 'wetting herself'. Menstruation is a kind of 'wetting'. So is involuntary urination. It is Fuaadah herself who associates these two kinds of wetting with her first sexual 'temptation', bearing in mind that this association of ideas is itself linked to erotic fantasies whose inevitable outcome provokes a third kind of 'wetting':

She lay on the bed gazing at the ceiling. She considered stretching out her hand and reaching for the telephone to ask for the five-figure number,[27] as she did every night before going to sleep. But she did not stretch out her hand. She pressed her head into the pillow telling herself: I must kick this habit.[28] But she didn't.

The ringing of the phone never sounded clear. It was always mixed with the sound of her heavy breathing in and out and the pounding of her heart. The ringing stopped and Fareed's voice[29] came over the line whispering into her ears. She felt his arms around her, his warm breath on her neck. She swooned and all that remained were two great burning lips.[30] She opened her eyes to look into his eyes. But he was not Fareed. He was someone else, the first man that she had loved.[31]

She was a small child. She forgets how old at the time, but she remembers that she was big enough to open her eyes every morning and find her bed dry. She hated wetting the bed. She thanked God that she was rid of it. But God was not deceived by her thanks and was quick to inflict a different but more serious kind of wetting on her. This time it was not colourless as before, the sheet drying white, but had a dark red colour which could only be removed by vigorous washing which scalded her fingers. Even then it never disappeared completely but left a pale yellow trace.

We shall only dwell on one point in this heavily symbolic extract: the shortness of the interval between the two 'wettings'. The first wetting, continuing until just before the onset of the second, betrays (as is accepted both by traditional psychological medicine and by psychoanalysis) a continuation of child-like masturbatory practices through the latency period up to puberty.[32] Young people who practise this auto-erotic activity often imagine that the resultant wetting is merely urine. The above quotation shows that such confusion is possible.

Fuaadah describes the first wetting as 'colourless'; 'as soon as the sheet dried it became white again'. However, this only applies to sexual wetting, not to wetting from urine. But whatever kind of wetting it is, it arouses in Fuaadah such an intense feeling of nausea that it can only be explained by the guilt surrounding her auto-erotic activity:

She moved her body under the cover. It weighed down on her as if it had turned to stone. She felt incredibly hot, sweat poured off her, soaking her body, and a warm sticky liquid flowed from her nose. She took a handkerchief from under her pillow and wiped her nose, feeling sick. Her nose was leaking like a worn-out tap, her body oozing with sweat. She is not a clean dry-stone wall, but a wall whose head and belly are being soaked from above and below by leaky taps — an involuntary nauseating wetting.

This wetting can move from below to above, and be projected onto the nose or any other bodily orifice, even the pores of the skin (let us remember the dance of salvation by the deserted Pyramids which left Fuaadah soaking wet). It can also be projected from the inside to the outside. This 'disgusting, nauseating' wetting is exactly the same as the father's wetting of the bathroom, despoiling the house which 'stayed clean all through the week except for Fridays'.[33]

In fact, it is exactly the same as the wetting projected onto the father's nose, which he 'blows a lot', soiling 'many handkerchiefs' contaminated 'with those small organisms harmful to man' ('germs'). Children can in turn easily see these 'germs' as referring to sperm. Indeed that 'foul-smelling' wetting can even be projected onto inanimate objects. The ministry building brings to Fuaadah's mind the image of the mother's womb, not only because of the shape but also because of the smell, which is difficult to distinguish from that of a 'toilet'. In any case, what is the womb? Isn't it 'a urinal' according to some theories of infantile sexuality? And in accordance with the same theories, does the father when making love to the mother do anything other than 'urinate' into her, or into her 'urinal'?

The reader who rejects these interpretations will find it difficult to contend with the 'urinous' atmosphere which pervades *The Absentee*. It is no coincidence that Fuaadah chooses to open a special laboratory for 'chemical analysis'. We shall see shortly that the only analysis she carries out here with any sense of 'pleasure' is that of her mother's urine.

At this point, we must pause at a scene in the novel which demonstrates the equation not only between the sex organs and urine, but also between the sex organs and a name. The scene shows clearly how some of the precepts of patriarchal society, when combined with the psychotic fixations of the individual libido, can lead not only to a neurotic but also to a psychotic attitude towards the sex organs. When Fuaadah Khaleel Saleem puts up a sign with her full name on it outside her laboratory and sees men stop outside the building to read the various signs:

> she imagined that they were looking at her name in particular. She shrank inside her coat, ashamed, imagining that the letters of her name were no longer scratches in black paint, but living entities like the limbs of her body. She didn't know why she imagined this but she sensed that, as the eyes of the men gazed on her name, they were gazing at her naked body.

The interpretation of this fantasy of nakedness — and it is here that the novel's socio-critical vein emerges — may be sought in 'an event which happened to her when she was in the first year of primary school':

> The theology teacher, with his thick curved nose like the neck of a swan, was standing in the classroom explaining to the young girls aged between six and eight the precepts of religion which stipulate that females should be bashful at all times. On that day he told them that the female must cover her body because it is a forbidden area, and must not speak in the presence of strange men because her voice too is forbidden. He also told them that a woman's name is a forbidden thing and should not be uttered in front of men who are strangers. He gave himself as an example, saying: When I find it necessary in highly exceptional circumstances to mention my wife's name in the presence of other men, I do not mention her real name but I use the plural form.
>
> Fuaadah was sitting listening, not understanding a word but reading the expressions on the teacher's face as he spoke. When he uttered the words 'forbidden parts', she did not understand their meaning but understood from the expression on his face that they signified something 'ugly and despicable'. She curled up at her desk feeling sorry for her female self. And the day would have passed peacefully like any other day had the teacher not chosen to ask her to summarize what he had said. She stood up trembling with fright, and as she stood, she didn't know

how, a flow of urine was involuntarily released from between her legs. The girls' eyes were all on her wet legs. She wanted to cry but she couldn't because she was too ashamed.

This externally imposed sinful nature not only of the sex organs but of the female body in general, and also of the name as a 'forbidden part',[34] allows the internally created sexual feelings of guilt (the taboo Oedipal feelings) ample scope for social rationalization. Fuaadah is unable to accept or know her sex organs even though she washes them every day; Bahiah Shaheen feels sick every time she accidentally catches sight of her sex organs in the bathroom. Oriental patriarchal society has a totally negative attitude towards female sexuality. Both Fuaadah and Bahiah see this attitude as running parallel to, reiterating and confirming their own negation of their sex organs, their feelings of disgust at their 'wetness' and the impossible myth of their existence without sex organs.

2. The Regressive Station: The basic premises underlying the three 'autobiographical' novels under analysis allow us to determine the approximate time of the commencement of the regressive station. In adolescence, those sexual urges which have been unable to break out of their Oedipal mould become a source of intolerable frustration. They also threaten to sweep away the entire structure of the ego. Fuaadah has this to say about the onset of puberty:

Her small body began to change. She felt the change creeping through her like a soft snake with a long thin tail which it wriggled in her chest and belly, biting her in different places in her body. The bites were painful and delicious.

On the same subject, the heroine of *Memoirs of a Woman Doctor*, the suppressor of her own femininity, speaks of that 'cowardly part of me which trembled with fear at the stronger part when I was awake, but then crept into my bed at night and filled the darkness around me with fantasies and illusions'. It is Bahiah Shaheen, on the other hand, who goes to the greatest lengths in describing the onset of puberty, even though projecting it onto her schoolmates: 'Moans, groans, sighs and gasps, a hidden burning desire buried within herself like a germ that sought to torture her body, rip it apart, destroy it so completely that nothing would remain.'

When up against this dangerous 'crushing', the first defensive measure resorted to is that of denial. It is not 'me' who is the adolescent (male or female): it is my parents (the two poles in the Oedipal fixture) who see me as such. It is not 'me' who thinks of sex and is torn by sexual desires, but my parents who are preoccupied with sex. Again it is Bahiah who goes to the extreme limits of this projective interpretation: the guise she denies herself is projected onto her parents, until it is them rather than her who are the adolescents, and them rather than her who are at fault for their sinful sexual fantasies:

> She had never felt that she was a girl or that she was eighteen. This used to be called the age of puberty. A suspicious word. At the mere sound of it fathers and mothers tremble with suppressed sexual desire, baring their teeth and shaking a warning finger at their sons and daughters. Other eyes look at them suspiciously, but mothers and fathers follow their own instincts free from suspicion.
>
> She knew they would interpret her escape from home in sexual terms alone, although at the time she had no sexual desire at all...
>
> ...she imagined that sexual desire was abnormal...
>
> But to them she was an adolescent. When she stood on the balcony to enjoy the sun her father would imagine that she was flaunting herself in front of their bald old neighbour. If she was late, absent-minded, drawing, thinking, having a bath, or looking in the mirror, the reason was all too obvious: a man. She later realized that parents thought of nothing but sex and imagined that their offspring were just like them.

Here we can formulate something akin to a law: the strength of sexual desires, and the extent to which they can be charged with taboo Oedipal desires, can be measured by the extent of the need to negate them. If, in spite of the psychological cost incurred in building them, the dams of denial are in danger of being swept away by the tides of instinctive drives (carrying an intolerable amount of Oedipal alluvium), then the road to regression is the only way passable.

Here we can discern three halts in the regressive station.

a. First, there is an initial, brief, transient pause at what we may call the *homosexual halt*. This halt is referred to in only two of the novels: *The Absentee* and *Woman at Point Zero*. Fuaadah talks of an 'unusual love' which has been burning in her heart ever since that 'historic day' when the female chemistry teacher says in front of the whole class, 'Fuaadah is someone else, different from all the other girls in the class.' However, the origins of this feeling lie further back in the novel. Even before that 'historic day', Fuaadah imagines that the deep, supremely confident glances of the chemistry teacher are directed 'at her alone amongst all the other girls in the class'. True, there is no 'material proof' of this, but 'she felt it, felt it strongly, especially when she used to bump into her in the school yard and she would look at her and smile. She didn't smile at all the girls. No, she didn't smile at all of them.'

Then comes that 'historic day':

Yes, Fuaadah began to love chemistry. It was not an ordinary love like that for geography, geometry and algebra, but an extraordinary love. She would sit in the chemistry class and her mind would experience a magnetic tremor attracting everything to her brain. The voice of the teacher, her words, her gestures, the specks of dust which whirled in the air, every atom, every shudder, every vibration, every movement, everything that transpired was picked up by her brain as a magnet would pick up iron filings from a wooden surface.

But as with every time that Fuaadah loves, hatred is always the other side of the coin. It is as though she can only feel love by confronting hatred, precisely as happens to Bahiah Shaheen who 'only saw white in confrontation with black'. Thus at the same time as all her feelings of love are mobilized by the chemistry teacher, a wave of hatred is generated that submerges all the other teachers without exception. Fuaadah has the following comment:

It was natural that after all this her brain turned towards

chemistry and that things around her began to take on chemical shapes and descriptions. It wasn't unusual for her to imagine sometimes that the history teacher was made of copper, the art teacher of lime and the head teacher of magnesium, that hydrogen peroxide emanated from the mouth of the Arabic teacher, and that the voice of the biology and hygiene teacher sounded like tin sheets rubbing against each other. One person alone was exempt. That was the chemistry teacher. Her voice and eyes, her hair, shoulders and arms, thighs and everything which was made up of living matter existed, moved and throbbed like the arteries of the heart. She was a living human being of flesh and blood who couldn't possibly be associated with a chemical formula.

It should be pointed out, however, that when we talk here of homosexual feelings, these appear to be of an affectionate type and are not sexual in the full meaning of the word. In other words, this is Platonic homosexuality. The strongest evidence for this is that the relationship's channel of communication is the ear:

But her voice [the chemistry teacher's] was the most noticeable thing about her. It was as sweet as an orange from the top of a tree, or a tender budding jasmine flower, unplucked and untouched. Fuaadah would sit in the chemistry class and open her eyes, ears, nose and the pores of her body to that sweet voice. Words entered her pores like a breath of warm, pure air.

This short passage, rare amongst the novels we have analysed for its affection, grace and gentleness, leaves no doubt that the penetration of sound through the ears is a symbol for the full love relationship between a man and a woman. The ear itself is susceptible to erotic investment (i.e. it can play the role of 'the erotogenic zone', to use Karl Abraham's term[35]). A clear example is that of Fuaadah, and Bahiah Shaheen before her, who deny their sex organs in the strict sense of the word, thereby liberating their sexual sensitivity from any one specific area and extending it to all parts of the body, especially its orifices and pores.

It is this generalized, non-specific sensitivity which Bahiah, in the 'magic key' passage quoted at the beginning of the present chapter, compares with 'particles of soft hot sand' which send shivers through her arms and body, seeping down to her thighs and rising to her neck and head. It is probably this which makes her speak of the 'unknown senses' in man, 'more able to sense than other known senses'. In Fuaadah's case in particular, the idea that her mother 'gave birth to her through her ear' facilitates erotic investment in this particular orifice.

Further evidence of the brief, fleeting pause at the homosexual halt is provided by a passage in *Woman at Point Zero*. What gives this quotation added significance is that it seems to have been grafted on to the novel with no artistic justification on the grounds of the heroine's development. Firdaus's uncle has sent her to a boarding school, where, in the full flush of adolescence, she has got to know the female teacher Iqbal. They meet on a bench in the courtyard where they have both gone, unable to sleep, on a pitch dark night. In describing their first meeting, Firdaus speaks of the light flowing through Iqbal's eyes as if coming from 'some unknown magical source which was neither on the earth nor in the heavens':

The night around us was deep, silent, motionless, with not a single sound or movement anywhere. Everything was steeped in an absolute darkness through which no ray of light penetrated, for in the sky was neither moon nor sun. My face was turned towards her, and my eyes looked into her eyes...

I held her eyes in mine, took her hand in mine. The feeling of our hands touching was strange, sudden. It was a feeling that made my body tremble with a deep, distant pleasure, more distant than the age of my remembered life, deeper than the consciousness I had carried with me throughout. I could feel it somewhere, like a part of my being which had been born with me when I was born, but had not grown with me when I had grown, like a part of my being that I had once known, but left behind when I was born...

At that moment a memory came to my mind. My lips opened to speak, but my voice failed to come through, as though no sooner did I remember than I had already forgotten. My heart faltered, stifled by a frightened, frenzied beating over something precious I was on the point of losing or had just lost, for ever.

My fingers held onto her hand with such violence that no force on earth, no matter how great, could tear it away from me.

This 'deep, distant pleasure' is 'more distant than the age of [her] remembered life'; it is no sooner remembered than forgotten, as though it is something which 'happened just once before, only to be lost for all time, or as though it had never happened at all'. This pleasure which brings Firdaus and the warden together cannot be, as the text shows, anything other than a 'race memory', the pleasure of an existence prior to existence, the pleasure of togetherness prior to separation, the pleasure of paradise lost, the pleasure of yearning to curl up afresh in the mother's womb, the pleasure of that moment to which Bahiah says she will 'dedicate her entire life until she dies in searching for it, or escaping from it'.

As we have already shown, in Fuaadah's case the symbiotic libido is necessarily of a homosexual nature. Whether or not we accept the interpretation according to which 'Miss Iqbal' is in the final analysis only a substitute womblike mother, Fuaadah's love for Iqbal is incontestably (though in the guise of affection) a woman's love for another woman.

The main question Firdaus asks herself in connection with her undeclared relationship with Iqbal is, 'But she's a woman. How could I be in love with a woman?' It is the same question that could have been posed by the one heroine (though under different names) of *The Absentee*, *Two Women in One* and *Memoirs of a Woman Doctor*. Since the road to homosexuality is not passable, given the alter ego's dignity and moral scruples,[36] Firdaus not only answers her question in the negative, but makes the positive affirmation, 'No, in fact I hate her.'

This transformation, this transfer to the opposite, is one of the ego's common defensive strategies. It partly explains the feelings of hostility towards 'the female species' which positively ooze from the three novels. There is no need here to review all the damning verdicts that are endlessly pronounced upon the female 'reptiles' by the single heroine of the three novels. Firdaus, the heroine of *Woman at Point Zero*, even prides herself on having 'become conscious of hating men' without being aware of the fact that she hates women just as much.

b. The second pause at the regressive station is longer than the first. It is what we will term the *anal father halt*. Here we would do well to remember Firdaus's father who drinks his glass of water, 'then belched loudly, expelling the air from the mouth or belly with a prolonged noise... Once over with his pipe he lay down, and a moment later the hut would resonate with his loud snoring.' We may also recall Bahiah Shaheen's description of men in a patriarchal family:

> All the men of the family met. They sat round the table devouring stuffed chicken. After lunch they sat smoking in the hall, picking their teeth with tooth-picks; their bellies swelling over their thighs like pregnant women and their fat, flabby bottoms filling the big bamboo chairs. Each would belch audibly, clear his throat and say something in a coarse, deep voice that was not his own.

Finally, let us remember Fuaadah's father who dirties 'the clean house', wetting the bathroom and lounge and disturbing the quiet of the place with his rough voice, and who 'coughed a lot, spat a lot, and cleared his nose loudly and abruptly'.

As in the previous halt, it is clear that the defensive procedure opted for by the ego is a reversion to the opposite. Just as the woman who would have been seen as a homosexual love object is ruled out by reversing potential love into outright hatred, the feelings for the father (who was once a taboo love object) have been reversed to make him an object of hatred typical of the anal-sadistic phase. The road to generalization from father to man has opened up. All men are father substitutes, and therefore anal. They are only fit to be the objects of contempt rather than of love. The supreme example is Muhammad el-Saati in *The Absentee*.

It is also worth mentioning Firdaus's picture of men, even before she knows them, when she is still young and her 'breasts were not yet rounded':

> [She] could hear them as they invoked Allah's name and called upon His blessings, or repeated His holy words in a subdued guttural tone. [She] would observe them nodding their heads, or rubbing their hands one against the other, or coughing, or

clearing their throats with a rasping noise, or constantly scratching under the armpits and between the thighs. [She] saw them as they watched what went on around them with wary, doubting, stealthy eyes, eyes ready to pounce, full of an aggressiveness that seemed strangely servile.

The heroine of *Memoirs of a Woman Doctor* prefers to escape into the imaginary world of dolls, away from 'those strange creatures with loud voices and moustaches called men'. No sooner does she hear the 'loathsome' word *marriage* than she visualizes 'a man with a big see-through belly with a table of food inside it'. It is as if, before knowing anything of men, she has associated 'the smell of the kitchen' with 'the smell of marriage. I hated the word [marriage] and I hated the smell of food.'

It is this hatred of 'the species of men', associated with the hatred of 'the species of women', which has produced that strange hybrid creature lacking sex organs and sexual desire. It has resulted in someone who has no sex objects, whether homo- or heterosexual, paternal or maternal — in other words, someone like Bahiah Shaheen. It is worth quoting once again a key passage from *Two Women in One*. With one stroke of the brush, it gives us an extraordinary picture that throws into relief the triple negation encapsulated in one being, the negation of sex organs, sexual desire and sex objects:

Since the time her mother had smacked her when she was three, she felt disgusted by the sight of her sexual organs in the bathroom, and would quickly avert her eyes. She was not even aware of being female. She did not consider Saleem male... When she was with him, she lost all desire for food as well as her sexual appetite...

Her sexual desire was shrinking despite her. She could feel it withdrawing from her, leaving her body on its own. Sometimes when she felt the need for it she would try to summon it up, but it refused to respond and never settled in her body...

Bahiah came to hate bath-days. When she undressed she looked with loathing at her sexual organs. She even hated God for creating them... One day she told her mother that she hated

God. Her mother gasped and slapped her face...

That night she heard her whispering to her father, 'The girl is not normal.'

Since she did not know what was normal, she imagined that sexual desire was abnormal. So she was disgusted when she saw men's sexual organs bulging under their trousers; she wanted to throw up when a man dug his elbow into her chest as she waited for the tram. She hated men with their trousers, their ugly protruding organs... their smell of onions and tobacco...

She knew her father was a man and so she hated him all the more. At night when his snoring stopped she would imagine that he had died. She did not love her mother, nor did she love women with their low-cut dresses, revealing breasts swollen with hidden desire, and their eyes made up with kohl, like slave maidens burning with lust. But their fat, closely-bound legs and their beaten eyes betrayed their everlasting frigidity.

c. The third halt at the regressive station is by far the longest in duration and the most serious in terms of its consequences. This *womblike mother halt*, covered by two entire novels (*Two Women in One* and *The Absentee*), is itself composed of two stages: regression towards the mother and running away from her. In *Two Women in One* we see the sweeping violence of Bahiah Shaheen's flight to the womblike mother. Fuaadah's flight in *The Absentee* is no less violent. It is as though psychological life were subject to the old law of physics which states that if body A applies a force to body B, then body B will exert a force equal in magnitude but opposite in direction on body A, regardless of the resistance of the environment or the inertia of the body itself.

The most extraordinary aspect of Fuaadah's relationship with her mother is that she lives it purely on a symbolic level, treating ciphers as though they were reality. This symbolism is the only possible alternative to an impossible real-life relationship. If such a relationship was achieved, it would inevitably have been both homosexual and taboo at one and the same time.

Symbolism is the language of the subconscious. When sexual life is repressed and forced to cower in the depths of the subconscious, it can of necessity only be expressed by means of symbols. We have already seen how the ministry's dreary flattened building comes to symbolize the mother's womb. Fuaadah's relationship to her laboratory can be understood from the same perspective, but with one crucial difference: the ministry building is not, after all, actually her mother's belly, but is 'like her mother's belly'.

The word 'like' implies a conscious distance between the two objects being compared. In Fuaadah's relationship with her laboratory, this distance no longer exists: there are no two sides to the comparison and the word 'like' is not used. In fact, there is no conscious process of comparison at all. Fuaadah does not realize that her relationship with the lab repeats or symbolizes her relationship with her mother. The symbol here is a complete substitute for the comparison. It becomes the primary premise, imposing itself with full independence; it is no longer a means of indirect expression, or a substitute for what it is supposed to symbolize. In a word, instead of becoming a symbol for reality, it has become reality itself.

Fuaadah has the idea of starting a lab at the very beginning of her relationship with the chemistry teacher, a loving relationship before love is recognized as such:

> It is an idea which saw the light of day a long time ago. It loomed over the horizon while she was sitting in the chemistry class at school. It wasn't very clear but it appeared as if through a mist. Her eyes were intently following the strange movements within the test-tube, watching the colours which suddenly appeared and disappeared, the strange-smelling gases and the residue at the bottom. A new compound which is the result of chemical interaction between two different substances, with new characteristics, a new shape, new powers. The chemistry lesson ends. She stays behind in the lab combining different substances and watching their interaction with astonishment, smelling the gases rising from the mouth of the test-tube and exclaiming joyfully, 'A new gas! Eureka!'

The stream of symbols in this cryptic text, though superficially innocent, suggest a transition from the school lab to a bedroom, and thence to a maternity hospital. It is as though all the secrets of sexuality and reproduction are revealed to Fuaadah and ourselves in one fell swoop. This may seem somewhat of an exaggeration, but the symbols and the sequence of events lend themselves to no other interpretation. The 'test-tube' immediately brings to mind the image of the mother's womb. The 'two different substances' whose interaction produces 'a new compound' with 'new characteristics' and a 'new shape' are unarguably the masculine and feminine elements. Their 'interaction' leaves a residue at the bottom of the test-tube that will soon develop into a new creature. No matter how many of its parents' characteristics it carries in its genes, it is this new-born creature that represents 'a new shape' and 'a new power'.

As to that other tiny creature who, on reaching puberty, will no longer be tiny, it will one day stand in amazement in front of the Sphinx. And on that day it will find that its joy would equal its amazement, if only it were to find the missing piece of the jigsaw puzzle and reconnect the severed bridge between the 'bedroom' and the 'maternity hospital'. It could then enter the adult world in triumph, just as Oedipus entered Thebes, echoing from the depths of his soul Archimedes' triumphant 'Eureka — I've found it!'

Furthermore, chemistry is not only the science of living matter; it is also, since its roots lie in alchemy, the science of magic properties. It is the science of the search for the philosopher's stone and of turning base metal into gold. Its magical properties give it a new and totally unexpected significance if it is applied to the relationship between the sexes. In this guise it appears to be the only way of overcoming the anatomical differences between male and female.

From the standpoint of the imaginary castration complex, chemistry can actually bring about a magical effect. If base metal can be turned into gold, then the female can turn into a male, or quasi-male. Moreover, she can move symbolically from the world of the non-possessors ('the world of circumscribed sky', in the words of the heroine of *Memoirs of a Woman Doctor*) to the world of the possessors ('the world of vast freedom').

Again our interpretation may appear arbitrary. But it is Fuaadah herself who gives chemistry its magical significance. She raises it from the level of chemical elements and interacting substances to that of confrontation between femininity and masculinity. She equates 'the great discovery' to which she will devote her life with the re-creation of that 'missing' or 'severed' organ which, once restored, will enable her to regain her usurped place in the world of men:

> One day the voice brought her the story of the discovery of radium. It had previously brought her the names of brilliant researchers and discoverers. She was chewing her nails while listening and repeating to herself, 'If I were a man, I could do all the things they did' — feeling deep down that these inventors were no more capable of discovery than she was. But they are men. Yes, a man can do things a woman cannot, simply because she is female. A man is no more capable, but he is male. It is as if masculinity were a pre-condition for discovery.
>
> But here is a woman who has discovered something, a woman like herself, not a man... she was prepared to accept that there was something around her waiting to be unveiled, discovered, something existing like sound, light, gases, steam or the radiation of uranium. Yes, something existing but which no one else knew of.

Chemistry, then, is another 'magic key'. Bahiah Shaheen likens the key to Saleem's flat to a 'life-raft' for a drowning woman. Fuaadah resorts to the same imagery in describing her laboratory: it is 'her only hope in life, the only life-raft to save her from loss and vacuum; the only life-line which guides her to chemical research and perhaps to the greatest discovery'.

This semi-psychotic relationship with chemistry needs to be unravelled and interpreted symbolically. This can only be done by examining the regimen of 'denial and challenge' that the heroine of *Memoirs of a Woman Doctor* sets herself at the end of her secondary schooling:

> I would reject my femininity, challenge my nature... prove to my mother and grandmother that I wasn't a woman like them... that I was more intelligent than my brother... than any man, and that I could do everything my father did and more.

It should be noted that this regimen has been drawn up in the image of the mother. It is to her mother that the heroine wants to prove that she can do what her father can do and more. And it is in the image of her mother alone that Fuaadah wants to open her laboratory. What is even more curious is that the only substance she ever analyses there is a specimen of her mother's urine.

Here we must recall the reproductive significance of urine to Fuaadah, who 'did not know why, but she always associated urinating with giving birth and felt that they must be related'. Nor does Fuaadah stop at mentioning 'the pleasure of analysing her mother's urine'. She then proceeds to the semi-psychotic analogy between her mother's urine and her sex organs, to the extent of defining 'art and the pleasure of urine analysis' as 'an act which depends on all the senses: smell, touch, sight and taste'.

The immediate question is whether Fuaadah's mother is prepared to give her daughter her urine for analysis. Fuaadah insists on her mother giving her a sample as the first substance to be tested in her lab. But with her mother's refusal, the castrating mask appears. The mother who denies her daughter her urine and the pleasure of examining it is the same woman who denies her husband her body and the pleasure of her response in sexual intercourse:

> Fuaadah looked at her mother and saw in her eyes a strange look, similar to the one she had noticed in the wedding picture. A tyrannical, sceptical look, bitterly lacking in confidence in the one standing in front of her. She felt the blood rushing to her brain and found herself saying unconsciously, 'I know why you refuse to let me do the analysis. You refuse because you have no confidence in my competence.' She raised her voice unconsciously and shouted, 'You don't trust me to do anything. That has always been your view, and that has always been your attitude towards my father.'

This identification of the 'castrated' daughter with the 'castrated' father betrays, at the very heart of the 'declared' love, an unconscious hatred of the castrating mother. This is far more deep-rooted than the hatred of the father, even in his anal image. This is because the hatred of the father is secondary; it is basically restricted to his preparedness to compete for possession of the mother. The hatred of the mother, on the other hand, is basic to the extent that it becomes primary: it is the mother who originally denied her daughter the possibility of competing with her father. Isn't it the mother who created her 'a daughter', in other words, a 'deficient' being, unable to possess the mother herself?[37]

Ever since she discovered the magical powers of chemical interactions, Fuaadah has dreamed that she will one day be able to appeal against the verdict of 'castration' to which she has been sentenced. This dream, or 'the research topic' as she calls it, is 'the only reason for her continuing to live'. Once she has her laboratory, the belief grows that she is within an ace of realizing her life's dream, and that she will inevitably discover 'the sought-after' under the lens of her microscope.

But by withholding the sample of urine, the mother has changed what was a provisional sentence into a final, irrevocable and absolute sentence against which there can be no appeal. It was the mother alone who put it into her daughter's head that she could one day become another 'Mme Curie', and who was confident that her daughter would be 'better than all the other girls' and would make 'the greatest discovery' — yet now she has withdrawn this confidence, revealing at the decisive moment that it was nothing but a will-o'-the-wisp:

Fuaadah looked into her mother's eyes and said, 'Why were you so confident?' Her mother replied quickly, 'Just like that, for no reason.' Fuaadah tried to fix her mother with her eyes and to catch the meaning of her expression and learn the secret of the certainty which was always there, but she couldn't see anything.

Is it anatomically preordained, then, that the 'test-tube should remain empty' and 'the research topic' be lost? Fuaadah is like someone who has had a final appeal turned down and is left with only one hope, an appeal for clemency. She now resorts to a regressive and highly primitive form of subjugation to her mother's insatiable demands. She will confront her by regressing to the state of a baby wanting to be breastfed: 'Her small finger moved involuntarily and crept over her upper lip and entered her mouth. She began to suck the end of it like a baby whose teeth have come through but who is still sucking at his mother's breast.'

In confronting the adult daughter who has regressed to the state of a suckling baby, the mother has no option but to regress in turn and become a feeding breast:

A long time elapsed and she was sitting on the sofa in the lounge, her head between her hands, the tip of her small finger between her teeth.

She supposed that her mother had left the lounge, but she did not know where she had gone to. After a little while her mother returned holding a small bottle filled with a yellow fluid. She stretched forward her thin perspiring hand, holding the bottle out to her daughter. Fuaadah raised her eyes to her, and an imprisoned tear dropped between them into her lap.

Any remaining doubts as to the reproductive significance of the mother's urine will be dispelled when we see the fate of the sample Fuaadah has managed to win from her mother. The subtext here is not 'the great pleasure' which Fuaadah feels while 'washing the test-tubes and preparing the chemicals and bottles'; but the discovery, whilst examining 'a small drop of cold urine' under her microscope, of a living, moving cell. This cell is 'egg-shaped, in fact it was actually an egg'. It is, more precisely, 'her mother's egg'.

The bottle could have contained albumin, or salts, or some germ. But instead it contains her 'mother's egg' — the secret of life, of fertility, of fertilization, of birth, of the two sexes and the difference between them; it is the secret she always wanted to know 'when she was tiny'. She had almost found her way to the right solution when she had guessed 'when tiny' that she was born 'from an opening in her mother's abdomen, and that the opening could have been the one from which she urinated or another adjacent opening'.

Her mother was responsible for the great anatomical 'handicap' by giving birth to a girl. It was also her mother who misled her, 'spoilt her natural feelings, and thwarted her awareness of a number of basic precepts' when 'she told her off when she reported her discovery that she believed she had been born from her ear'. Ever since that day Fuaadah had begun to establish fanciful and confused relationships between things, particularly those related to sexual 'secrets':

She spent a long time trying to establish a relationship between the hearing of voices and birth. She was sometimes sceptical about the ear being created for hearing, and was inclined to believe that it was created for women to urinate from after marriage.

Thus it is the mother who digs the first spadeful from the semi-psychotic trench which Fuaadah is to dig for herself in order to find a way out of this sexual no-man's land.[38] Fuaadah's tragedy, if we can use this term, lies precisely in the trench which she has hollowed out of the rock of reality, and its inevitable transformation into no-man's land itself. This is what she subconsciously drags with her into her lab with 'its empty test-tubes' and 'her mother's egg' under the microscope.

It may be instructive to look more closely at this 'egg'. According to Fuaadah, her mother is sixty-five. Now a woman of this age is well past child-bearing. Moreover the mother has had a hysterectomy. Even if we assume that it is only the womb that has removed, leaving an ovary or ovaries, the 'egg' from such an ovary would be dead *in situ* as it would not have access to the Fallopian tubes.

Even if we were to assume the impossible, and imagine that the mother is still fertile, her 'egg' could not have showed up in the urine as the urethra and bladder are a closed system to which the ovaries have no access. A chemical analyst like Fuaadah cannot delude herself into believing that the sample of her mother's urine actually contains an egg — unless she subscribes to the theory of infantile sexuality which postulates a relationship between urination and birth.

In fact, it is precisely this theory to which Fuaadah subscribed when 'she was tiny'. Consequently, her scientific blunder resurrects her infantile attitude towards her mother. It also reflects an infantile desire to heal the narcissistic wound which has caused adult confusion.[39] Finally (though no less importantly), it reveals the buried desire to assume the father's role *vis-à-vis* the mother, and to prove her ability to do 'everything her father can do and more'. In a word, this is fertilizing 'her egg' even if it is only in a test-tube and under the lens of a microscope.

But it is precisely here, more than anywhere else, that the

impossibility of effecting a regimen which challenges anatomical destiny emerges and its intrinsic illogicality is confirmed. The dream to which Fuaadah has devoted herself and her life has dispersed and been dissipated — on the very day she is due to put it into practice. Her mother's imaginary egg has changed nothing in the reality of 'nothingness' within her head as in the test-tube. Her feelings of emptiness and loss of the 'research topic' are only finally confirmed once Saati has shattered her privacy in the laboratory and 'spoilt for her the pleasure of analysing her mother's urine'.

It all comes to an end the very next day, as the 'great pleasure' has left only a residue of bitterness:

She entered the lab and put on her white apron, and arranged the bottles of salts and acids on the table. She lit the burner and pressed the metal handle to hold the test-tube. But she did not pick it up. She left it in the wooden stand, with its gaping open mouth. She gazed at the empty test-tube for a few seconds, then sat down with her head in her hands. Where will she begin? She doesn't know, doesn't know! Chemistry evaporated from her brain. All the ideas which used to crowd her head are gone! Where to? She doesn't know, doesn't know.

Once again, it is the great absence, the whistling of silence, the emptiness of the great depths, which reveal an insubstantial existence. As with every disappointment or failure, a large charge of self-guilt is released from the conscious. The failed ego explains away failure as some sort of just punishment. It is not the mother who is evil, nor is it her 'fierce, tyrannical' gaze. The eyes are those of the 'egg' looking at Fuaadah 'gently as her mother would'. Here is the evil Fuaadah treating 'her mother's egg' differently from the way her gentle mother treated her when she 'herself was this egg thirty years ago'. Her mother 'did not put her in a bottle and stop it up with a cork' but, on the contrary, used her womb to provide her with a warm haven and a secure refuge. It is Fuaadah who is evil, who then 'grabbed with her teeth at her mother's flesh as a louse sticks to the scalp, sucking up her cells and syphoning off her blood'.

Yes, it is the evil Fuaadah who deserves to be punished. And the punishment should naturally fit the crime. Since she grabbed with her teeth at her mother's body and sucked its blood, then let a louse suck up her cells and syphon off her blood, and let that louse be Muhammad el-Saati. In the depths of her subconscious, she has coveted her mother's body in a taboo manner and wanted to fertilize her egg in a sinful fashion — for this she deserves to be punished severely. Then let her submit her body to a taboo possession by Saati, and let an abominable anal father fertilize her in a no less abominable, sinful fashion.

If and when Saati fulfils this role, Fuaadah will be able to return to her room from the quiet spot near the Pyramids, carrying that 'horrible rusty smell', that 'burning bitterness' 'in her entrails, cells and blood'. She will be able to look with 'her two blood-shot eyes' at the picture of her mother hanging on the wall, and wonder:

> Won't her mother now give up that crushing look? Hasn't she done penance enough for her sin? Hasn't she filled her body with that burning bitter bile? Hasn't she immersed her body in that concentrated rusty bitterness? Is there greater sorrow than this? Has there ever been a mother who has died and been granted more grief than this? Has ever a mother left behind her a daughter to tolerate such poison? Is there any more faithfulness to motherhood than this? Is there any greater restitution of a daughter's debts than this?

But are we faced with an atonement on the part of the daughter or a new criminalization of the mother? Or rather, are we hostages in a vicious circle where love leads to hatred, and hatred to love, in a continuous concentric movement which endlessly repeats itself?

3. The Restorative Station: This concentric chain can be broken at at least one of its links. Here the ego regresses to the most primitive stages of its existence, to the phase where it is indistinguishable from the mother and its symbiotic co-existence with her, in a word to the phase of the non-ego. But it is merely a defensive measure which aims to maintain the ego's existence and protect it from more serious dangers which threaten to uproot it.

The non-ego is not a negation of the ego, but a protective shield and a mask to disguise it. If it becomes apparent to the ego that the shield itself is poisoned and the mask suffocating, it may well take the defensive counter-measure of ripping off both the shield and the mask, and attempting to restore and reconstruct itself by undertaking a regressive journey.

Just as the breast-fed baby discovers itself and its own distinct ego through its discovery of the existence of the external world and through learning to differentiate between the elements it contains, so does the regressive ego. If it feels in danger of being totally and effectively crushed and annihilated, it may return to the objects of the external world, valuing and hanging onto them as the only life-line.

The Absentee is no ordinary love story. There are virtually none of the purple passages generally to be found in novels bemoaning the absence of a loved one. Fuaadah's crisis as a result of Fareed's absence is an existential one. Indeed, it is a crisis of identity rather than an emotional crisis. Like Saleem Ibraheem in the case of Bahiah Shaheen, Fareed causes things to be present by his presence and absent by his absence. As Bahiah says in *Two Women in One*, in Saleem's absence 'things around her would lose their existence and reality. When he returned... a strange feeling of the truth of things and of existence coursed through her body.'

Thus the anxiety Fareed creates by his absence is no common anxiety. It is ontological, in all the criteria and controls which allow the ego to be distinct and to differentiate between reality and illusion, certainty and doubt:

But where is Fareed? He is absent. As long as he is absent, how can she distinguish dreams from reality? If he had left even a small piece of paper with his handwriting on, it would know, yes the piece of paper would know, but she, with her head, with her arms and legs, is powerless. Her body can do nothing, nor can her mind. Everything in her head is reduced to a dumb humming. Everything is crushed within her to become a constant, shrill whistling like the sound of silence.

I think, therefore I am. I feel, therefore I exist. But in the shadow of Fareed's absence, even this existential proof seems to have lost its explanatory power. How many times has Fuaadah 'touched her own thighs looking for proof of her existence'? How can she take her feelings in particular as proof of her existence as long as she doubts the feelings themselves? Are feelings 'reality or a myth'? What prevents feelings from becoming illusions, from becoming 'an imperceptible movement in her head, like illusions, like dreams, like hidden powers'? Can her 'scientific brain' believe in these 'tricks'?

The intellectual proof fares no better than the emotional one. Ideas refuse to come from her head. And even if they do, they come up against a 'thick wall, thicker than the bones of her head'. How can the brain actually reason as long as it has 'solidified and become a metallic mass'?

Fareed is one option in a choice between this and madness or non-existence. Without Fareed, it seems as if Fuaadah is destined to go round 'in circles', continually revolving until she vanishes and is crushed: 'Going round and getting crushed, and nothing else, nothing else.'

Passive and lazy, Fuaadah is slipping into non-existence. Before she is totally drowned in nothingness, however, she issues one last SOS to Fareed — or if not to him as 'flesh and blood', then to his essence, 'that special warm and extraordinary smell' which:

arrives just before he does, and stays with her after he leaves, permeating her clothes, her hair and the folds of skin between her fingers as if it was another person with her, or as though the smell emanated from her and not from him.

If it isn't his essence, or even his nose, it is at least the sound of the phone ringing. Although it is 'a dumb, shrill bell', she knows the sound 'issues from Fareed's telephone, ringing in Fareed's house, crashing out over Fareed's desk, colliding with the big sofa where they had often lounged side by side, and disturbing the air which they had both breathed in and out'.

This ontological anxiety, together with the sorrowful attachment to the few remaining things of the external world and its objects, are what give to the atmosphere of *The Absentee*, polluted as it is by the smells of vomit, urine and rusty bitterness, a certain poetic flavour. It pervades the novel as the perfume of jasmine transcends the smell of the manure with which it is fertilized.

Though the novel is painted in less vivid colours than those of *Two Women in One*, the descent — like the ascent — has its own magic, and particularly its own sense of tragedy. What makes the reader more sympathetic towards Fuaadah is that in her descent, she rids herself of the elitist aura with which Bahiah Shaheen surrounds herself both on taking off and on flying aloft. In fact, when stirred to anger, the ego can be as captivating as when it is full to overflowing — just as the timidity with which the ego restores itself may be more deserving of sympathy than its outbursts when intent on self-destruction. Finally, the model of the 'inferior man' represented by Fuaadah is nevertheless more human than that of the Superman to which Bahiah Shaheen aspires.

5
...And Other Stories

'I admit to you that my unconscious is stronger than my conscious mind and most of the time I obey it.'

Nawal el-Saadawi
(*A Modern Love Letter*[1])

Nawal el-Saadawi's short stories, and even some of her novellas such as *The Thread*[2] and *Ring a Ring o' Roses*,[3] may be seen as adding a new dimension to the art of the short story. With their 'autobiographical flavour', they relive, recall or at times merely describe various different positions or attitudes in the stream of psychological development of a heroine who is struggling to reach her own personal fulfilment.

The dead narrator of *The Greatest Crime* says:

But I am no longer like you. The experience of death has given me an inhuman courage and I no longer need to section off the phases of my life nor to erect a thick wall to separate one from the other. I was able to acquire such a view of the disjointed and fragmented phases of your lives only after I left the earth.

This image would appear to support the psychoanalytic interpretation advanced in the previous chapters. Picasso's paintings are often scattered with unnaturally transposed human organs. Similarly, Saadawi's short stories expose us to only parts of a disjointed psychological pattern, not connected by any obvious organic link. It is a series of stations through which the train of psychological development has passed, picking up or offloading baggage without considering whether these stops are main stations, halts, bypasses or termini.

In the previous chapters, we have undertaken an in-depth analysis of several of Saadawi's novels in an attempt to 'rechart' the train journey. Our brief review of some of her short stories, however, will merely indicate some of the stations, or points en route, leaving it to the preceding lengthy analysis to join them up.

A New Theory of Infantile Sexuality

We are not here referring to the theory alluded to by the heroine of *The Absentee*,[4] and adopted by the heroine of the suggestively entitled *Nobody Tells Her Anything*,[5] according to which, 'small children are born from the ears of women'; or rather, 'not from their ears' but 'their noses'. We are referring instead to the more intriguing theory which, for elitist reasons that will become apparent in the following quotation, maintains that it is the father and not the mother who gives birth:

> At school whenever I heard girls referring to the fact that it was their mothers who had given birth to them, I used to reply that it was my father who had given birth to me. I used to hear them laugh but I didn't care. In fact I secretly felt proud that whereas all the other girls had been born of women, a man had given birth to me.[6]

Another Theory of Infantile Sexuality

The novella *Ring a Ring o' Roses* springs another surprise on us. On the one hand, it confirms the 'typological' theory of infantile sexuality: this holds that children are all conceived as one sex, only to be distinguished later as male or female by a conscious adult interference that runs counter to nature. Not content with this view, the novella even asserts that 'the faces of children are sexless like those of old people' and that 'A girl's foot cannot be distinguished from a boy's because feet in childhood are as sexless as faces, particularly if the feet are bare, as shoes are the only indication of sex.' Not only does the theory insist on the uniformity of sex; it also insists on the uniformity of its origins:

166

Hameedo cannot conceive of life without Hameeda. She is not an ordinary sister, but his twin. Twins are of two types, one type nurtured separately but simultaneously in the womb, and the other coming as male and female from one ovum. Hameedo and Hameeda grew together in the womb as if they were one foetus. At the beginning they were only one cell, then everything split into two. The most minute of features was divided, so that it became impossible to tell them apart. Even their mother confused Hameedo and Hameeda.

This exceptional similarity, even to the point of a shared identity, is stressed in order to deny any natural anatomical differences between the two sexes. Any such differences are seen as merely social/conventional. This explains the choice of the dual name (Hameedo = Hameeda), which, had it not been for the feminine case ending, would have signified one being:

The fact is that one dot can change a meaning radically, particularly in Arabic. A male becomes female merely by the addition of a dot or hyphen, and so on. Female names are only distinguished from the male by their feminine case ending, e.g. Ameen–Ameena, Zuhair–Zuhaira, Hameedo–Hameeda. Thus at the stroke of a pen, a man becomes a woman.

But it goes beyond a 'stroke of the pen' to include anatomical differences. It is here that we see the startling new theory of infantile sexuality. The typological assumption takes as its starting-point the oneness of physical origin, concluding that a girl is merely a 'castrated boy'. The 'updated version', on the other hand, refutes this assumption of castration, or rather reverses it by maintaining that the boy was originally a girl before the addition of an extra artificial organ, which made him male.

Thus Hameedo is initially so confused by his striking resemblance to Hameeda that he 'would hide behind a wall and lift his galabiyah, exposing his thighs, looking between them, and realizing on seeing a narrow cleft that he was Hameeda'. The original form of humanity, then, is the one 'with a cleft'. Only at a later stage, and as a result of artificial implantation, does the male child 'gain an organ'. Thus Hameedo leaves the unisex world of children for the male world only when he discovers 'in the pocket of his robe something hidden, something hard, dangling between his thighs, an alien member', 'like an artificial arm or a transplanted organ'.

By the same token, the reverse is true. It is not the female rejecting her femininity who needs to prove that she is a man who can do what men can or even more. On the contrary, it is Hameedo (who 'sometimes likes to think of himself as a woman') who bears the onus of having to 'prove that he is not a woman' and who, like Adam after having committed the original sin, discovers that 'an ugly organ' has grown in place of 'the old cleft'.

Re-Enactment of Foetal Omnipotence

Narcissistic role-playing may lead to child-like attitudes in adult life. It may also be one of the main contributory factors in a regression towards the phase of womblike existence and the foetal ego, characterized by a sense of imagined omniscience and omnipotence. This narcissistic role-playing is the other feature which finds new expression in *In Camera*:

> I always felt that you, my daughter, were capable of anything, of moving mountains or of crumbling rocks, even though your body is small and weak like mine. But when your tiny feet used to kick the walls of my stomach, I'd say to myself: God, what strength and power is there inside my body? Your movements were strong while you were still a foetus and shook me from inside, like a volcano shakes the earth. And yet I knew that you were as small as I was, your bones as delicate as your father's, as tall and slim as your grandmother, your feet as large as the feet of prophets.

Re-Enactment of the Father's Sexual Aggression during Life in the Womb

Another re-enactment related to life in the womb is where the child imagines that, even as a foetus, it was subjected to periodic and recurrent sexual aggression by the father. This role-playing has three characteristics. First, it is usually a feminine and not a masculine activity. Second, it ultimately denies the sexual role of the mother in relation to the father: the girl reserves this role for herself, as it is the occupant of the womb with whom the father is copulating and not the mother. Third, it conveys an anal vision of copulation: the foetus is seen as occupying the womb like a human being does in the world — head uppermost and bottom down. But it is to the buttocks that the aggression is ultimately directed:

Unlike normal people, her life did not begin on the day she was born but many days previously. It began as a small entity inside her mother's womb. She was still a foetus, but nevertheless she could feel, see and perhaps even smell too. She could not see anything worth mentioning except pitch-black day and night, although sometimes a faint glow would filter through from an unidentifiable source below. Everything around her was moist and dark, conveying security and continuity of growth, except for the occasional odd event.

This event would begin with a strange sound which might have emanated from her mother and filtered through from the outside. But she could never catch the words. They were not identifiable as words but rather as a humming sound or a roar or a sob, violent sobbing, as her mother's body used to shake and quake violently. All was well apart from the fact that it made her grab the shaking walls around her, sinking her thin fingers into them to hang on. It felt as if she could be shaken from her grip to fall into the well: not a well of still waters but rather a maelstrom of swirling waters with, at its vortex, a deep, dark hole signifying death.

She remained in a sitting position, hanging onto the wall, glued to it as a louse to the scalp. Her sharp eyes would quiver under her closed eyelids in anticipation of the thing about to rise from the hole. She would hold her breath when that long sharp instrument with its gleaming point thrust itself towards her. She would shiver and curl up, thrusting herself deep into the sticky folds of the wall. The tapered end swayed and probed around her, searching in its blindness like a wild beast sniffing out its prey. Its sharp end bumped into her bottom, causing her cells to shrink away from the bleeding and reform around the wound,[7] enfolding it in her belly.[8]

Return to the Mother's Womb

In at least one short story (*The Greatest Crime*), we are again presented with the sort of overwhelming yearning experienced by Bahiah Shaheen in *Two Women in One*.[9] In her desire for reunion with her mother so that their identities can merge, the heroine of *The Greatest Crime* longs to abolish the distance separating her body from the ego, to regain those 'foetal senses' which 'felt nothing but warmth' and 'smelt nothing but milk', at that stage of existence in which all life is reduced to a mother's womb or a mother's breast:

> I used to be frightened of two things: darkness and death. I'd slip out of my small bed in the middle of the night and creep into my mother's bed. I'd bury myself in her warm body and cling to her as hard as I could. I'd curl up to make my whole body smaller and try to shrink to the size of a foetus which could return to its mother's womb. My whole body shook with this fervent desire and trembled as in a fever. I thought nothing could save me from imminent death in the darkness other than disappearing inside that warm and tender womb which would enclose me alone.[10]

What is new this time, however, is not this burning desire *per se* but its explicit link with pleasure (by definition taboo here) and with delusions of grandeur, characteristic of the foetal phase in the development of the ego:

> Anyone seeing me at that moment, curled up like a foetus, would have understood that this desire was real and that it was violent, that it was not so much a desire to escape death but rather to get close to my mother, so close as to stick to her, to merge my body into hers so that she and I could become one. I loved her so much that the obliteration of my body in hers was not obliteration, was not death, was not painful, was not frightening, but was the peak of my life, the climax of my pleasure, was security and total comfort.[11]

The Father as Intruder in Competition over the Mother

In the dual relationship between a mother and her child, the Oedipal triangle cannot function or even be visualized. The father necessarily takes on the role of the intruder who both hates and is hated in accordance with the anal conception of hatred:

In such a state, I was oblivious of the presence of my father who lay beside my mother with his huge body, his long black moustache trembling with the movement of his upper lip, his lower lip drooping under the pressure of a loud snore, a long thread of white spittle drooling slowly from the corner of his mouth and over his chin. Despite his deep sleep, from which it appeared to me at the time he would never awake, he opened his eyes. And although I could not see him (because I was curled up like a foetus), I noticed the look which flashed across his eyes and immediately vanished. At that time, I didn't know whether it had disappeared of its own accord or whether he had made it disappear, but I now know that it was he who did it. Despite the dark which immersed the bedroom and although I was unable to raise my eyes to his, that look was powerful enough to penetrate my skull like an arrow. Despite the pain of that penetration, despite the fear of it, despite the pitch-dark, and although it disappeared in a flash and there returned to his eyes the look of a loving father, despite all that, I knew the meaning of that look. It was the look of a man expressing hatred.

My father was a civilized man and like all civilized men of our time, who can control and hide their real feelings and display other feelings to show how they've progressed, like all of them, my father was able to hide his real desire to grasp my neck with his large fat fingers and fling me far away. His hand did in fact move towards me, but he resisted the movement so that it moved like the hand of a civilized father, patting his child on the shoulder. With a slow, quiet movement, he separated my body from the body of my mother and I found myself on the cold edge of the bed whilst he occupied my warm place.[12]

In the light of this passage, it is not difficult to appreciate the significance of the 'greatest crime' referred to in the title:

The first crime in the life of humanity was not that Cain slaughtered Abel but that Adam killed my mother. He killed her because I loved her and did not love him. And I wish he had realized that I could have loved him had he loved me. But my father was incapable of loving. Even though I was a child, I understood that he did not love me. And he did not love my mother. He loved only to satisfy himself.[13]

An Anal Vision of the World

A direct line leads from the anal father to the anal man and the anal world. As we have seen, this generalization is first postulated by Firdaus in *Woman at Point Zero*:[14] 'the fathers, the uncles, the husbands and men of all professions'. The theme is continued by Hameeda, who is attacked for the first time by 'a huge body which smelt of tobacco' and that looks like those of 'her father, brother, uncle, cousin or any other man'.[15] As in the previous novels and all the short stories, all men — whether husbands, lovers, prostitutes' clients, officials or family men — are portrayed as having 'a hairy chest like that of a monkey and a prominent belly like that of a pregnant woman'.[16] In *In Camera*, the generalization takes on an even more extreme and categorical form:

> Her eyes began to make out the bodies sitting on that elevated place, above each head a body, smooth heads without hair, in the light as red as monkeys' rumps. They must all be males, for however old a woman grew, her head could never look like a monkey's rump.

As the heroine of *A Modern Love Letter* maintains, the world is made by men and for men, and the hatred unleashed by males on the world they have created expresses itself anally. As this world is governed by two great drives — hunger and love, to quote the poet Schiller — it is at the level of the stomach and sex[17] that the male's anal ugliness is most apparent. It is in close proximity to rubbish bins and refuse tips that males find copulation most appealing. Narjas, the heroine of *The Picture*,[18] catches her father having sex with the servant Nabawiyah next to a refuse bin in just this way:

> She saw something moving on the kitchen floor. She looked at it closely. The pupils of her eyes widened, settling on a naked heap of flesh rolling on the floor, with two heads. One was Nabawiyah's with its long locks of hair, the other was her

father's with its prominent curved nose. Her gaze froze on the big naked heap rolling until Nabawiyah's head reached the floor and hit the refuse bin and her father's head rose and banged on the underside of the sink. But soon they swapped places, with Nabawiyah's head hitting the sink and her father's head falling into the rubbish.

In turn, Hameeda's master always fancies having sex with her next to the rubbish bin like a rooting pig:

He was dazzled by the movement of live flesh like a pig suddenly released from a refuse tip where it had lived for years on scraps and bits and pieces of offal. Leaping forward lustfully, he dropped his clothes. His overheated body touched the cool floor, sopping wet from the mop. His flabby, sagging muscles contracted and an electric current flowed up his spine. Life seeped into his five senses and his quivering nose began stealthily to sniff the odour of the refuse from under the sink. With all his strength he drew a deep breath and filled his lungs with the putrid smell of the rubbish. The stink[19] suffused his body and with it seeped in an old childhood memory of his first sexual pleasure.[20]

After the bedroom, it is in the dining-room that the disgusting ugliness of the male world is represented as a vast cesspit:

...the dining room, with its table surrounded by nine mouths opening and closing in pairs of swollen jawbones, the upper jaw ruminating on the lower jaw, teeth like millstones grinding and crushing. In the sink, piles of empty plates accumulate topped by a layer of solidified fat, its drain blocked by scraps of food.

The refuse bin is filled to the brim with more scraps of uneaten food. As man's social position rises, so does the amount of refuse he accumulates. The stomach which is crammed full from above naturally has to dispose of more. Her master's stomach being unarguably the largest, the amount of refuse he accumulates is naturally more than anyone else. His servants pile it in metal-sided carts and it is carried away to a distant place in the desert where it forms a huge pyramid to be marvelled at by tourists.[21]

The Idealized Father

Alongside the image of the crude and despicable father, 'only living to eat and to satisfy himself', from some of the short stories (and in a way unparalleled in the novels) there emerges an idealized picture of a sensitive, loving father who fills the house 'with activity, joy and life', in the words of the heroine of *And Love Died*.[22] When his daughter looks into his black eyes full of 'strength and proof of affection', 'the world shines in her eyes' and everything seems 'delightful' to her.[23] When she walks beside him in the street, she 'feels proud': she sees 'all eyes directed at her father' and 'all lips open with prayers to her father', 'her small ears almost catching a whisper from among the passers-by: this is the man who has absolute authority and this is his daughter walking beside him'.[24]

The roughness of the father and the grossness of his body will subsequently turn into objects of an anal form of hatred. Yet in these extracts, these very features seem to encapsulate his lovable characteristics, making him an object of affection. For the heroine of *And Love Died*, the father, 'the strong, the powerful, the mighty, the giant whose height stretches to heaven', is 'her sight, her hearing and her life'.

The heroine of *The Thread* confirms this when she says:

A stage of my life passed during which I saw my father as tall and slim, his shoes treading firmly on the ground. The sound of his heels on the pavement still rings in my ears, step by step, firmly and rhythmically. I used to listen to my father's voice when he spoke. His voice was rough like that of all men, but it was a gentle roughness. I felt it in my ears particularly when he used to call me by my name. I loved this period of my life for no apparent reason. I loved my father's big hand in mine and his fingers holding mine. I loved him most when he used to walk beside me in the street carrying my heavy school bag. I was short, almost touching the ground, and so I could see his large feet when he walked. One foot moved after the other, slowly, firmly and rhythmically as though it knew precisely the distance in front and behind it, and as if it knew exactly where to position itself for the next step, placing itself with all its enormity and planting itself firmly with all its weight. Everything was magical, or seemed to be magical with hindsight.

In the same vein, the heroine of *The Picture* recreates the image of the great fatherly hand, charged with affection and emotional sentiments commensurate with or even larger than life. But she does this only after she has added two features which will later become objects of an extreme and violent hatred, contributing to the anal image of the father. The features she adds are his hair and his smell:

When they crossed the street, her father would hold her hand and his fingers would enfold her tiny ones. Her heart would beat faster and her breath pant and she would tilt her head to rub against him. No sooner do her lips touch his large hairy hand than that strong distinctive smell assails her nostrils, the distinctive smell of her father. She does not know exactly what it is but she can smell it wherever he goes.

When she enters his room, she smells it in every corner, in the bed, in the wardrobe, on his clothes. Sometimes she buries her head in his clothes to breathe it in even more deeply. She may kiss his clothes, burying her face in them, while kneeling before the large portrait of him over the bed, as if in prayer. It is not the sort of prayer she rattles through quickly to a God she has never seen, but a real prayer to a real God she can see with her own eyes, hear with her own ears, and smell with her own nose.

This passage, which reveals all too clearly the borderline separating affection from sexual love, carries the idealization of the father to its ultimate limits, that is, to deification. God is always the great father, in fact the greatest. While the heroine of *The Thread* does not go as far as to compare her father to God (as does the heroine of *The Picture*), she nevertheless endows him with one of God's main attributes — omnipotence: 'I believed that my father, unlike other men, could do anything he wanted.'

It is this 'ability to do anything he wanted' ascribed to the father which reveals a somewhat unusual attitude that links not only the heroine of *And Love Died* to that of *The Thread*, but also these two to that other father-deifying heroine, Amira, in *The Defiant* by Amina el-Sa'id.[25] This attitude rejects the possibility of the father being ill, although it is a biological law applicable to all other human beings. The heroine of *And Love Died* covers her father's face with a sheet and locks the door of the room because: 'I don't want anyone to see my father in bed, pale and weak... Weakness is like the private parts of the body. I don't want anyone to see my father's private parts.'

In her turn the heroine of *The Thread* says, 'I knew nothing about illness. I may sometimes have heard the word or seen sick people, but it happened far away from me, in the lives of others at the other end of life where neither my father nor I were to be found.' In order to spare her father any illness or pain, this particular heroine goes so far as to put an end to his life.

The Father as Taboo Object

In as much as the inversion to the opposite represents one of the ego's main defensive priorities, changing the father's image from ideal to anal can be explained in only one way: the father himself has at an earlier phase represented a taboo love object. In view of the danger to the ego represented by taboo objects, and the intolerable feeling of guilt, this taboo object of love must subsequently be inverted into a main object of hatred.

It is from this perspective that Saadawi's short stories fill in the gaps left by the novels. The novels are not only devoid of references to the ideal father (that is, the father as an object of love in its positive sense); they are also devoid or almost devoid of references to the taboo father (i.e. as an object of love in the sexual sense). The exception is Bahiah Shaheen in *Two Women in One* who feels sick if she accidentally catches sight of her sex organs, and who can accept her nakedness and sexuality only in reference to her father.

A similar reference is found in *Memoirs of a Woman Doctor*.[26] The young woman whose 'cowardly self' sneaks into bed at night to fill it with 'fantasies and illusions' tells us openly that the fantasy which prevents her sleeping is of:

Long powerful arms [which] encircled my waist. A man's face...
with eyes like my father's and a mouth like my cousin's, but
he wasn't either of them. Who was he? ...Where would I find
him... the spectre of a man lodged firmly in my imagination?
I knew the look in his eyes, the timbre of his voice, the shape
of his fingers, the warmth of his breath, the depths of his heart
and mind. I knew, I knew. I can't tell how, but I knew.

This fantasy is recognized by the depths of the subconscious
but is unrecognized on its surface, since the conscious ego is
unaware of it. It is nothing other than the father object which has
to be suppressed and can thus only exist as a fantasy. And it is this
very fantasy which takes on flesh and blood in the short stories.
The shy heroine of *And Love Died* says only that, after the death
of her father, she finds herself incapable of loving even those on
whom she used to project her love for her father:

She arrived at his house without too much trouble. He opened
the door. It was the first time I had seen him since my father's
death. I don't fully know what impression seeing him in his
house left me with. Have the good looks I loved been lost, or
has the death of my father dissipated the appearance of life and
everything in it, including him?

However, the heroines of both *The Picture* and *The Thread* are
more frank and go much further than that. Narjas, the heroine of
the first story, likes taking off her clothes and standing naked in
front of her father's picture:

She found herself in front of the mirror. She turned round. Her
eyes widened in surprise to see two small mounds quivering
under her skirt. Her hand reached round to her back, exploring,
and her trembling fingers encountered two soft fleshy orbs. She
too had buttocks. What shape are they? Are they round or oval?
Are they prominent and attractive? She lifted her skirt behind
to expose them and twisted her head to look, but they turned
as her body turned and always remained hidden behind her.
As she turned her head the upper part of her body moved
with it. Every time her torso moved, the lower half moved

177

with it. That infuriated her and made her even more determined to see her own backside. She pulled her skirt up until she was completely exposed behind. She planted her feet firmly on the ground, turned her head and began eying her body. As she was turning her head in front of the mirror with her back naked from top to bottom, her eyes suddenly met those of her father. She trembled. She knew that they were not really his eyes but those of the picture on the wall. But her small body continued to shake and she was incapable of tearing her eyes away.

In fact Narjas not only enjoys gazing into her father's eyes as they stare from the picture at her naked back.[27] She also enjoys masturbating under his gaze, making sure that, from his room, he can hear the sounds of her panting breath and the squeaking of her bed shaking beneath her buttocks:

> While she was lying back, her prominent buttocks rubbed against the bed. A delicious new tremor ran through her body. Her trembling fingers reached behind her. Two round masses of flesh squeezed between her and the bed. She turned over waiting for the feeling to go away so that she could sleep, but her buttocks rose in the air as her abdomen was pushed down by the weight of her body.
>
> She turned onto her side but they still rubbed against the bed with every breath she took. She stopped breathing for a minute but her breaths were still chasing and following each other at a rapid pace, making her small body quiver spasmodically in the process, shaking the bed and making a faint creaking noise which she imagined was clearly audible in the still of the night, loud enough to reach the ears of her father, who, although asleep in his room, would no doubt understand the source of the noise and its real reason.

This sarcastic, semi–caricatural tone is deliberately introduced in *The Picture* to lighten the force of the 'subtext'. It shows a daughter with only her father to relate her femininity to — a stance that is generally absent in the works we have analysed so far. *The Thread*, however, presents a more dramatic scenario. It shows a daughter who discovers that she is female only in relation to her father, and who recognizes the anatomical distinction between the sexes only in relation to his masculinity:

> Until this day, I didn't divide people into different sexes, men and women. The whole world full of men and women was one sex; my father and I were another. I thought that my father was the same sex as me, and that he was not a man, nor I a woman. But my ignorance was not total. It was interspersed by fleeting glimpses of light. These glimpses did not occur arbitrarily. There was always a reason.
>
> Once I woke up trembling in the middle of the night after a nightmare. I left my room as I used to when a child and I went to my father's room. The cover had fallen off while he was asleep and left him completely naked. It wasn't the first time that I had seen him naked. I used to catch sight of him changing his clothes. As soon as he saw me he would turn round and put on his trousers.
>
> But this time my eyes froze on his body, as if I was discovering for the first time in my life that he was male. This masculinity struck me as strange, turning him in my eyes into a stranger whom I had never seen before. When I looked at my own body I was overtaken by the most peculiar sensation that I was a woman, a being of a sex other than man.

Disgust with Sex

When sexual feelings are associated so strongly with taboo objects, and consequently with feelings of guilt, it is not uncommon for the instinctive love of sex to change into a neurotic loathing of it. From this perspective, Saadawi's short stories join forces with the novels in emphasizing the disgusting nature of sexual intercourse. Dawlat, the heroine of *The Thread*, says that once she has seen her father naked, he becomes 'the reason for her being terrified', even though he was once a source of security. Her view of the naked body then becomes so horrifying and evokes such feelings of disgust that the 'mid-point' of her body, 'in the small triangle under her abdomen', becomes a point where bitterness settles, breathing into her a:

> warm and bitter [breath] like poison, flowing up to my throat

179

and mixing with my saliva. I try to spit it out but it is unspittable. I try to vomit it up to empty my guts, but it remains, filling me with salty water like that of the sea.

The heroine of *A Modern Love Letter* publicly declares her hatred of the world of men because 'nothing in it can amuse a woman other than that sort of amusement which neither amuses nor gratifies me and which only shows life in its ugliness and man in his baseness'.

The two most important principles of life, which supposedly give pleasure when they come together, meet only as the aggressive hissing of the male and the servile groaning of the female.[28] The ugliest scene imaginable is that of copulation, its music an obligato of 'snoring reminiscent of the trickling of water in an ancient water-wheel drawn by a sick and worn-out ox'.[29]

The proposed blueprint for women's behaviour entails one of two alternatives. First, there is the example of the heroine of *The Man with the Buttons*,[30] who, when she knows that 'that thing was going to happen', presents her husband with 'a body as still as the waters of a pool, cold and still as death'. The second alternative is that adopted by the heroine of *Lying*,[31] who essentially refuses to take part in the game of 'lying' otherwise known as sexual intercourse. She rejects man 'as violently and irrevocably as we would fight off a disease, death or any other calamity in order not to be destroyed by its onslaught'.

Rejecting Anatomical Pre-Destiny

This is seen most clearly in the heroine of *A Private Letter to an Artist Friend*: 'Is it my destiny… not to be a female? …Or is it really my destiny to be a person before being a female? …I am a person by nature and not a female.' But the heroine fails to ask herself the following question: can a human being exist without being either male or female? From this perspective, is there any meaning to 'before' and 'after'? One is not a human being 'before' or 'after' being male or female. One is a human being whether male or female. Maleness and femaleness are to humanity as like is to like — as interdependent as a parasite and its host, a symbiotic relationship.

Rejection of the Male

Rejecting femininity necessarily implies a rejection of masculinity. The woman is only a woman in relation to man. A woman who rejects man has in effect rejected her female body. By relegating femininity to a secondary rather than a primary consideration, and by demoting it from a biological fact to a social factor, the gap is bridged between these two rejections. The heroine of *A Private Letter to an Artist Friend* says, 'since childhood I have rejected my femininity because it was not me, not of my making, but rather that of a world full of masculinity'.

There is no doubt that femininity has social implications. But to reduce it to its artificial and partial implications is to refute its innate biological nature.[32] Femininity, like masculinity, needs neither the ego nor others to create it. At least this is usually the case, as long as it is considered a primary given. But despite the heroine's social rationalizations for the rejection of her femininity,[33] the rejection *per se* will be valid only when the refusal of masculinity as a biological phenomenon is also accepted.

The heroine of *A Private Letter to an Artist Friend* seems to have taken up the rejection of men as a hobby, with all the pleasures this implies:

> Refusal for me is as easy and natural as the air I breathe. But for him, refusal was hard, harder than death.
>
> It has always puzzled me why men are unable to cope with refusal, especially the refusal of a woman. I see the face of one of them, from which the blood ebbs away until it becomes as white as death. Does this refusal expose his real face to himself, so that he realizes for the first time that it is a dead face? Or that he is refused within himself as well and is suddenly unable to cope with both refusals together?[34]

This rejection can clearly be interpreted in terms of castration, even if this is expressly denied by the heroine of *A Modern Love Letter*:

> It is not... that I kill or castrate men, but I am always able to stare a man in the eyes and can always see the muscle around his mouth or his fingers quiver. It may only be quick and last

no longer than a moment or two, but it is always enough for me to see it and to bend his will to mine. His muscular power, even the power of all men in the world, is incapable of making the muscles of my hand yield under his.

Elitism

Given that masculinity and femininity are equally rejected as domains for the choice of love objects, what is the way out and where does the solution lie? In fact, there is more than one solution. This can be deduced in particular from *A Modern Love Letter* and *A Private Letter to an Artist Friend*. The common denominator in these various solutions is that they can all be categorized under one heading, namely, that of 'elitism'.

This elitism is obvious in the choice of love object, in the alignment with the quality of life rather than its quantity, in the wish to be unique and totally distinct from the mass of humanity, in the waging of a great war under the slogan 'Me alone against all others', and in the choice of a destiny that is felt to be unique and extraordinary.

The bulk of these elitist options are defined and expressed, both here and in Saadawi's novels, in that massive transformation from the level of anatomical differences between the sexes to that of a qualitative difference from the rest of humanity.

Hypersensitivity to the Inflation of the Ego

When the ego is forced to fight an impossible battle, or to take part in a 'no-win' situation, it has only one alternative if it is to escape madness or annihilation: it must use itself and its full potential as a protective shield. We see this model of an inflated, shielded and indestructible ego in the heroine of *A Private Letter to an Artist Friend*:

I realized that the world had fragmented everything, fragmented humanity into master and slave, fragmented the individual into mind and body, the body into reputable and disreputable parts. I realized that the world had fragmented everything, apart from myself. Had fragmented men, women, children, rulers and ruled.

The Worship of Paradox

For such a protected ego to sever 'the thread between doubt and certainty' and prove that 'the world is wrong' and that it alone 'was right', it must conduct its life to a different rhythm from that of everyone else. This rhythm is achieved through living a paradox: as the heroine of *Two Women in One* puts it, 'We feel alive only when we face death.' The heroine of *A Private Letter to an Artist Friend* expresses it as follows:

> Most of the time I don't know the difference between living and dying. At times my life seems to me like death, whilst at others, death suddenly appears to me to be the only hope for living...
> But since I am basically dead, I'm not afraid of death. And because I don't fear death, people are afraid of me. That is the only reason that I come out alive from every battle and remain on earth.

Quality versus Quantity

Paradox is thus one of the most powerful forms of expressing the ego's feelings of power and immunity. Similarly, the juxtaposition of quality and quantity is one of the most potent means of expressing the ego's feelings of fullness and richness, and particularly its belief in its ability to reverse a qualitative anatomical fate and turn it into a qualitative ontological fate. This is governed not by the ego's openness and receptiveness but by its exclusivity:

> How often, amongst the millions of heartbeats, is there a real one? Every minute the heart beats about seventy times, four thousand times an hour, three million times a month. How often does the heart beat in a lifetime? Do any of us recognize a true heartbeat amongst the millions?...
> Contrary to what they taught me, I realized that the sum of my life did not amount to the number of years between the date of my birth and my death. I realized for certain that there is a heartbeat other than that of the heart and that the sum total of my whole life may be the one true heartbeat I manage to grasp amongst the millions of untrue ones...
> I don't measure time in terms of years. My whole life, in

my view, may not be equal to one moment which I feel with
my mind and body and with all my reserve energy.[35]

Heroism

The law of 'quality versus quantity' is in the final analysis a law
of heroism. Is heroism anything other than the minority defeating
the majority, or at least resisting it unto death? There is one
difference, however. The minority here is not a minority as such
but a single monadic unit:

> It was not the first time I'd witnessed a man's failure. There are
> many men but the number of failures is greater and, in the end, I
> was only one woman...
>
> I noticed you once, when I was walking at my normal fast
> pace. I was angry with that supervisor and when I'm angry I
> begin to walk faster. Anger shows me heading for a new battle.
> I mustn't waste time along the way, each second of my life
> becomes valuable and the feeling of time passing becomes so
> oppressive that I must run, scared that death will catch up with
> me before I can enter into combat, as though it is the last battle
> of my life and after it I will die...
>
> That day you asked me about my anger, so I told you. I
> hadn't told anyone before and didn't know what to say. Even
> if I had known, I wouldn't have been able to speak, for there
> was nobody to hear me or to believe me had I spoken. And
> what could I have said? That the whole world was in the wrong
> and I alone was in the right? That the world was mad and I
> alone was sane?[36]

Schizophrenia

The hero of *The Death of His Excellency the Ex-Minister* says, 'Is
there any other world in which a person lives apart from that of
people, unless God has taken him?' This is precisely the
predicament in which the heroine of *A Modern Love Letter* finds
herself. She is forced to live in the world despite knowing that it
is a world of mad people and she is the only sane person in it. But
for a human being to judge that he (or she) is the only sane person
in a mad world, isn't he really condemning himself to the role of
the only lunatic in a sane world? If the bridges between the ego

and others are cut off, is there any way to cross them other than through schizophrenia?

> And that's my dilemma. I want to be a separate entity and at the same time I want to be an inseparable part of others. This contradiction tears me apart, splitting me into two, one part inside myself far from others, the other part outside myself in the heart of others. One part is quiet and immobile and observes the other, or is it the other which observes me?[37]

Searching for the Alter Ego

If the world of others is rejected on the grounds that it is a world of lunatics, and if the world of the ego is intolerable on the grounds that it is a schizophrenic world, then what is the way out? As in the cases of Bahiah Shaheen and Fuaadah Saleem, the only life-raft is the objective relationship, provided that it is given new significance. The other party in this relationship is not the 'other' but the 'alter ego'. It is not another person but the 'self' itself, as if this has become two 'selves', or as though it were the self reflected in a mirror:

> I look around me, searching for others like me... looking for another person who can tell me, 'Yes, you're in the right and the world is in the wrong. You tell the truth and the world tells lies.'[38]

It is axiomatic that this sought-after counterpart must, like the seeker, be of the stuff rarity is made of:

> But despite being a woman, despite being only one woman, I had realized that amongst the multitude of men there was at least one who was not defeated. I realized that with every step I took, with every movement or turn I made, be it merely a momentary head movement walking down some street or other, whether consciously or unconsciously, willingly or unwillingly, with mind or body or both together, I realized that I was searching for that man. I also realized that he was not the only man, that there were perhaps two or three or four, maybe no more than could be counted on the fingers of one hand, but

they were there, albeit rare, and as long as they were there, I had to search for them.[39]

Art

If searching for one's alter ego is love, and if love and nothing but love is the way towards being unique, and if uniqueness is the final ontological goal, we can then understand why love cannot be the goal. We can also understand why there is something which exists beyond love, something nobler, more complete and more precious within the perspective of the assertion of the self and its quality of uniqueness. This explains why the following extract, for example, puts the 'pleasure of art' over and above the 'pleasure of love' and before any other pleasure:

Since the time I was born I have felt letters coursing through my veins like the circulation of blood. When I hold a pen, the whole world disappears along with the pleasures of food and love and sex and death.[40]

No matter how voluntary and selective, love still has (as the heroine of *A Modern Love Letter* puts it) an involuntary side which leads to rebelliousness. No matter how superior it is in relation to mere anatomy, love cannot cancel out the coincidence of birth. In turn, it is art alone which can fulfil a personal destiny (as opposed to the impersonal destiny of fate) and bypass the accident of birth: 'art was my choice and will but... I am female by chance'.

This art is clearly elitist: 'When I pick up my pen, what I write is not for people in general to read but rather for one particular person, for him alone to read, separate from all the rest.'[41]

It is not difficult to trace this artistic elitism to its source, namely, egoism. The ego's self-aggrandizement sometimes reaches such a level as to reverse the equation of art itself. The majority of artists want their art to be what they themselves, with their egos, cannot be. They want it to be richer and more fulfilled than they themselves have been. But the heroine of *A Private Letter to an Artist Friend* speaks of the relationship between the ego and art as follows: 'the words on the page seem to me inadequate, lesser and weaker than myself'.[42]

Deriding Mediocrity and Praising Madness

In the conclusion to our analysis of *Two Women in One*, and by way of self-criticism, we referred to Wilhelm Reich's words of praise for the schizophrenic who carries within him the seeds of another Nietzsche or Van Gogh, and Reich's deriding of the 'normal man', the 'well-adapted', the 'socially integrated'. Similarly, the heroine of *A Modern Love Letter* scorns what she calls 'the middle position'. Thus she pre-empts all possible criticism of her own elitism, since her critics suffer from:

> a halfway position between something and nothing, when a person loves and doesn't love, is angry and is not angry, hates and doesn't hate, speaks and doesn't speak, and always holds the rope in the centre. It is that fluid moderate position in everything which psychologists praise and to which they give the name mental health. Such health, in their view, consists of moderation in all things — in intelligence, in enthusiasm, in love, in hate, in ambition, in honesty.
>
> And because honesty knows no moderation, so a person must lie to a certain extent to win the stamp of mental health from psychologists.

6
Nawal el-Saadawi's
Reply

Georges Tarabishi has undeniably put a great amount of hard work into his book *Woman Against Her Sex*.[1] I can therefore have nothing but respect for this Arab writer and critic's enthusiasm for the writings of Arab women and for his penetrating literary and scientific analysis. After all, nothing is more demoralizing for a woman than to produce literary or scientific work which no one feels worthy of criticism.

It is even more demoralizing, however, when criticism degenerates into a kind of subjective personal attack. My scientific and literary works have already been subject to this kind of vilification, and I have never bothered to refute it. Time is too precious. In any case, I have always chosen to write freely and deliberately without looking back or replying to criticism. In this case, however, friends who had given me Tarabishi's book to read suggested that I respond. I read the book for the first time in London in April 1987, although it had been published in Beirut three years earlier.

The first thing to note is that Tarabishi has not addressed himself to all my novels but has made a specific selection, including *Memoirs of a Woman Doctor*, *Woman at Point Zero*, *Two Women in One* and *The Absentee*.[2] Of course he is free to choose as he wishes but I cannot help wondering why he has not chosen to include *The Death of the Only Man on Earth* or *Ring a Ring o' Roses*,[3] to which he makes only passing reference.

It is my belief that Tarabishi has only selected those works which substantiate the foregone conclusions around which his book revolves. He has adopted a Freudian analysis of sick, neurotic women in order to prove that my heroines are all, without exception, suffering from the castration complex, phallic envy, the Oedipus complex, or any of the other psychological complexes likely to be suffered by a woman who rejects her femininity (in accordance with Freud's definition of femininity). We are led to believe that, since Nawal el-Saadawi is the author of these novels, it follows quite naturally that she shares her heroines' neuroses.

Tarabishi considers his four chosen novels as 'autobiographical' because one heroine is a 'woman doctor', another a 'student of science and chemistry' and the third a 'medical student'. As to the fourth heroine, 'the prostitute' in *Woman at Point Zero*, we are informed that the authoress expresses a desire to identify with her!

I should like to make it clear at the outset that the literary critic has no right to confuse a novel with an autobiography. So long as the writer does not state that the book is autobiographical, then no one has the right to say otherwise. I have not yet written about my personal life, apart from a few sections in *Memoirs in the Women's Prison*.[4] Other than this, I have never mentioned my life, my childhood or my relationship with my mother and father. If I have chosen the character of a woman doctor in *Memoirs of a Woman Doctor*, this in no way means that the woman doctor is Nawal el-Saadawi. If this were the case, I should have stated that these were my memoirs and not a novel.

I should like this first point to be crystal clear in the mind of the reader so that there is no confusion between my life and that of the heroines of my novels. That the author expresses her admiration for one of her heroines (as in *Woman at Point Zero*) in no way means that the heroine is the author herself. I fully believe that had the novels been written by a man, Tarabishi would not have found the same need to identify the author with his heroes. This is one of the problems facing women writers. I have published a large number of stories about the lives of women, whether from the countryside or the city, and for every story there has been a critic who holds that the heroine is the authoress herself disguised in another persona.

In order to assure Tarabishi that my writing is not autobiographical, I should like to point out that my father, for example, had a completely different personality to that of the father

in the four novels analysed. For the most part, the father in
novels is absent; and when he is at home, he is loud-mouthed
domineering towards his wife and daughters. My own father
contrast, was an exceptional human being, who always showed
me great affection and fatherly love. I remember, for example,
one particularly cold winter when he denied himself a badly needed
new suit in order to buy me a new winter coat.

My father also had a particularly soft voice. Never in my life
did I hear him shout at my mother or even raise his voice in anger.
In fact, I thought all men treated their wives gently and with
mutual respect. Perhaps this explains why, when I got married for
the first time and heard my husband yelling at me, I started to
think of him as abnormal. My father's example was always in my
mind, and his relationship with my mother represented an ideal
of married life. Since then, I have come across a number of husbands
and wives whose married lives are totally different from the
relationship enjoyed by my mother and father. Naturally this has
had an effect on me artistically and from a literary point of view,
precisely because these couples lacked any basis of love, gentleness
or mutual respect. It is perhaps for this reason that they imposed
themselves on my literary works more forcefully than the
profoundly human relationship between my parents.

After all, human relationships without any problems are less
interesting, at least from the artistic and literary point of view,
than those beset by difficulties. This is why I have never written
an autobiography. On the whole, my private life has never been
spoilt by bad relationships. I have always had enough courage to
break them off before they could affect me.

In a word, I can say that I was invincible in the face of the
authority of a father or husband, unlike most women in our part
of the world or elsewhere. If art and literature only spring from
an artist's subjective life, I could not have written a single story,
nor could I have written so much about the authority of the father
and the oppression of the mother. These issues are of far greater
importance than one individual's private life.

In fact, I would maintain that the freedom I experienced through
my mother and father, and the freedom I enjoy as a wife and
mother, are what helped me see the flaws in the freedom of others.
It is also this freedom which has helped me see how limited the

political and social freedoms are in my own country. For example, the freedom allowed me as a child was greater than the freedom granted to me as a writer by the head of state, and greater than that granted to me by my first husband when I was in the prime of life. It is this which sparked off the rebellion against my first husband, against the head of state and against any dictator at work who failed to provide me with the freedom to which I had been accustomed by my mother and father.

I should also like to make it clear to the reader that I am a simple woman, extremely simple, to the point of naivety. Perhaps this has been my pride and my downfall at one and the same time. A woman writer, particularly if she is also a doctor, cannot, in the eyes of the critics, be a simple, naive woman. She must be, they would have us believe, a complicated, multifaceted personality, riddled with as many complexes (Oedipus, phallic, castration, etc) as she has talents. Let's face it, some artists and men of letters find a particular satisfaction in confessing to their neuroses and insanity before the critics. Some even think of madness as an art form. After all, Freud believed that art springs from the subconscious.

I must say that I do not see it like that. I believe, rather, that art springs from the 'greater conscious' or the 'higher conscious', not the subconscious. However, this is another story and another book. The truth is that I was amazed by Tarabishi's book. I had previously read his study of my novel *Two Women in One* in an issue of *The Journal of Arabic Studies*. In this literary study, his attitude to the heroine Bahiah is clearly positive. She is described as rich in feelings — the phrase used is 'a mountain of feelings'. In his latest book, however, and having subsequently read and translated a number of books by Freud, Tarabishi has redefined his view of Bahiah. He now sees her as a neurotic suffering from a phallic complex, an anal-erotic complex and birth trauma, in addition to castration and Oedipus complexes, and so on.

After translating more than ten of Freud's works, the change in Tarabishi's viewpoint is hardly surprising. Perhaps he sees himself as another Freud; he has begun to analyse the heroes and heroines of my novels in much the same way as Freud analysed Leonardo da Vinci. If 'art' to Freud is a kind of madness or neurosis, the mind boggles at what might become of the characters created by the artist's 'insane' imagination.

In no way do I mean to denigrate madness or the insane. Among them I have found many who are truer to themselves and possessed of more humanity than the so-called sane. But I do not consider art to be a form of madness or neurosis. On the contrary, I consider it a sign of a higher degree of mental health than the traditional concept (which both Freud and Tarabishi define as the ability to adapt to the world[5]).

As I see it, mental health does not mean adapting and adjusting to the world and its social systems. Indeed, art is a kind of revolt against the injustice of these very societies. In my work there are revolutionary heroines rebelling against the concepts of femininity, masculinity, obedience, honour, morals, and so on. But this rebellion in no way implies psychological illness or neurosis. Before getting down to brass tacks, I have one reservation about the type of literary criticism which confuses art and psychology, and attempts to analyse literary characters in the light of certain theoretical concepts that properly belong in the realm of psychology. In my opinion, such analyses do not fall within the sphere of literary criticism.

I am not here to defend the heroines of my novels: they are quite capable of defending themselves through their own personalities. Nor do I feel obliged to prove that these are great heroines who are in the pink of psychological health (whatever the differences between the various schools of psychology in defining this concept). My intention here is to articulate the fundamental differences between my own viewpoint and that of Tarabishi (via Freud) regarding the concepts of the female and femininity, and those of love, sexuality and the psychology of women.

Right from the beginning of the book, Tarabishi prejudges my view of the world. He implies that I am being true neither to myself nor to my revolt against my condition as a colonized subject. Instead, my view is branded as a process of identification with the colonizer, an act of internalizing the enemy ideology. Subsequently he maintains, 'Our criticism will be biased in favour of the woman who is inside the woman, so that the criticism can better focus on reaching the man who is inside the woman.'[6]

Thus we see how the author differentiates between what he sees as 'femininity' and 'masculinity' in one and the same woman. This definition of femininity is obviously based on Freudian criteria. In fact, Tarabishi admits that he is biased towards this femininity in a woman, further confessing that he is against any 'masculinity' in a woman — again basing his definition of masculinity on Freud. Having noted this obvious bias, it is only to be expected that any positive action on the part of my heroines will be taken as a function of masculinity, aggression and violence or as a woman's rejection of her own femininity or nature.

Tarabishi does not claim that this female nature is a 'divine law' come down from heaven as holy writ (as do other critics who believe in the correlation between divine law and biological law). He does, however, replace divine law by Freudian law. If a woman, Tarabishi argues, refuses to die by man's sword and instead brandishes her own sword in his face in self-defence, then she is no longer considered a normal human being, defending herself: she is seen as psychologically sick, masquerading under an aggressive masculinity, swapping her feminine gentleness for a crown of thorns to engage in a war between the sexes.

Tarabishi goes on to say, 'If women have any mission at all, it is to win the war by annulling it and not by arming themselves in their turn with thorns and a gun.' He quotes Germaine Greer (on whom he confers the epithet 'militant') as saying that women must tame and humanize the penis so that it is no longer a weapon forged of steel but one of flesh. To which Tarabishi adds, 'Women must also humanize the world.'[7]

No doubt these words have a noble, compassionate ring, reflecting a hatred of violence and war. But if one studies them more deeply, it is soon obvious that they are mere words, devoid of any real meaning. How can a man's penis be changed from a lethal weapon into an organ of flesh and blood? Yet although Tarabishi marvels at these words, my heroines actually put them into practice.

Firdaus, the heroine of *Woman at Point Zero*, is described by Tarabishi as a neurotic, a prostitute who 'avenges herself on every man for the gift she expected from her father and never received' and who devotes her entire life to the collective castration of all men.[8] Yet Firdaus seeks all her life to humanize men's penises, attempting to change them from a destructive weapon into a human organ capable of love and the exchange of human emotions. The evidence for this is that Firdaus is always open to a man's love. In love, she will down her weapons and give her all without asking for anything in return. Had Firdaus been Germaine Greer, Tarabishi would have fallen at her feet and granted her the title of 'militant'. As it is, Tarabishi, like all men in the Third World, seems more impressed by women writers from the alien New World or Europe. Arab women, on the other hand, even if they achieve as much as their foreign counterparts and write as well as them, and perhaps with more depth, are not regarded as of equal status.

Why on earth has Tarabishi only cited a foreigner writing in English? Isn't there one Arab woman worthy of quoting? This startling omission indicates that Tarabishi has never read the works of Arab women writers. If he had done so, he would never have equated them with the works of Germaine Greer or any other foreign writer. I have nothing against foreign writers but I am against this 'xenophilia' and the ideological idolatry of all that is 'foreign'.

Tarabishi's judgement of my heroines is duplicitous. This is because he has been converted to the Freudian duality or schism between the concepts of femininity and masculinity. This view regards femininity as a set of fixed characteristics, including weakness, submission, infatuation with violent man and seeking hopelessly to have a penis — and replacing this with a baby and becoming absorbed in the role of motherhood as the only way of coping with this natural disaster. In addition, Tarabishi subscribes to Freud's theories of the Oedipus, Electra and castration complexes, on which Freud and his disciples built their ideas of the psychology of women and their sexual nature.

Since 1920 this school of psychoanalysis has been divided on the question of the understanding of women and their psychological make-up. Newer and more sophisticated ideas have emerged, critical of the traditional Freudian thinking which saw the penis, or the penile phase, as a pivotal point in psychoanalysis, rivalled in importance only by the castration complex. New psychological research in the last half of the century has made it clear that the concept of woman is much more profound, both physically and psychologically, than that previously delineated by limited masculine views.

Here I will summarize some of the basic Freudian ideas on femininity, women and sex, which Tarabishi himself has translated into Arabic from Freud's 'Three Essays on the Theory of Sexuality'.[9] First, we should be aware of the fact that Freud always talks about 'males' as if they were the entire human race and only mentions women or girls when he is remarking that they lack a penis, as if they were a male manqué. Freud writes:

The assumption that all human beings have the same (male) form of genital is the first of the many remarkable and momentous sexual theories of children...

Little girls do not resort to denial of this kind when they see that boys' genitals are formed differently from their own. They are ready to recognize them immediately and are overcome by envy for the penis — an envy culminating in the wish, which is so important in its consequences, to be boys themselves...

We are justified in speaking of a castration complex in women as well. Both male and female children form a theory that women no less then men originally had a penis, but that they have lost it by castration. The conviction which is finally reached by males that women have no penis often leads them to an enduringly low opinion of the other sex.

Freud then insists on the masculine aspect of sexual activity in female children, stating:

The sexuality of little girls is of a wholly masculine character. Indeed, if we were able to give a more definite connotation to the concepts of 'masculine' and 'feminine', it would even be possible to maintain that libido is invariably and necessarily of a masculine nature...[10]

For Freud, therefore, it must follow that the sexual development of a female child hinges on the repression of masculine sexual activity. This is in direct contrast to what happens to a male child, who develops sexually by increasing this activity. If, then, the clitoris in the girl is the point around which the libido revolves, the girl's development into a mature, psychologically healthy woman must take place in the following way, we are told:

when erotogenic susceptibility to stimulation has been successfully transferred by a woman from the clitoris to the vaginal orifice, it implies that she has adopted a new leading zone for the purposes of her later sexual activity. A man, on the other hand, retains his leading zone unchanged from childhood. The fact that women change their leading erotogenic zone in this way, together with the wave of repression at puberty, which, as it were, puts aside their childish masculinity, are the chief determinants of the greater proneness of women to neurosis and especially to hysteria. These determinants, therefore, are intimately related to the essence of femininity.[11]

In these paragraphs, I quote passages from Freud that Tarabishi himself has translated into Arabic. They show clearly how Freud distinguishes between masculinity and femininity. The libido, or sexual activity, is masculine in its identity. If the girl does not rid herself of this positively masculine trait, she will never achieve maturity and will always be a prey to sickness and neurosis.

According to Freud's theories about the penis, humanity is divided not into male and female but into those who possess a penis and those who do not (i.e. women who once had a penis but lost it as a result of being castrated). These ideas were opposed by a number of Freud's pupils within his own school of psychoanalysis. Among them was Jacques Lacan, who attempted to study the relationship of sex to language and tried to develop Freud's theories further, particularly those related to the Oedipus and castration complexes.[12]

In his study of linguistic expression in girls and boys, Lacan concludes that the penis theory is counter-intuitive in both cases. It is a contradictory theory which omits a number of important considerations relating to psychological health. Freud appears to have forgotten the relationship of the female child to her mother and concentrated solely on his conception of the Oedipus complex, in other words, the relationship of the male child to his mother and of the female child to her father. But what of the relationship of the female child to her mother?

Freud does mention that the female child, like the male child, first desires her mother, then progresses to desiring her father when she discovers that he possesses the male organ her mother lacks.

In adulthood, the male child transfers his desire for his mother to another female. The female child, on the other hand, must transfer her desire for her mother to someone of the male sex, a totally different sex to that of the mother. Thus the female child's task is more difficult than that of the male child, in seeking to move from the mother's sex to that of the father.

For Freud, the distinction between the sexes hinges on the existence or non-existence of the penis. The male child is seen as loving himself (narcissism) because of his possession of this marvellous object. The female child, on the other hand, despises herself, her mother and other members of her sex because they are deprived of this majestic organ. Thus Freud's conception of narcissism revolves around the penis. It is purely penile narcissism.

The woman's frigidity arises from her vision of the vagina as 'an empty penis'. All women are frigid because of this penile division between people. The woman who escapes this by some divine intervention, if the clitoral orgasm has not died within her, becomes, in Freud's view, aggressive, neurotic and unfeminine, indeed masculine, as she has never progressed from infantile masculine activity.

It is impossible to accept Freud's notion that any sexual feeling, desire or orgasm is transferred from the clitoris to the vagina as a woman matures. Remnants of this fallacy still persist in legends or the tradition of artistic imagination only because all women know that there is no difference between a clitoral and a vaginal orgasm and that this separation is arbitrary and may even be purely theoretical.

The last half of this century has seen a number of books published about women. They attempt to shed new light on 'femininity' and on the differences between femininity and masculinity, whether psychologically, sexually or sociologically. It is well known that it is men themselves who laid the foundations of modern psychology and sexology. And it is only recently that women have started writing about themselves. It was men alone who determined the place of sexual desire. It was they who saw an apple as symbolizing a woman's cheek, a pear the breast, and cherries the lips, for example. Desire, or the libido, or positive sexual desire, has been seen as a purely masculine desire. The woman has become 'the thing', 'the vessel of this desire', 'the sex object'. It was impossible for women to enjoy the same freedom as men in expressing positive desire or the feminine libido.

This is perhaps the most important discovery to strike male researchers in psychology and sexology. They imagined the libido to be masculine as Freud willed it to be. Here the libido means a positive approach not only to sexual desire but to life in general. A positive personality is positive in all things, not only in the domain of sex. The new writings by women underlining women's positive attitude towards life and sex are the very things which give Freud's pupils a 'birth trauma' or 'the shock of the new'! This may explain the harsh judgement to which some of my heroines (Firdaus, Bahiah Shaheen, Fuaadah and others) have been subjected.

Tarabishi sees these heroines through purely Freudian eyes — a view which cannot possibly humanize women. The problem is not that Firdaus has failed to humanize the world but that Tarabishi has failed to humanize Firdaus. Firdaus prefers to die on the gallows rather than live as a sex object or a commodity. Tarabishi maintains that women have no need to fight. Instead they should win the war by annulling it. This is an elegant turn of phrase, but he has omitted to tell us how women can possibly annul a war when they still have no political, military or social power, whether collectively or individually. Without this power, how can a woman stop the war or annul it?

Tarabishi never mentions how this can be achieved. He would probably have us believe that women can stop the war through love, poetry and songs. This may be an effective fantasy, but reality is something else.

Tarabishi's is the duplicitous logic which glorifies the philosophy of non-violence only to justify another kind of violence. I am against this philosophy of double standards, which leads to further aggression and war rather than their abolition. Humanity necessitates justice and justice demands that if someone points a gun at me, I do more than present him with a flower and my chest as a target.

When the pimp brandishes a knife in her face, Firdaus (in *Woman at Point Zero*) behaves in a logical and humane way by turning the knife on him in defence of her humanity and life. So what angers Tarabishi about this just reaction? Is it because the perpetrator is a female and femininity stipulates that the female should smile sweetly into the face of her killer and colonizer?

The highest indication of humanity is not non-violence in the face of violence or weakness in the face of strength, but a balance of power which would eliminate violence and war. War will never be abolished until there is a correct balance of power between countries, and there are no more weak unarmed countries in contrast to armed countries. The same holds true for men and women. There will be no really human relationships between them without an equal balance of power. Power here means social, economic and intellectual power as much as personal and psychological power. It is only then that the penis will change from a weapon of aggression and usurpation into a force of humanity, of flesh and blood, such as dreamed of by Germaine Greer.

Humanizing[13] the penis is closely bound up with humanizing the political, economic and social systems which govern the state and the family. In order to achieve an equal balance of power, there must be a just distribution of authority and wealth, regardless of a person's sex, colour, race or creed. In short, the humanizing of the penis necessitates the abolition of all forms of slavery and exploitation, at the level of both the state and the family, both within countries and at an international level.

This global view of the problems of war and violence allows us to understand why Firdaus wields the knife and kills her pimp. It is not because she hates men, envies them for possessing a penis or wants to take revenge on them for the forbidden gift she had expected from her father. Nor is it because she has a desire for collective castration. She is not a criminal but a woman forced to resort to murder.

In spite of having translated the bulk of Freud's works into Arabic, Freud has obviously not read Jacques Lacan, the most important of Freud's disciples at the present time. I do not belong to Lacan's school, but I believe him to be more modern and up-to-date than Freud. He does not harbour the same hatred as Tarabishi, nor does he sing of love, peace and an end to war. Tarabishi is shocked when Firdaus proclaims her hatred of men. He sees this hatred as a deviation from normal femininity. Lacan, on the other hand, maintains that the person who does not know hatred cannot know love, and since God does not know hatred he is the most ignorant of all.

Tarabishi subscribes to Karl Abraham's views on sexual frigidity in the prostitute, believing this frigidity to be an essential behavioural pre-condition. Indeed, he sees it as a professional and defensive activity. In the case of Firdaus, however, he sees frigidity as aggressive and offensive:

> To the prostitute, frigidity is secondary; to Firdaus, by contrast, it is a primary condition. The prostitute becomes frigid in order to practise her profession; Firdaus, on the other hand, has chosen to be a prostitute in order to practise frigidity, because, to use Karl Abraham's terminology, it is 'castrating'.[14]

Here Tarabishi ignores the novel from start to finish. The average reader (never mind the specialist critic) soon becomes aware while reading this simple, uncomplicated and unambiguous tale that Firdaus has not 'chosen' to become a prostitute. The opposite is true. Throughout the novel Firdaus fights against becoming a prostitute. In fact, even while practising the profession, she is not a prostitute in the moral sense. She continues to seek human dignity and freedom right up to her death. These are Firdaus's words verbatim as Tarabishi quotes them in his book. Yet he completely ignores their real meaning:

> I had never experienced suffering such as this... Perhaps as a prostitute I had known so deep a humiliation that nothing really counted. When the street becomes your life, you no longer expect anything, hope for anything. But I expected something from love. With love I began to imagine that I had become a human being. When I was a prostitute, I never gave anything for nothing, but always took something in return. But in love I gave my body and soul, my mind and all the effort I could muster, freely. I never asked for anything, gave everything I had, abandoned myself totally, dropped all my weapons, lowered all my defences, and bared my flesh. But when I was a prostitute I protected myself, fought back at every moment, was never off guard.[15]

Could there be any clearer way of showing that Firdaus subscribes to the ideals of humanity, peace and love? She does not take part in the war between the sexes, nor does she hate men or take revenge on them by collective castration, as Tarabishi would have it. Instead of sympathizing with her when all doors are closed in her face and all roads blocked, he accuses her of harbouring the wrong within her. He refuses to accept that it is the social system which turns women into goods and chattels in the markets of marriage, work and love (as indeed it also changes men, though in a different way).

The main difference between Tarabishi (and other Freudians) and myself is that they turn what I see as social, economic, religious and political problems into merely biological problems within the woman herself. As Tarabishi sees it, even political and economic struggles between countries acquire biological significance, inside the body of the human being. The struggle between man and woman for human dignity and freedom becomes explicable in terms of the sex organs. Even Firdaus's natural human desire to achieve a minimum of privacy by having a private toilet with a door that locks becomes, in Tarabishi's eyes, one of the sick manifestations of the 'anal complex'.[16]

Even Freud himself would not have reduced Firdaus's human desires in such a perverse, flawed way, attributing everything in life to the anal complex or the castration complex! Even the normal human desire to be economically independent from others, and to have at least a banknote to buy food in order not to be provided for, insulted and dominated by one's husband or other people, becomes in Tarabishi's twisted view a clear confirmation of the theory of anal eroticism. In this connection he makes the following comment:

> It is a banknote. That may very well be so, but ever since Freud discovered anal eroticism we have known that the equation *money = penis* is one of the principal symbolic equations governing the anal complex. It is Firdaus, not us, who wonders, 'Was it possible that a mere piece of paper could make such a change?' It is Firdaus, not us, who associates the banknote with the genitals and forbidden pleasure.[17]

Tarabishi persists with his flawed, one-sided interpretation of Firdaus. He also continues to condemn the victim and acquit the real perpetrator of the crime. This is the philosophy of slavery which has evolved in all world religions ever since the slave system first appeared. Firdaus will always be in the wrong even if all paths are blocked to her. If she loves a revolutionary and then discovers him to be false, she is the one to be condemned.

In Tarabishi's opinion, Firdaus is hostile to all men without exception, including revolutionaries.[18] He does not attempt to understand why the love between Firdaus and her 'revolutionary' failed. Was she the one who exacerbated their differences and started to be unfaithful or was it he who left her for another woman with status and authority (the daughter of the president of the company)? Tarabishi does not examine these basic reasons for the failure of their love affair. He ignores the man's unfaithfulness and has no hesitation in accusing Firdaus of suffering from an anal complex, a castration complex and a hatred of all men *in toto*.

What Tarabishi fails to understand is that the political climate in the Arab world has produced a number of false revolutions bandying the slogans of justice and socialism, only to murder or imprison the genuine socialists and seekers after justice. In the shadow of such false revolutions, new breeds of revolutionaries have sprung up, mouthing the slogans of revolution, but in fact oppressing and exploiting those under their domination. This schism between words and deeds is prevalent in our part of the world.

But Tarabishi does not touch on these important matters which exert such an influence on Firdaus's life. He is constantly genuflecting before Freud's holy gospel, looking at Firdaus's body as if through a microscope, pinpointing only the opening of the vagina or discovering the absence of a penis. No wonder he sees Firdaus's yearning for freedom and justice as merely an attempt to castrate her father![19] As for Bahiah Shaheen's struggle to achieve freedom and justice, these are seen only as a desire to possess the mother. Thus all human relations in the life of these heroines are reduced to child-like Freudian emotions neither more nor less than the Oedipus complex.

When the pimp raises his knife to kill Firdaus, she raises her knife and kills him instead. She explains this by saying, 'I might not kill a mosquito, but I can kill a man.' Tarabishi misunderstands the wider human implications of this utterance. What Firdaus is saying is that she is not a murderess by nature, so much so that she is incapable of killing a mosquito. Mosquitos do not threaten her life even if she is bitten by them. But she could kill a man if he threatened her life. Tarabishi is blind to these meanings and takes this to be yet another proof of Firdaus's psychological illness, labelling it 'an identification with the father in the anal-sadistic phase of pre-sexual organization'.[20]

I couldn't help laughing when I came across the complicated phrases such as 'pre-sexual organization' with which Tarabishi interprets Firdaus's plain and simple statement, 'I might not kill a mosquito, but I can kill a man.' He brands Firdaus as a sick neurotic, saying:

> Neurosis can be defined as the lost ability to adjust to reality, whether positively or negatively, by accepting or rejecting it, perpetuating or changing it. Can we then imagine a more neurotic condition than that of a woman who chooses to be a prostitute and a murderess in order to wage a war of the sexes, reassert herself and win 'the crown of a princess' in a society of men?[21]

Here we discover his problems with understanding the meaning of neurosis and his rigid adherence to the Freudian definition, which sees neurosis as a kind of inability to come to terms with reality. Had Firdaus been satisfied and reconciled with her role as a prostitute and succumbed to the domination of the pimp, she would no doubt have become in Tarabishi's eyes a normal, psychologically healthy and well-adjusted woman.

Tarabishi insists that it is Firdaus herself who chooses prostitution and murder in order to perpetuate the war between the sexes. This is patently untrue, as Firdaus chooses neither prostitution not murder. She does not want to participate in the war between the sexes, or any other war. She wants simply to live a life of love, faithfulness, work, freedom and independence. To achieve this she knocks on door after door. If all doors are shut in her face, she tries other avenues. She continues this search, striving, resisting, right up to the end. When she refuses to ask for a pardon, this is because she sees herself as a human being and not a criminal.

In *Memoirs of a Woman Doctor* the heroine would have rebelled against her femininity had it not been the kind of femininity which prevents her from going out and finding a place in society. Tarabishi is astonished that the heroine feels no pride when her breasts make an appearance, compensating her for the lack of a penis! She is supposed to feel 'proud' of acquiring these lumps of flesh rather than the other lost piece. This is the 'narcissistic compensation' which any normal girl would feel, according to the gospel of Freud and Tarabishi.

But the question is not that of substituting one lump of flesh for another. It is, rather, the political, social, moral and religious significance of this or that piece of flesh. Does the girl enjoy the same rights as the person who possesses the male organ when she actually acquires her own new lumps of flesh, the breasts? The answer is a categorical 'No!' On the contrary, her social rights and freedoms are reduced the moment she sprouts breasts and enters adolescence and puberty. She enjoys more freedom as a child than as an adolescent. Similarly, she has more rights as a young girl than when she is a wife or a mother.

The heroine of *Memoirs of a Woman Doctor* is not a female who wants to be male, as Tarabishi maintains, but a female who wants to be a free human being, enjoying the same freedoms as men and more. Her revolt relates to her desire to possess freedom *per se* and not to her desire to possess a male organ in order to become a man or a quasi-man. Her long hair is perceived by Tarabishi in a similar way to the emergence of the breasts — as a source of narcissistic compensation for the absence of the penis, and something which a girl should cherish and be proud of.

But I don't see it like that. I see long hair as a personal matter, or a particular fashion of the times. There are men who grow their hair long, just as there are women who prefer short hair. I personally prefer long hair in the winter as it keeps my head and neck warm, and short hair in the summer as it is more practical, cooler and easier when I go swimming. Thus there is no correlation between femininity and the length of one's hair.

The heroine of *Memoirs of a Woman Doctor* is not denying that she is female. She doesn't want to be a male with a male organ.

The evidence for this is that she never sings the praises of this much-vaunted organ, and that she loves a man who treats her as a human being, not as a pair of breasts, thighs or lips. There is nothing shameful about a woman demanding scientific and intellectual superiority, dreaming that one day she will achieve recognized social status, as indeed happens to the heroine of *Memoirs of a Woman Doctor*. This is not anti-femininity or anti-men, but it is a natural desire in a rational human being, and the woman *is* a natural human being.

The desire to achieve social and intellectual superiority does not mean that she aspires to be a Superman. She wants to be a woman who rises above the position she has been allocated by society. Society imposes on women the role of wife and mother. Freud believes that the woman creates 'children' and not 'ideas' because this is nature. I believe, on the contrary, that nature gives to women as human beings a creative brain, and the right to play a social, economic, political and cultural role in society.

The main struggle in the novel revolves around unjust laws and social conditions which oppress women intellectually, ideologically and sexually. It is a moral, political and social struggle and not a biological struggle against the organs of the body, whether masculine or feminine. When the heroine of *Memoirs of a Woman Doctor* is pleased to hear her father telling his friends how well she is doing at school, this is not a form of identification with the aggressor, as Tarabishi would have it. [22] It is a way of asserting herself as a thinking, intelligent human being and not merely a kitchen utensil or a maid-of-all-work.

There is nothing deviant about a young girl hating the kitchen with its smell of onion and garlic, [23] and preferring to read books instead. On the contrary, I see this as quite normal. I don't think there are many women *or* men who are wild about cooking onions and garlic. By the same token, if the heroine of *Memoirs of a Woman Doctor* hates sex or sexual relations with men who see her as just a sex object, this is not because she hates sex as such and lives without sex organs, struggling against a castration complex. It is rather that she prefers living without sexual satisfaction to being enslaved by a man in order to achieve it.

This is normal. Most men and women who enjoy free will and human dignity prefer being deprived of pleasure to being demeaned and enslaved because of it. This is a personal matter to do with the degree of willpower and awareness and has nothing to do with maleness or femaleness, masculinity or femininity. In prison, for example, there are men and women who put up with sexual deprivation for the sake of their revolutionary ideals. And there are men and women who are incapable of suppressing their desires, or living for a higher ideal. It is, I repeat, to do with the personality of the individual and nothing to do with masculinity or femininity.

Tarabishi takes the heroine of *Memoirs of a Woman Doctor* to task for saying that her childhood stays alive within her in spite of her transition to adolescence and puberty. He takes this as evidence of her neurosis and as showing that the child within her has not satisfied its desires: 'Desires which can be repressed are desires which can be stifled.'[24]

Here I must differ with Tarabishi and say that repression is what allows most people to forget their childhood and start differentiating between the various stages of their life. Life is a series of interwoven events. The brave, creative person is the one who admits that he is a child, a youth and an old person all at once. The capacity to be creative and innovative lies in the ability to hang onto childhood, alongside youth, maturity and old age.

In the dissecting room, when the heroine of *Memoirs of a Woman Doctor* feels nauseated by the sight of the corpses, particularly that of a naked man, Tarabishi takes this as evidence of a 'hatred fixated in the anal-sadistic phase of pre-sexual organization'.[25] He muses, 'Is the corpse of a woman less ugly?' This is a strange question because it indicates that Tarabishi has not read the novel carefully enough to realize that the point is not whether a dead man or a dead woman is more ugly; the problem lies in the glaring contrast between the man's elevated status when he is alive and his equality with that of the woman when they are both on a dissecting table, thus proving that it is society alone that elevates the man.

When the man in the novel changes after marriage from an affectionate lover into a boorish, loud-mouthed, domineering husband, no fault is found with him or the marriage laws which allow a husband to be the legal master of his wife. On the contrary, Tarabishi believes that the fault lies with the heroine, to whom the husband appears in the image of 'the anal man, heir to the base father on whom the hatred pertaining to the anal-sadistic phase has been fixated in the phase of pre-sexual organization'.[26] In the novel it is clear that the heroine wants to live a normal life with love and work, and free from problems and battles. But the battles are imposed on her by a patriarchal, classist society. Tarabishi fails to see this. He imagines the she creates the battles for herself, lest her 'reserves of narcissistic sustenance should run out'.[27]

When the heroine says that society looks at her with eyes as sharp as daggers, Tarabishi is ready with his psychoanalytic accusation: 'the tools of persecution mania are nearly always the organs of the reproductive system'.[28] I was not aware that daggers were organs of the reproductive system, but Tarabishi maintains that swords and daggers are blatantly masculine sexual symbols.

Tarabishi takes the heroine to task when she says that her sustenance springs from herself and her will and not from her job, her profession or the money she earns. He accuses her of narcissism and egoism, regardless of the fact that the most important elements of psychological health in human beings are willpower and the strength which springs from the inner self, not from one's position, profession or income.

In Tarabishi's eyes, all human traits turn into faults. He accuses both the heroine of *Memoirs of a Woman Doctor* and Firdaus, the heroine of *Woman at Point Zero*, of rejecting the idea that work can be a democratic, non-elitist path to the liberation of women.[29] This is simply untrue, as both heroines try to find the kind of work which will give them human respect and dignity. But work in a class-conscious patriarchal society does not always lead to human respect and dignity. On the contrary, it is sometimes demeaning, denying human beings the right to dignity and respect. This is what Firdaus finds when she works as a secretary for a company, and also when she turns to prostitution, a profession, like all others, created by this same class-ridden patriarchal society.

The problem is not simply that of a woman going out to work; it is, rather, the concept of work, the type of work and the moral and material rewards for work. Work can be a way of liberating women, but it can also be a way of further enslaving and demeaning them. At the end of *Memoirs of a Woman Doctor*, the heroine falls in love with an artist who recognizes the human being in her and she in him. They exchange love in its real sense, as a high point of human experience, mind and body united and indivisible.

Tarabishi dismisses this as the height of narcissistic satiety.[30] No doubt the ending disappoints him as it discounts his theory of a neurotic heroine who is confirmed in her hatred of all men.

The heroine of *Memoirs of a Woman Doctor* does not open her surgery to death through the medium of abortion. She treats people who are sick. She intervenes to save the poor, unmarried pregnant girl who begs for her help because she knows that the girl is innocent and that the real criminal is at large, protected by society. The question, then, is not that she lives by performing abortions but that, through the girl who appeals to her, she is debating the problem of rape. When young girls are subjected to rape, they are then abandoned to carry their burden of shame alone, while the male aggressor escapes unscathed.

Tarabishi, however, ignores these ideological considerations and tries to portray the doctor's surgery in the novel as an abortion racket, saying, 'The doctor's duty... is not to renege on his Hippocratic oath and carry out an abortion, but to struggle within the existing legal and medical structures to legalize and legislate for abortion.'[31]

Tarabishi's ability to twist the facts in the novel and turn the doctor's humanity and rescuing of the wretched girl into something inhumane, into a violation of the Hippocratic oath and an elitist solution to abortion, in no way surprises me. Apparently he would prefer the doctor to refuse the abortion until she has struggled through the medical and legal red tape, or until the authorities have legalized abortion. His words here are nothing but empty, unrealistic slogans. Such phrases as 'the democratic and radical solution to the problem' are simply used as a cover for inaction, a failure to confront the problem, and an unwillingness to make sacrifices in order to help a suffering fellow human being.

Any problem, whether abortion or anything else, affects the human being first and foremost. A legal or political struggle through existing channels is of course necessary at some point, but the solution must also alleviate individual suffering. High-flown phrases about democracy are too often used as an excuse to avoid offering practical help to the creature caught in the trap, perhaps for fear of the moral, legal or social consequences.

Of course, I cannot respect any doctor who deals in and profits from the practice of abortion. But I respect all doctors who expose themselves to danger in order to abort a woman or girl impregnated against her will, and who do not perform abortions for financial gain. This is the difference between the attitude of doctors who traffic in their profession and the noble humanitarian attitude of the heroine of *Memoirs of a Woman Doctor*. In my opinion, the struggle to solve social problems such as abortion requires collective action and must be waged through the relevant institutions in order to change the law. It also demands individual struggle to solve the problem on the level of the individual. Social reform requires personal reform, and vice versa. The two are indivisible.

In his analysis of *Two Women in One* and *The Absentee*, Tarabishi attempts to mete out the same treatment to the heroines as he did to those of the other two novels. He condemns them as neurotic women suffering from penis envy, anal eroticism, and so on. Despite my profound differences with Tarabishi over his Freudian view of these heroines, I cannot but admire his inventiveness in using the criteria of psychoanalysis in his analysis. In spite of this having led to a number of arbitrary and at times contradictory diagnoses, I cannot deny that I derived a great deal of pleasure from reading the book. It was instructive in that it increased my distrust of psychoanalysis in the diagnosis of psychological illness, let alone in its ability to prescribe a cure.

The book also increased my confidence in myself as a writer when my heroines were shown to have anal-erotic complexes, penis envy complexes, pre-sexual complexes, and so on, something which had never occurred to me. I cannot but be grateful to Tarabishi for shedding light on some of the hidden aspects of my characters. Whether these aspects are real or imaginary, their undercurrents will inspire me in future novels, especially as my characters always seem to be totally independent of me and beyond my domination or control.

In spite of my anger at some of the unjust and aggressive parts of Tarabishi's book, I was pleased with other parts, such as the end of the analysis of Bahiah Shaheen (the heroine of *Two Women in One*) where he says, 'In the hundred or so pages of the story of her life, Bahiah tells us as much as one thousand pages of ordinary history.'[32]

Another pleasing part comes at the end of the analysis of

Fuaadah, the heroine of *The Absentee*, where Tarabishi speaks of the 'poetic flavour' that 'pervades the novel as the perfume of jasmine transcends the smell of the manure with which it is fertilized'.[33] I cannot find more elegant words than these with which to conclude my reply to Tarabishi. I only wish he had written more about the poetic sensitivity within a work of literature. But beauty is instead ascribed to ontological anxiety and a desperate grasping for what remains of the external world and its denizens.

That is as may be. But what human being (whether male or female) does not suffer from anxiety, especially when living in a society deprived of justice, freedom and basic human rights? Why does Tarabishi turn this anxiety into a kind of psychological illness or neurosis? Why must he try to interpret this anxiety as an expression of childhood complexes, sexual repression, birth trauma or lack of a penis? And why doesn't he attempt to relate this anxiety in the life of the heroines to social and political causes?

This is where the true question lies. I cannot deny that anxiety or psychological illness may in some people be ascribable to biological or sexual events in childhood and that it is sometimes not possible to separate biological from social causes. But I believe that Tarabishi has ignored social and political events in the lives of my heroines and overplayed the sexual and biological causes and childhood psychological complexes.

In conclusion, I must reiterate my appreciation of Tarabishi's efforts in re-envisioning the characters in my novels in the light of psychoanalysis. I hope he will subsequently see fit to do the same in the light of a social and political analysis, thus enabling us to see all the facets of the characters. It is surely unjust to judge a revolutionary hero or heroine as psychologically sick or neurotic merely because we have not studied the social and political conditions which forged such characters and which forced them to take the path of struggle and rebellion.

Nawal el-Saadawi
London, April 1987

7
A Clarification
by the Author

I fully expected this to be a highly constructive confrontation between a novelist and her critic. In the event, Nawal el-Saadawi's reply has unfortunately taken the form of a polemic rather than a dialogue. She argues the case against psychoanalysis as though it were an ideological cause rather than a scientific discipline. It seems to me, therefore, that it is necessary to make the following three clarifications:

1. I have been scrupulously careful to deal with Saadawi's novels as such. My analysis never claimed to deal with the personality of the writer but only with the personalities of her heroines. If I used the expression 'autobiographical novel', this was only a reference to the kind of 'subjective novel' whose reliance on essentially 'non-identifiable elements' of a biographical nature distinguishes it from the 'objective novel'. Nevertheless, a novel is only a novel; it is fiction, not an autobiography. I cannot help remarking, however, that Saadawi's heated, passionate defence of her heroines would be mystifying if we did not postulate that the motivation for such a defence is the author's own identification with them.

2. In trivializing my analyses, Saadawi has taken my quotations out of context. It would indeed have been ludicrous for me to have taken Firdaus's remark 'I might not kill a mosquito, but I can kill a man' as indicating her identification with her father. What I said was that what points to such an identification is her love of legislation and the pleasure she takes in proposing laws for her own sex.

3. Saadawi accuses me of suffering from 'xenophilia' or undue deference to the views of foreign writers simply because I quote Germaine Greer. Such an accusation can only derive from a misguided sense of nationalism. Moreover, Saadawi herself does not apply this precept to her own works. In her theoretical studies, she cites dozens of foreign supporters of feminism, both male and female, without ever giving a single quote from the Arab-Islamic world.

Georges Tarabishi
Paris, June 1987

Notes

Introduction

1. Georges Tarabishi, *The Oedipus Complex in the Arabic Novel* (Dar al-Tali'a, Beirut, 1982; in Arabic).

2. Also Tawfiq el-Hakim's plays.

3. Georges Tarabishi, *Manhood and the Ideology of Manhood in the Arabic Novel* (Dar al-Tali'a, Beirut, 1983; in Arabic).

4. Several of Nawal el-Saadawi's novels and short stories have been translated into English: *Woman at Point Zero* (Zed Books, London, 1983); *Two Women in One* (Saqi Books, London, 1985); *Death of an Ex-Minister* (Methuen, London, 1987); and *Memoirs of a Woman Doctor* (Saqi Books, London, 1988).

5. For example, Tawfiq el-Hakim says, 'Woman is undoubtedly the flower shining in the orchard of our human existence, a flower which has its own freshness and perfume, but which also has its thorns.' *Under the Sun of Ideas* (Maktabat al-Adab, Cairo, n.d.; in Arabic).

Chapter 1

1. Karl Abraham, 'Manifestations of the Female Castration Complex', *Selected Papers of Karl Abraham* (L. & V. Woolf for Institute for Psycho-Analysis, London, 1927), ch. 22.

2. Nawal el-Saadawi, *Woman at Point Zero* (Zed Books, London, 1983).

3. Nawal el-Saadawi has published the results of this research in her book *Women and Psychological Conflict* (al-Mu'assasa al-Arabia lil-Dirasat wal-Nashr, Beirut, n.d.; in Arabic).

4. Or 'female and male' so that the word order is not misconstrued as a rank ordering of values.

5. 'You are criminals, all of you: the fathers, the uncles, the husbands, the pimps, the lawyers, the doctors, the journalists, and all men of all professions.'

6. In this description of men, it is not difficult to detect what in psychoanalysis is referred to as 'the anal complex'. This is a particularly significant point in the writings of Nawal el-Saadawi to which we shall return in detail.

7. This birth from a 'non-father', or from a different father, provides us with early evidence of the neurosis of the heroine of *Woman at Point Zero*. Firdaus, for her part, has her own 'family story' with which she proves the truth of Freud's partial law which stipulates that neurotics as well as the mentally deranged have a compulsion, under the influence of the Oedipus complex and its derivations, to amend their family trees in their imagination. This is a point to which Firdaus repeatedly returns: 'Back in my father's house I stared at the mud walls like a stranger who had never entered it before. I looked around almost in surprise, as though I had not been born here, but had suddenly dropped from the skies, or emerged from somewhere deep down in the earth, to find myself in a place where I did not belong, in a home which was not mine, born from a father who was not my father, and from a mother who was not my mother.'

8. On the relationship between meanness (and wealth in general) and the anal phase of pre-sexual organization, see Sigmund Freud: 'On Transformations of Instinct as Exemplified in Anal Eroticism' in *The Complete Psychological Works of Sigmund Freud*, vol. 17 (Hogarth Press, London, 1955); 'Character and Anal Eroticism' in *Complete Psychological Works*, vol. 9; and the 'Rat Man' in *Complete Psychological Works*, vol. 10.

9. There is an intentional pun in the choice of the procuress's name: *sharifa* in Arabic means 'honourable'. There is a similar reason behind the choice of Salah el Dine as Sharifa's surname.

10. This is a phrase used by one of Hannah Minah's heroes. Incidentally, Minah's heroes (el-Turusi in *The Sail and Wind* and Salih Hazzum in *A Sailor's Tale*) reflect this equation. These men prove their masculinity by insisting that even prostitutes be brought to a climax. They are therefore made of the same stuff as Firdaus, only they are in the opposing enemy camp.

11. To dwell on the prostitute's alleged freedom, and value it so highly, also reveals what we have termed the 'anal complex'.

12. We shall return to this elitist attitude towards all other members of the female sex.

13. 'As I turned over in bed a thought flashed through my mind. Revolutionary men with principles were not really different from the rest. They used their cleverness to get, in return for principles, what other men buy with their money. Revolution for them is like sex for us. Something to be abused. Something to be sold.'

Notes

14. If blindness is analogous to castration, as shown by the psychoanalytic interpretation of the Oedipus legend, could we not reverse the equation and say, as the text before us proves, that 'seeing' is equivalent to victory over castration and the regaining of the lost organ?

15. Bahiah Shaheen, the heroine of Nawal el-Saadawi's *Two Women in One* (Saqi Books, London, 1985), also flouts the system in a provocative manner. But contrary to Firdaus, Bahiah dreams of re-establishing contact with the universe only so as to perish in it. Bahiah Shaheen is not really the antithesis of Firdaus, however. Rather, it is that the universe represents the mother to the former and the father to the latter. Thus the severance and establishment of contact are equivalent and complementary: they are two facets of the same phallocentrism. It is as if by severing all contact with the universe, Firdaus castrates her father, whereas by establishing contact with the universe, Bahiah possesses her mother.

16. An example of this legislation: 'Yes, exactly like a snake. Life is a snake. They are the same, Firdaus. If the snake realizes you are not a snake, it will bite you. And if life knows you have no sting, it will devour you.' This compulsive tendency to legislate shows signs of the subconscious identification on the part of all women with the role of the father, the legislator *par excellence*. Bearing in mind that laws a–c below are all based on the principle of hatred, we can be even more precise and say: it is an identification with the father in the anal-sadistic phase of pre-sexual organization:

a. 'I became aware of the fact that I hated men.'
b. 'I knew I hated him as only a woman can hate a man.'
c. 'I might not kill a mosquito, but I can kill a man.'

Chapter 2

1. An English edition of Nawal el-Saadawi's *Memoirs of a Woman Doctor* will be published by Saqi Books (London) in 1988. The title is given as *Memoirs...* in subsequent references throughout the present chapter.

2. We note that the origin of the free-flowing hair is leaving it unbound and allowing it to grow. But the interpretation, or the hallucinatory interpretation as we are inclined to maintain, reverses the facts: to the extent of taking it for granted that the hair which can really be said to qualify as 'free' is the cut hair, i.e. the boy's.

3. These titles are all included in *The Complete Works of Nawal el-Saadawi* (al-Mu'assasa al-Arabia lil-Dirasat wal-Nashr, Beirut, 1986; in Arabic).

4. The Church in the Middle Ages forbade women from entering a place of worship during menstruation. In Judaism, the woman is considered unclean during this period. Whoever touches her, or even the

place where she has been sitting, will be impure until sunset. Her husband is not allowed to approach her without the say-so of a female witness who has seen her washing. Until the last century, 'In the bath-houses of countries inhabited by Jews, there used to be a woman from the Israelites whose function was to grant certificates of cleanliness to the Jewish women who came to bathe.' See our introduction to Muhammad Jameel Bayham's *Women in Islam and in Western Civilization* (Dar al-Tali'a, Beirut, 1980; in Arabic), p. 44.

5. This is a true autobiographical event, told or retold by the writer in her personal capacity and not in the role of narrator as follows: 'I took to my room for four consecutive days, not having the courage to face my father or brother or even the house-boy. When I had to go to the bathroom I would look around me for fear of anyone seeing me. Before I left it I would wash the floor thoroughly as if to remove the traces of a terrible crime, then I would wash my hands and arms with soap and water dozens of times, to obliterate any after-effects from the smell of that dirty blood.' (Saadawi, *Woman and Sex*, p. 48.)

6. Interpretation and nothing but interpretation again! A human being lives under the domination of his 'involuntary muscles' not only for days but all his life. Nevertheless it does not occur to the heroine of *Memoirs*... to protest. Her protest is only levelled at the operation of 'involuntary muscular activity' as far as this is connected with the rejected feminine function.

7. As in the elegant title of one of Hemingway's stories, we notice that 'to have and have not' is the bourgeois equivalent of the eternal Shakespearian formula, 'to be or not to be'.

8. We will return later to this male criterionism.

9. 'Since childhood, I'd been immersed in a series of endless battles.'

10. Usually Freud only mentions the 'castration complex' in general terms. In the following, however, we prefer to be more specific and speak of an 'imaginary castration complex'. The general concept of the complex suggests that it is a primary formation, while actually it is a secondary formation — although it is a psycho-sociological creation rather than a natural creation even if it becomes a part of genetic inheritance. The origins of a woman are her being a woman and not the fact that she is some deficient male. The criterion of her identity is 'by origin' and not 'by proxy'. 'Deficient maleness' is the product of sheer imagination, generally fixated not only by the predominance of the male value system in patriarchal society but by the internalization of this predominance through the priority of the defensive 'identification with the aggressor'. Doesn't the heroine of *Memoirs*... present us with an example of this identification when she says: 'I was used to meeting most of my father's friends and

bringing them coffee. Sometimes I sat with them and heard my father telling them how well I was doing at school. This always made me feel elated and I thought that since my father had acknowledged my intelligence he would extricate me from the depressing world of women, reeking of onions and marriage.'

11. In the literature of psychoanalysis, envy and revenge are considered natural traits characteristic of the anal-sadistic phase in the development of the libido.

12. The most convincing proof of the childishness of the revengeful spirit lies in the fact that it is not susceptible to the law of time. No wonder that the theme of most stories about revenge revolves around the idea that this revenge may be wreaked after ten or twenty years or even after a lifetime.

13. That the 'needle' by virtue of its shape, size and function (that of penetrating the flesh) takes on a flagrant symbolic significance is not surprising. What is more surprising, however, is that the eyes are also accorded such significance. In fact, Karl Abraham, as far back as 1913, talked of 'the sexual significance of the eyes' under what he termed 'neurotic photophobia'.

If the comparison between the doctor's needle and his eyes is predetermined by the insistence on describing them as 'penetrating' ('penetrating' also being the function of the needle), *Woman at Point Zero* (Zed Books, London, 1983), in turn, presents us with a case which is typical of male sexual symbolism pertaining to the eye. Firdaus, the heroine who has developed, as it were, penetration phobia (practising prostitution is her defence against this phobia) is literally forced, after running away from her uncle's house (having overheard the conspiracy to marry her off to Sheikh Mahmoud) to put an end to her flight and turn tail and accept her destiny as a wife to the despicable man with the pustulous lip. This is because of nothing other than the fright which she experiences in the street from two piercing eyes like a knife which follow her everywhere, causing an intolerable neurotic fear. In describing the terror which the eyes inspire in her (we apologize in advance for the length of the quotation) she says: 'A shudder passed through my body, like the fear of death, or like death itself. I tensed the muscles in my back and face to stay the shiver and overcome this feeling of terror which had swept my whole being. For after all, I was not confronted with a hand holding a knife or a razor, but only with two eyes, nothing but two eyes. I swallowed with an effort, and thrust one leg forward. I was able to move my body a few steps away from the eyes, but I felt them on my back, boring through me from behind. I noticed a small shop lit up by a glaring light, and hastened my pace towards it. I stepped inside and hid amidst the little crowd. A few moments later I came out and looked up and down the street cautiously. When I was sure the eyes had gone, I ran quickly down the pavement. Now I had but one thought in my mind. How to reach my uncle's house in the shortest possible time.

'Once back I do not know how I put up with life in my uncle's house, nor do I remember how I became Sheikh Mahmoud's wife. All I know is that anything I would have to face in the world had become less frightening than the vision of those two eyes, which sent a cold shiver running through my spine whenever I remembered them. I had no idea what colour they were, green or black, or something else. Nor could I recall their shape, whether they were large, wide-open eyes, or just two narrow slits. But whenever I walked in the street, whether by day or by night, I would look around me carefully as though I expected the two eyes to rise up suddenly through some opening in the ground and confront me.'

14. While it is not difficult to see in this description of man a typical example of hatred fixated in the anal-sadistic phase of pre-sexual organization, we submit here again the possibility of a neurotic interpretation. Is the corpse of a woman less 'ugly' than that of a man, objectively and anatomically speaking? Even if she isn't covered by hair on the outside, isn't she surely as putrescent on the inside?

15. In accordance with the precepts of psychoanalysis, this is a sublimated castration complex.

16. Before her, the heroine of *Woman at Point Zero* preferred being a prostitute to being 'somebody's wife'.

17. 'The feeling of emptiness took root in me and the giant found he had space to move. The throng of ideas and images inside me dispersed and the giant spread out his arms and legs and began lazily to yawn and stretch...

'But the nights had grown long, and the nocturnal phantoms had taken up position around the bed again and the bed itself had become vast and cold and frightening. The giant didn't want to go back to sleep.'

18. Nothing is more indicative of the subconscious sexual origin of this battle with 'society at large' than the weapons of society being such flagrantly male sexual metaphors: 'swords', 'guns', 'machine-guns'. Later on, the heroine adds: 'Society casts on me looks as sharp as daggers, and lavishes on my face lewd tongues like burning knives which resemble lashes from a horse whip.' Here again we find confirmation of the psychological discovery that the tools of persecution mania are nearly always the organs of the reproductive system.

19. Previously we saw Firdaus, the heroine of *Woman at Point Zero*, as someone else who refuses to see work as a democratic, non-elitist path to the liberation of women.

20. This transformation from negativity to positivity in the objective choice, that is the refusal of the self which absolutely esteems itself to be an object of the choice and its insistence on being the very self in that choice, finds with the novelist an ideological rationalization which is beyond reproach. She considers this transformation at the level of women's liberation. It has become a woman's right to go through 'the experience of choosing a man' after it had been the case in patriarchal society that love did not mean anything more than her right to be chosen by a man.

21. This is precisely the programme that Firdaus, the heroine of *Woman at Point Zero*, has actually put into practice: hatred of man to the point of death or murder. This woman who chooses to be the angel of death and its tool, the sickle, sees the struggle through to its conclusion between the two principles of life and death (the biophilia and the necrophilia, to use Fromm's terminology) and confers on it the force of law: 'My life means their death. My death means their life. They want to live... I have triumphed over both life and death because I no longer desire to live, nor do I any longer fear to die.'

22. We will see that Bahiah Shaheen, the heroine of *Two Women in One*, suffers from what, in a previous study, we defined as 'fear of the common herd'. (See 'The Female of Nawal el-Saadawi and the Uniqueness Legend' in our *Literature from Within* (Dar al-Tali'a, Beirut, 1981; in Arabic), 2nd edn, pp. 10-50.)

23. Let us note that the mind itself, under the influence of an obsession with death, changes into a 'steel cell'.

24. The final words of one fascinated by death, the heroine of *Woman at Point Zero*, are: 'Now I am waiting for them. After a little while they will come to take me away. Tomorrow morning I shall no longer be here. I will be in a place which no one knows. This journey to an unknown destination, to a place unknown to all those who live on this earth... fills me with pride.'

25. Note that the romantic myth of 'nature' first saw the light of day in the nineteenth century, precisely the century which witnessed the expansion of the Industrial Revolution which contributed, and is still contributing, to sustaining anal eroticism. This revolution has also regressively engendered an unprecedented need to go out into the countryside and seek refuge in its 'purity'.

26. Let us remember that the name which is so important to her is that of her father.

Chapter 3

1. Nawal el-Saadawi, *Two Women in One* (Saqi Books, London, 1985).
2. An English edition of Nawal el-Saadawi's *Memoirs of a Woman Doctor*

is to be published by Saqi Books in 1988. (The title is given as *Memoirs*...
throughout the rest of this chapter.)

3. Why is Bahiah not circumcized? Are we to believe that it is just by
chance that she escaped a practice which, though abhorred, is prevalent
throughout Egypt? With a courage unprecedented in modern Arabic
writing, Saadawi opens her book *The Hidden Face of Eve: Women in the
Arab World* (Zed Press, London, 1980) with the scene of her own
circumcision and that of her sister, saying that no girl, whether from the
city or the countryside, escaped this appalling practice. How then has
Bahiah managed to avoid it?

In order to understand this point (to which we shall return later), it is
important to remember that the excised organ in circumcision is the
clitoris. For those women who reject their own femininity, however, the
clitoris is not a female organ but the equivalent of the penis. It is thus a
factor which determines maleness and not femaleness. Given that Bahiah
rejects not only 'the life of a woman' but also her gender, she has to be
spared Umm Muhammad's razor, even if only notionally.

4. This anal hatred finds its expression in a blatant self-identification
which speaks for itself. In one of the scenes set in the dissecting room,
where Bahiah sees a 'male organ' for the first time, the only words she
can find to describe it are 'a wrinkled piece of black skin like old excrement'.

5. Female circumcision does not kill sexual desire. It partially paralyses
a woman's ability to achieve physical satisfaction, however, as it denies
clitoral orgasm, leaving her only the possibility of vaginal orgasm.

6. We shall return shortly to the significance of the colour black for
Bahiah Shaheen.

7. We shall see that the universe and her mother's womb are one and
the same thing to Bahiah.

8. In dreams, symbols and fantasies, a policeman often substitutes for
the father. In Bahiah's case, this is definitely so. In her own words: 'Her
father stood like a vast, high barrier between her and her real self, blocking
her way, guarding the entrance to the house with the bulk of his body,
his loud coarse voice, huge palms and wide eyes... When she drew her
father, she gave him two red eyes and a black handlebar moustache, huge
hands and fingers coiled round a long stick.

'Her father did not have a black handlebar moustache. But on her way
to and from school every day, she would see the policeman in his street-
corner wooden shelter. All she saw of his face was a black handlebar
moustache. She always quickened her step when she passed him, and
sometimes ran home without stopping.'

9. The primal scene is the parents making love, as witnessed by the
child for the first time, or rather as the child imagines it.

10. This entire scene represents the projection of Bahiah's memories or fantasies of rape onto the painting she has exhibited at the medical college. Even if she hides behind the guise of a child, there are still a number of clues as to her real identity. Among these are 'the lost handbag' and 'the tiny fingers red and swollen from the sharp end of the ruler'.

All one can say here is that projecting the imaginary rape onto the image of a small boy and not a girl (Bahiah) necessarily defines a vision of the primal scene which is anal as well as sadistic.

11. Bahiah prefers to be without sexual desire and sex organs to being sexually 'sinful'. The one and only time she 'sins' (with Saleem Ibraheem), she would prefer in her imagination to die rather than have her sin discovered by her father: 'She shuddered as in a dream: she knew she would willingly sacrifice all the years of her life to spare her father that shock, that she did not mind dying or being seen naked if only her father would never see or know.'

12. The first sentence of the novel.

13. In his classic book *The Trauma of Birth* (Kegan Paul, Trench, Trubner & Co., London, 1929), Otto Rank argues that all anxiety neuroses stem from this event, and that neurotic feelings of confinement (claustrophobia) are due to this severance. To this he ascribes the longing to return to one's origin.

14. In this and all subsequent references to 'minted human beings', anal eroticism re-emerges and the world again appears as a vast cesspit. By using the analogy of minting money, one is in effect alluding to defecation. Money — the dirt of this life, according to an Arabic proverb — is the closest equivalent to faeces in the collective unconscious, as revealed by psychoanalysis over half a century ago.

15. In the works of the Egyptian school of realism (for example, the early stories of Yousif Idris), the human world also seems to be denied any value. But Saadawi's novels and short stories do not in any way belong to that school. The aim of the author of *Two Women in One* is to pour scorn on this world, while the aim of the realists is protest. The realists depict humanity as transmuted or 'minted' only in order to condemn the oppressive socio-economic conditions which prevent man from achieving his true potential as a human being.

16. Hannah Minah is another novelist who cries out, 'I hate ordinariness. Kill the ordinary!' (See our study *Manhood and the Ideology of Manhood in the Arabic Novel* (Dar al-Tali'a, Beirut, 1983; in Arabic).) But what a difference between the narcissism of Nawal el-Saadawi's heroines and that of Hannah Minah's heroes. With the latter such narcissism is secondary, and their need for the world of others is crucial if not vital. Indeed, it is only in the mirror of such a world that they can

see themselves as heroes.

Narcissism in the heroine of *Two Women in One*, on the other hand, is primary. Bahiah only experiences her full potential at the expense of the death of objects in the external world, and by regressing into the phase of the narcissistic bond with the mother where the objects of the external world, i.e. human beings, have no existence.

17. Essentially this is the sort of logic which maintains that thirty seconds can make up for half a century: ' ...thirty seconds can change the course of a life; in thirty seconds a bomb can explode, transforming the face of the city and the earth. Life's crucial events happen all of a sudden, sometimes in the twinkling of an eye. Insignificant things occur slowly, taking their time, sometimes even dragging on for a lifetime.'

18. In a comparable narcissistic use of the body, the heroine of *Memoirs...* acts similarly. When confronting the students, she raises her head and stares at them with her eyes 'like slinging back their arrows'.

19. Since the text itself adopts the metaphor of the river, we might add that a river loses its way in two instances: when it dries up and when it floods. The flow of Bahiah's river seems to get lost twice: first, in the dryness of the external world and, second, in the flooding of the internal world precisely at the expense of that drying up. Dams which regulate the flow of a river have two advantages here: first, they prevent it from drying up in the hot season and, second, they stop it flooding in the rainy season.

20. 'She kicked him in the stomach and he fell to the floor, wiping his eyes in surprise and disbelief. This strong foot could not possibly belong to a female. For a female's foot, from his experience with prostitutes, was so soft and small that he could bend it with one hand. But this foot was as firm and strong as a bullet.'

21. In his book *Thalassa: a Theory of Genitality* (The Psychoanalytic Quarterly, New York, 1938), Sandor Ferenczi was the first to interpret the ecstasy and transport of coition as a partially successful attempt on the part of the ego to return to the mother's body. Otto Rank in turn adapted this interpretation by holding that the act of sexual love is an attempt partially to recreate the primary position between mother and baby and to overcome the trauma of birth. (See his *Trauma of Birth*.)

22. 'The Schizophrenic Split', a chapter Wilhelm Reich wrote in English in 1948 and which was included in the third, revised edition of his book *Character Analysis* (Vision Press, London, 1969).

Chapter 4

1. In Nawal el-Saadawi's *Two Women in One* (Saqi Books, London, 1985).

2. Quoting this passage in its entirety allows us to interpret it in the light of our adopted methodology. Regardless of its size, it is abundantly clear that the 'key' symbolizes the male reproductive organ, as opposed to the 'padlock' which symbolizes the female. This derives not only from the function of the key, but also from its shape (see the description at the beginning of the quotation). Moreover, this 'magic' key can also expand (see the second paragraph), generate heat and diffuse feelings of pleasure which radiate throughout the body in concentric circles from where it lies (see the first paragraph).

It should be pointed out that when Saleem hands over his key to Bahiah, he reinforces this surrender by accepting a passive role (he is reduced to 'waiting'), leaving her to take the initiative. From the point of view of the castration complex, this seems to be role-reversal. What was his has become hers, thereby moving from the possessors' camp to that of the non-possessors. The explanation behind the glow that illuminates Bahiah is her belief that this 'magical' transference is 'as visible as the sun' to all eyes.

3. Nawal el-Saadawi, *The Absentee*, 2nd edn (Dar al-Adab, Beirut, 1980; in Arabic).

4. 'Her breath came in great gulps as if she were drowning. Life around her had turned into permanent liquidity, water above and below, and her hands and feet found no solid purchase.

'She reached out with shaking, panicky fingers as though thrashing in the water for a lifeline. When her hand touched the edge of her pocket, her fingers curled around the metal key and gripped it firmly, as if to make sure it was really there; its solidity seemed to reassure her that something in life was tangible, something could be grasped in the fingers.'

5. Or 'ten thousand, nine hundred and fifty days', as Fuaadah loves to calculate.

6. An English translation of Nawal el-Saadawi's *Memoirs of a Woman Doctor* is to be published by Saqi Books (London) in 1988.

7. We can perhaps put forward the following hypothesis: the feeling of 'take-off' that Bahiah Shaheen experiences has to be followed by a 'landing' — something that Fuaadah Khaleel Saleem in turn experiences. This law of alternating or cyclical motion applies to the majority of unintegrated psychological cases.

8. We shall return to this 'urination' theme later.

9. Or 'the good breast' and 'the bad breast', to use Melanie Klein's terminology.

10. The smell of jasmine, on the other hand, evokes 'the meaning of her meeting with Fareed', 'the touch of his lips on her neck' and 'the taste of his kisses in her mouth'. We may note incidentally that the mouth (the

oral phase according to Freud, and specifically according to Melanie Klein) is the child's first means of distinguishing between 'the good breast' and 'the bad breast'. As such, it is an important source of both pleasure and restriction, and of the simultaneous internalization and symbolic destruction of the mother object. As we shall see, the need to vomit almost becomes a compulsion with the heroine of *The Absentee*.

11. Firdaus kills her pimp because she wants to be 'amongst the masters and not the slaves'. The doctor/writer of *Memoirs of a Woman Doctor* leaves her husband just because it occurs to him one day to say, 'I'm the man.' Her alter ego keeps repeating, 'I wouldn't let a man so much as touch my hand if I didn't want him to, even if I was shut up within four high walls with him.' Bahiah adopts the scornful slogan, 'A man's brain is not in his head but between his legs.' When her husband parades his manhood before her, she does not hesitate to 'kick him in the stomach' so that he falls to the ground, 'wiping his eyes in surprise and disbelief'.

12. It is true that the father could also be an object of co-existing love and hatred. However, this is only secondary, whereas the mother remains the primary object.

13. The spider typically symbolizes the evil mother.

14. Salvation from what? From 'the fence of reason', as Fuaadah says when attempting to rationalize it, and from 'the fence of the mother', as we would prefer to interpret it.

15. Note that in Arabic *al-rahma* (compassion) is derived directly from *al-rahm* (the womb). The Arabic expression 'the linking to or severance from the womb' is used metaphorically to refer to those who uphold or sever family relations respectively.

16. Italics ours.

17. We do not have an exact description of the real father in this novel, but Bahiah Shaheen (in *Two Women in One*) speaks about her father as sitting in his 'large bamboo chair'. She insists on presenting him as having a 'huge body': 'He would turn up at home, with his tall, bulky frame, his straight back, and those big strong hands.'

18. Saati immediately notices the resemblance between Fuaadah and his daughter. Although he is old enough to be her father, this does not stop him coveting her from the first glance, and eventually seducing her. He is therefore, in a sense, a fornicator with the forbidden, and is committing incest. In fact, what encourages Fuaadah's identification of Saati with her father is that she sees the fatherly function only from the perspective of the taboo object.

19. This 'confession' is suspect, since the rest of the novel implies the contrary. All the other indications are that Fuaadah has always been preoccupied with 'the things that women (particularly mothers) do before

giving birth'.

20. Note that the libido connected with the symbiotic phase is necessarily of a homosexual nature when it brings together a mother and a daughter.

21. See pp. 19–20 of the present book.

22. We shall return to this 'wetting' theme later.

23. The reader who becomes impatient with the large number of possible interpretations of a single act, or even a single symbol, would do well to remember that the law of dialectics underlies psychological life just as much as social and economic life, for example.

24. This brings to mind the child with the small red fingers swollen from 'the sharp edge of the ruler' in Bahiah Shaheen's painting.

25. Note the connection between the ideal father and his eyes. Let us recall how important Bahiah Shaheen's and Fuaadah's eyes are to them, and also remember that what attracts Bahiah to Saleem and Fuaadah to Fareed are the eyes. Similarly, when the heroine of *Memoirs...* finally meets her 'extraordinary man', the musician, she is constantly speculating, 'What's in this man's eyes?'

26. The punitive interpretation of menstruation explains the fact that a large number of girls drop masturbation at the exact moment of the onset of puberty.

27. This is Fareed's phone number which he no longer answers.

28. Note the ambiguity of this sentence.

29. She is fantasizing, of course.

30. Note the ambiguity of this sentence also.

31. Without dwelling on the details of this first 'temptation', it is worth noting that masturbatory fantasies are often associated with the first real or imagined sexual temptation. Note also that Fuaadah's selective memory cuts out the lower half of the first man's body. The heroine of *The Absentee* is also an excellent psychological study of the influence of memory monitoring (selectivity): 'Why do all these old images remain in her memory alongside the memories of the first man? Why do they remain when more important and more recent images have vanished? But she believes that there is a chemical interaction occurring between the various memory cells which obliterates some of the images while bringing others into focus, distorting yet others, leaving some parts and wiping out others. Yes, some parts are obliterated, like the lower half of the body of the first man in her life. Why obliterate it? She doesn't know; she never mentions his lower half.'

32. Incontinence may not merely be the result of child-like infantile masturbation, but may also indicate the child's desire to remain in the cocoon of his bed, not to grow up, to remain close to his mother and her

body. In other words, it reveals a desire to achieve what Margaret Mahler terms 'symbiotic psychosis with the mother'. This is an extremely important point in the case of Fuaadah, whom we found under the name of Bahiah Shaheen, harbouring an overwhelming desire to return to the mother's womb.

33. Note that children who watch everything related to the intimate relations between their parents may well guess that bathing is a prelude or a conclusion to lovemaking. They may also correctly surmise that the appointed day for this is usually the weekend (in Muslim households, a Friday).

34. Etymologically, the Arabic *al-'awra* is a crack in the land in which to hide, or anything which brings shame, or any organ bashfully covered up. But *al-'awra* is not merely a word in a dictionary: it determines a whole psychology and sums up in one word the entire philosophy of degrading and suppressing women in Oriental patriarchal societies.

35. See, for example, Karl Abraham's article, 'The Ear and Auditory Passage as Erotogenic Zones' (1913) in his *Selected Papers on Psychoanalysis* (Hogarth Press, London, 1949).

36. Probably also given the inferiority of the sex object (i.e. the woman) as seen by the one who thinks it beneath her to be a woman, in other words, a 'deficient being'. It is therefore inevitable that she also thinks it beneath her to have as a love object someone who suffers from the same deficiency as she does, the imaginary castration complex.

37. If we take into consideration the situation peculiar to Egypt, where female circumcision is still prevalent, we can find additional indications of the primary image of the terrifying castrating mother. It is usually the mother who supervises the circumcision of her daughter. Firdaus in *Woman at Point Zero* has this to say about her mother: 'So one day I asked my mother about him [her father]. How was it that she had given birth to me without a father? First she beat me. Then she brought a woman who was carrying a small knife or maybe a razor blade. They cut off a piece of flesh from between my thighs.' In *Two Women in One* Bahiah's mother is the person who brings Umm Muhammad with her sharp razor to cut off 'that small thing between the thighs of her sister Fawziah'.

38. In fact the school, that second mother, is partly responsible for the neurotic or semi-psychotic nature of the theories of infantile sexuality. From this standpoint, Fuaadah's criticism of the school is legitimate, reasoned and sound, even if it interrupts the flow of the narrative: 'Fuaadah kept searching for the location of the opening from which she had emerged into the world. She thought they would learn about it in the history class, or geography or biology. But they taught her everything but that. She had a lesson on hens, and how they lay and hatch eggs, a lesson on fish

and how they procreate, a lesson on crocodiles, on snakes, on all living creatures except man. They even studied bees and their methods of fertilization. Can bees be more important than ourselves? Before the end of the year she put up her hand to ask the biology teacher. The teacher took this to be rudeness and punished her by making her stand against the wall with her arms raised. As she stood gazing at the wall, Fuaadah wondered why when plants, insects and animals fertilize each other it is considered a science, but when man does the same thing, it is considered an aberration and a punishable offence.'

39. Fuaadah's alter ego says that her mother is the reason: 'Maybe if she had been born without a mother, she would have understood everything by herself.'

Chapter 5
1. The following short stories by Nawal el-Saadawi are available in English in a collection entitled *Death of an Ex-Minister* (Methuen, London, 1987): *A Modern Love Letter*, *The Greatest Crime*, *In Camera*, *A Private Letter to an Artist Friend* and *The Death of His Excellency the Ex-Minister*. The others mentioned in this chapter are so far available only in Arabic.

2. An anthology of Nawal el-Saadawi's short stories, *She Was the Weakest*, was published by Dar al-Adab (Beirut) in 1979. This had previously been published in Cairo in 1972 under the title *The Thread and the Wall* and included, in addition to all the stories in *She Was the Weakest*, two other works: *The Thread* and *The Eye of Life*. These were published as two novellas in a separate edition entitled *The Thread and the Eye of Life* (Dar al-Adab, Beirut, 1981). All these editions are in Arabic.

3. Nawal el-Saadawi, *Ring a Ring o' Roses* (Dar al-Adab, Beirut, 1978; in Arabic).

4. Nawal el-Saadawi, *The Absentee*, 2nd edn (Dar al-Adab, Beirut, 1980; in Arabic).

5. In *She Was the Weakest*.

6. *The Thread and the Eye of Life*.

7. Fuaadah's dreams of a rape-like ravishment by the father-beast also include her taking refuge in the amniotic fluid: 'She felt the water surrounding her on all sides as though she was swimming in the sea, a deep and vast sea, and although she didn't know how to swim, she was swimming extremely well. The water was warm and fresh. She saw a great fish swimming under the surface, opening its massive jaws lined with two rows of sharp teeth. The beast approached, its gaping maw like a deep underground cave. She tried to run but she couldn't. She screamed in terror and opened her eyes.'

8. *The Thread and the Eye of Life*.

9. Nawal el-Saadawi, *Two Women in One* (Saqi Books, London, 1985).

10. *The Greatest Crime*.

11. Ibid.

12. Ibid.

13. Ibid.

14. Nawal el-Saadawi, *Woman at Point Zero* (Zed Books, London, 1983).

15. *Ring a Ring o' Roses*.

16. *She Was the Weakest*.

17. We may note that a woman's existence in this world — a world not of her making — is often reduced to the domains of kitchen and bed.

18. In *She Was the Weakest*.

19. This interpretation of anal eroticism, categorically linking it to the first sexual pleasure felt in childhood, is almost identical to the view of psychoanalysis.

20. *Ring a Ring o' Roses*.

21. Ibid.

22. In Nawal el-Saadawi's first collection of short stories, *Little Affection* (Roz al-Yousif, Cairo, in *The Golden Book* series, n.d.; in Arabic).

23. *The Thread and the Eye of Life*.

24. *She Was the Weakest*.

25. See Georges Tarabishi, *The Oedipus Complex in the Arabic Novel* (Dar al-Tali'a, Beirut, 1982; in Arabic).

26. An English edition of Nawal el-Saadawi's *Memoirs of a Woman Doctor* is to be published by Saqi Books (London) in 1988.

27. Another reference to the anal-erotic fixation.

28. See *Ring a Ring o' Roses*.

29. Ibid. In *Two Women in One*, Bahiah Shaheen, during her days of clandestine struggle, gives us the following image of two older people having sex in an adjacent room: 'He was an old man whose lungs had been destroyed by smoking. He had bled his life away in the beds of four frigid, virtuous wives... He had only one wife left, an old woman who propped herself against the wall, made him black tea and set up the water pipe for him in the evening. He would lie near her in the wooden bed and bury his thick fingers between her sagging breasts. Their thin bodies would shake wearily and their cold stagnant breath would be visited by a faint glimmer of warmth, soon to disappear like a death rattle, leaving them like two corpses in their old wooden bed.'

30. In *She Was the Weakest*.

31. Ibid.

32. From the standpoint of psychoanalysis, Simone de Beauvoir's definition of woman as 'not a being but a becoming' has undoubtedly played a critical and enlightening role. However, this definition seems to

us to be wrong or at least in need of correction. Obviously, this will not be achieved by reversing it ('Woman is a being and not a becoming') but, in our opinion, by modifying it to read: 'Woman is a being *and* a becoming.'

. 33. Note incidentally that the social rationalization behind the process of rejecting femininity betrays irrational premises in the quotation itself. Given that it is a rationalization, it is by definition adult behaviour. But we are told that the rejection started 'in childhood'.

34. Firdaus, a professional at the game of rejecting the male, also says, ' ...so from time to time I said no. As a result my price kept going up. A man cannot stand being rejected by a woman, because deep down inside he feels a rejection of himself. No one can stand this double rejection.'

35. *A Private Letter to an Artist Friend.*

36. Ibid.

37. *A Modern Love Letter.*

38. Ibid.

39. Ibid.

40. Ibid.

41. Ibid.

42. This does not preclude the fact that the ego's delusions of grandeur (together with its shielding of itself) is a secondary formulation, and that one of its priorities is defending itself.

Chapter 6

1. Georges Tarabishi's *Woman Against Her Sex* was first published in Arabic in Beirut (Dar al-Tali'a, 1984). In addition to a criticism of some of my novels and short stories (translated here in the present Saqi edition), the Arabic edition includes a final chapter in which Tarabishi criticizes some of my theoretical works.

2. An English translation of my *Memoirs of a Woman Doctor* will be published by Saqi Books (London) in 1988. Translations of *Woman at Point Zero* and *Two Women in One* are both available in English (published by Zed Books, London, 1983, and Saqi Books, London, 1985, respectively). *The Absentee* is so far available only in Arabic (2nd edn, Dar al-Adab, Beirut, 1980).

3. Nawal el-Saadawi, *Ring a Ring o' Roses* (Dar al-Adab, Beirut, 1978; in Arabic); *The Death of the Only Man on Earth* (Dar al-Adab, Beirut, n.d.; in Arabic).

4. Nawal el-Saadawi, *Memoirs in the Women's Prison* (Dar al-Mustaqbal al-Arabi, Cairo, 1982; in Arabic).

5. See p. 33 of the present book.

6. Ibid., p. 10.

7. Ibid., p. 11.

8. Ibid., p. 13. Tarabishi bases his view on Karl Abraham, who sees frigidity as a pre-condition for the behaviour of the female prostitute because she yearns to take revenge on her father (the Electra complex) through castrating men.

9. Sigmund Freud, 'Three Essays on the Theory of Sexuality' in *The Complete Psychological Works of Sigmund Freud*, vol. 7 (Hogarth Press, London, 1955).

10. Ibid.

11. Ibid.

12. Juliet Mitchell & Jacqueline Rose (eds.), *Feminine Sexuality: Jacques Lacan and the École Freudienne* (Macmillan, London, 1982).

13. Tarabishi seems to use the word 'humanize' as meaning 'change into humanity or a human being'.

14. See p. 23 of the present book.

15. Ibid., p. 26.

16. Ibid., p. 216, n. 11.

17. Ibid., p. 28.

18. Ibid., pp. 26-7.

19. Ibid., ch. 1, *passim*.

20. Ibid., p. 217, n. 16.

21. Ibid., p. 33.

22. Ibid., p. 218, n. 10.

23. Ibid., p. 37.

24. Ibid., p. 57.

25. Ibid., p. 220, n. 14.

26. Ibid., p. 50.

27. Ibid., p. 52.

28. Ibid., p. 220, n. 18.

29. Ibid., pp. 25 and 53.

30. Ibid., p. 55.

31. Ibid., p. 69.

32. Ibid., p. 107.

33. Ibid., pp.162-3.